Is It Really Too Much to Ask?

Is It Really Too Much To Ask?

The World According to Clarkson
Volume Five

JEREMY CLARKSON

MICHAEL JOSEPH
an imprint of
PENGUIN BOOKS

MICHAEL JOSEPH

Published by the Penguin Group
Penguin Books Ltd, 80 Strand, London WC2R 0RL, England
Penguin Group (USA) Inc., 375 Hudson Street, New York, New York 10014, USA
Penguin Group (Canada), 90 Eglinton Avenue East, Suite 700, Toronto, Ontario, Canada M4P 2Y3
(a division of Pearson Penguin Canada Inc.)
Penguin Ireland, 25 St Stephen's Green, Dublin 2, Ireland (a division of Penguin Books Ltd)
Penguin Group (Australia), 707 Collins Street, Melbourne, Victoria 3008, Australia
(a division of Pearson Australia Group Pty Ltd)
Penguin Books India Pvt Ltd, 11 Community Centre, Panchsheel Park, New Delhi – 110 017, India
Penguin Group (NZ), 67 Apollo Drive, Rosedale, Auckland 0632, New Zealand
(a division of Pearson New Zealand Ltd)
Penguin Books (South Africa) (Pty) Ltd, Block D, Rosebank Office Park,
181 Jan Smuts Avenue, Parktown North, Gauteng 2193, South Africa

Penguin Books Ltd, Registered Offices: 80 Strand, London WC2R 0RL, England

www.penguin.com

First published 2013
002

Set in 13.5/16pt Garamond MT Std
Typeset by Jouve (UK), Milton Keynes
Printed in Great Britain by Clays Ltd, St Ives plc

A CIP catalogue record for this book is available from the British Library

HARDBACK ISBN: 978–0–718–17867–3
PAPERBACK ISBN: 978–0–718–17868–0

www.greenpenguin.co.uk

MIX
Paper from
responsible sources
FSC
www.fsc.org   FSC™ C018179

Penguin Books is committed to a sustainable
future for our business, our readers and our planet.
This book is made from Forest Stewardship
Council™ certified paper.

In loving memory of Caro

Contents

x **Contents**

Hounded by the ash cloud on my escape

On Thursday morning I woke up in Colditz Castle, drove to Poland and found that I couldn't fly back to England as planned because all of northern Europe was shrouded in a cloud of ash that was thick enough to bring down a jetliner. But, mysteriously, not so thick that it was actually visible.

Brussels, then. That would be the answer. We'd drive at 180mph on the limit-free autobahns to Berlin, fly to Belgium and catch the Eurostar to London.

This, however, turned out to be ambitious, because the only vehicle we could lay our hands on was a knackered Volkswagen van that had a top speed of four. So Prague, then. That was nearer. Yes. We'd start from there instead.

Unfortunately, the index of our map was broken down into countries. And we didn't actually know which country we were in. We'd see a sign for Lückendorf, so I'd look it up in the index. But would it be filed under Germany, Poland or the Czech Republic? And how would it be spelt? The Germans may call it Lückendorf but the Poles might call it something entirely different. In much the same way that people in India call Bombay 'Bombay'. But the BBC insists on calling it 'Mumbai'.

By the time I'd decided Lückendorf doesn't really exist, we'd found a sign for Bogatynia and that doesn't seem to exist, either. The confusion meant that pretty soon we were on a farm track, our path blocked by a tractor that seemed to be scooping mud from a field and putting it on to the road. This encouraged us, since it seemed like a very un-German thing to do and all the Poles are in my bathroom at the moment. We had, therefore, to be near Praha, as the BBC doesn't call it. But should.

We were, and our worries seemed to be over. But they weren't. By this stage the invisible cloud of ash had settled on Belgium and Brussels airport was closed. No matter, we decided. We shall go to Paris and catch the train from there.

Oh, no, we wouldn't. We learnt that all the Eurostar trains were chock-full but we figured that would be okay. We'd fly to Paris, rent a car and we'd drive home in that. Job done.

To celebrate, we went for a beer. I had a lot, if I'm honest, because I wanted to be too drunk to drive this last leg. I had so many that after a while Barclaycard decided it'd be fun to cancel my credit card. And I couldn't phone to explain that if it didn't turn the credit back on again, I'd come round to its offices with an axe. Because by this stage my phone was out of bullets. And then we found that our plane was due to land at Charles de Gaulle just five minutes before that shut down, too. Any delay would be catastrophic.

Normally, people getting on to a plane are fairly polite. We're happy to stand in the aisle for hours while people try to fit the dishwasher they've bought into the overhead locker. I chose not to be so patient on this occasion, though, and as a result there were many injuries. But because of the violence, the plane took off on time and landed just before the Paris shutdown was due to begin.

By now I was Cardiff-on-a-Saturday-night drunk. And fairly desperate for a pee. But not so desperate that I failed to realize the gravity of the situation at Charles de Gaulle. You know those last moments in *Titanic* when the ship is finally going down? Well, it was nothing like that. It was worse.

In the baggage claim was a pretty girl asking if anyone could give her a lift to North Jutland. In the main concourse were businessmen begging rides to Amsterdam. And everyone was being approached by dodgy-looking North Africans with gold teeth and promises of taxis to anywhere. For you, my friend, special price.

Of particular note were the queues of people pointing and shouting at airline staff as though they were responsible somehow for the eruption. This seemed like an odd thing to do. I very much encourage assault, verbal or otherwise, on useless members of staff who won't help. But yelling will not bring order to the planet's mantle.

It's funny, isn't it? The airports had only been closed for six hours and society was cracking up. Not that I cared much about this because we had secured the last rental car in the whole airport and were in a rush to catch the midnight train from Calais. This meant there was no time for a pee.

By Senlis, my bladder was very full. By Lille, the pressure had become so great the contents had turned to amber. Ever peed from the window of a moving car? I have. It came out as pebbles. But it was worth it because at three in the morning I climbed into my own bed at home. Five countries. Planes. Trains and automobiles. And all because Mother Nature burped.

There is a warning here, because on the volcanic explosivity index (VEI) – which goes from one to eight – the eruption at Eyjafjallajokull will probably be classified as a two. And yet it shut down every airport in northern Europe. There are much bigger volcanoes in Iceland. They could, in theory, shut the whole world down for years.

Let's not forget that back in 1980 Mount St Helens in Washington state blew with a VEI rating of five. It was a huge blast but only local air traffic was affected.

What's changed, of course, is our attitude to safety, brought about in the main by our fear of being sued. Could volcanic ash bring down a jetliner? Fifteen-hundred miles from the scene of the volcano itself, it is extremely unlikely, but so long as there are lawyers, licking their lips at the prospect of proving the crash could have been avoided, air traffic controllers are bound to push the big button labelled 'Stop'.

It won't be a volcano that ends man's existence on this planet. It'll be the no-win no-fee lawyers. They are the ones who brought Europe to a halt last week. They are the ones who made a simple trip from Berlin to London into a five-country, all-day hammer blow on your licence fee. They are the ones who must be stopped.

18 April 2010

Help, Mr Spock, I need you to pilot my hi-tech new flat

In the olden days it was easy to make a television work. You plugged an aerial cable into the back, then bashed the top with your fist until, eventually, Hughie Green stopped jumping up and down. Things have changed. Have you tried to make a modern TV work? It cannot be done. No, don't argue: it can't. You have to get a man round and then it still won't work because you have absolutely no idea what to press on the remote-control device. I am looking now at the plipper thing for the TV in my office. It has thirty-two buttons on it, including one marked 'COMPO/(rgb 8)'.

Any idea what that does? I haven't. I do understand the one marked 'Power', but this does not actually turn the television on. So far as I can tell, nothing does, which is why, for three years, it has been off. Frankly, for getting the news I'd have been better off building a chain of beacons.

Then there is the world of the mobile phone. Sometimes my wife asks me to answer her Raspberry and not once in a year have I been able to do so before the caller rings off. To my way of thinking, it's not a communication device. It's a sex toy for geeks. A laptop enthusiast's Rabbit.

However, my life took a dramatic turn for the worse last week because I took delivery of a new flat in London. It's been done up by a developer and fitted with every single item from every single gadget magazine in the universe. This means I cannot operate a single thing. Nothing, d'you hear? Nothing at all.

Let us take, for example, the old-fashioned pleasure of

making a cup of coffee. For many years this involved putting some water in a kettle and boiling it. But now kettles are seen as messy, which is why my new flat has a multi-buttoned aluminium panel set into the wall. The idea is that you fill it with beans and the boiling water is instant. Sounds great, but the instruction book is 400 pages long and I'm sorry, but if I waded through that, my longing for a cup of coffee would be replaced by a fervent need for a quart of Armagnac.

The coffee machine, though, is the tip of the iceberg. There's a music system that can beam any radio station in the world into any room. Last night I selected a classic rock station from San Francisco and was enjoying very much the non-stop stream of Supertramp, until I wanted to go to bed. This meant turning the system off and, for me at least, that is impossible.

Normally, of course, you just hit the offending electronic good with a hammer or throw it on the floor – this works well for alarm clocks in hotel rooms – but I was holding a remote-control device. Smashing that into a million pieces, I realized, would not stop the noise. I needed to find the actual box and I couldn't. So the only solution was to fly to California . . . and burn the radio station down.

I considered it but in the end went to bed to 'The Logical Song'. The irony was not lost on me. This morning the station was playing 'Dreamer'. The irony was lost on me there, though. In a boiling torrent of rage. It's not just the music system and the kettle, either.

The extractor fan above the hob has seven settings. Why? What's wrong with off and on? I can't think of anything that's less in need of seven settings . . . apart from maybe a pacemaker.

Other things? Well, I can't open the garage door – it's remote control, obviously – and the entry phone doesn't appear to be connected to the front door. That means there's an increased chance it's connected to air traffic control at Heathrow and, as a result, I daren't go near it.

Burglar alarm? Nope. Television? Nope. Broadband? Not a chance. And the cooker? Hmm, you could use its controls to remotely pilot a US Air Force spy drone. But to make a shepherd's pie? Not in a million years. And, of course, I can't contact the man who installed any of this stuff because he's in Aspen. People who install high-tech equipment are always in bloody Aspen. This is because they're always American.

They go to gadget shows in Las Vegas, get completely carried away and then come to Europe to install systems that no one over here can understand. We've only just got over drawbridges, for Christ's sake. Then they disappear and the people who made the various bits and pieces go bust. Which means you're left in a house that has everything – and nothing at all.

In a desperate attempt to turn everything off, I thought I'd find the fuse box. Fuse box? To an American gadgeteer, a fuse box is as Victorian as a horse and carriage. So, in my new flat, the fuse box is a fuse room. And it's not hard to find, because you can hear the circuitry humming from a hundred yards away. Or you could if you weren't being deafened by 'Even in the Quietest Moments'.

Then you open the door and, Holy Mother of God, it's like stepping on to the bridge of the *Starship Enterprise*. I am not joking. There are rows and rows of switches and thousands of tiny blinking green lights. Thousands? Yes. Thousands.

I have been on the flight deck of a modern Airbus jetliner and I assure you there are fewer switches and lights up there than there are in the bowels of my three-bedroom flat. It's so scary that you don't dare touch anything in case, when you come out again, you are in Chicago.

Apparently this is not unusual. Many modern properties have rooms such as this, full of warp cores and modems and circuit breakers. The fans needed to keep it all cool would propel a military hovercraft; the power needed just to power itself would light Leeds; and it's all for no purpose whatsoever because no one in the real world understands any of it.

As I sat on the floor, then, with no heating, no kettle, no freezer, no television, no broadband, no light and no hope any time soon of turning the situation around, a profound thought wafted into my head. Our endless pursuit of a high-tech future seems to have taken us back to the Stone Age.

2 May 2010

Traffic storm troopers won't let me buy a bra

Now that the general election is over, we can turn our attention to one of the most important issues in our lives today: my local cobbler has closed down. I can't say that I ever used it because that would be a lie; I didn't, but I liked having it there. A genial old man in a brown coat, stitching up battered clogs, reminded me of a time when we didn't simply throw our training shoes away because they went out of fashion or because our football team signed a sponsorship deal with Puma. Waste Not. Want Not. It wasn't called that, but it should have been.

The florist has gone, too. I can't say I ever used that, either, mainly because the girl who runs the rival business on the high street is much prettier. But, again, I liked having it there. I liked living in a town that had two florists and now I don't any more.

Other shops that have closed down in the past couple of years include the hi-fi shop, the bra shop, the children's clothing shop, both off-licences and the delicatessen. Now, I should explain at this point that I did use the deli. Once. I bought some cheese there and it was very nice. Not so nice, sadly, that I actually bought more, but I liked the idea, should I be in town buying some stamps or getting my shoes mended, that if I were overcome by a need for a spot of Wensleydale, I could sally forth etc. and get some. And now, I can't.

Obviously, I am writing about Chipping Norton, and this news, you may think, would be of some interest in the

Chipping Norton Gazette. But we have no such thing. And, anyway, I bet exactly the same thing is going on in your town; that it's now just a bland, featureless desert of estate agents, fast-food joints and charity shops.

I know that charity shops perform a vital service. I am aware of this and I wish them all the very best as they leach into the premises once occupied by butchers, bakers and candlestick makers. The trouble is, I hate them.

I never want to buy a Victorian teapot. And I don't like to be reminded when I go into town that it's still possible. A Victorian teapot is no good when you want cheese or a romper suit. A Victorian teapot is no good even if you want a cup of tea. So I don't want one, even if it's only 3d – as it usually says on the label in these places.

I suppose, if push came to shove, I'd rather have a charity shop than a set of whitewashed windows that sit like broken teeth in the gums of the high street, reminding their former owners of their failure. However, what I really want is the cobbler back. And the bra shop and the florist and at least one of the offies.

They won't be back, though. They're gone for good. And it's a worry because when you take away a town centre's independent retailers, you take away its soul. You also take away the reason for going there. And then what? Why live cheek by jowl in the flabby doughnut when there's no jam in the centre?

I do not intend to dwell on the consequences here because I'm more interested in stopping the rot. And to do that, we need to work out why, all of a sudden, so many small shops are shutting up for good.

Some, of course, blame the recession. But many of these places had signs above the door saying they were established in 1890. That means they'd survived recessions in the past, and wars and diphtheria.

The most common scapegoat is the supermarket or the out-of-town retail park. People say that it is much cheaper to buy cheese from Asda than it is to buy it from a chap in an apron in your local deli. This is true. But if it's cheapness you want, then surely it'd be best to make the cheese yourself. All you need is some milk, some rennet and the bassist from Blur.

No. I suspect the reason we choose to visit a supermarket rather than flog around a town that was designed by King Alfred is that it's so much more convenient.

And that, I think, is where a solution to the problem of urban decay can be found. Realistically, we can never do anything to reverse the spread of supermarkets, but we can level the playing field. We just have to make town-centre shopping easier. And that can be achieved by getting rid of traffic wardens. Or civil enforcement officers, as they are now called. And how Russian is that?

Whatever they're called, I'm not suggesting they should be put in a vat and melted down, but if this were necessary, then so be it. The fact is, they have to go. All of them.

Every single time I go into my local town, I get a parking ticket. I'm driving along, I am suddenly consumed by a need for a bra, I park in a perfectly sensible place that causes no inconvenience to anyone, pop into the shop, find it's selling only Victorian teapots, come out again . . . and blam. I've been done. If they put that much effort into catching terrorists, nothing would ever explode ever again.

In Oxford I work on the basis that I'm going to be done anyway, so I just park right outside where I want to be. The last time I went there, I parked in a bus lane and went to watch a film. The fine was the same as if I'd made an effort.

It's as though towns don't want people to stop and shop. And, of course, many don't – those run by people who still cling to the outdated and now completely discredited theory that man causes global warming, for example. They would rather the locals stayed at home and beat themselves with twigs. But even enlightened boroughs continue to employ civil storm troopers. Which means they are employing a body of people whose sole job is to kill the town.

Do they think that, if left to our own devices, we'd all park on zebra crossings for a year? If they do, it means they don't trust us. And if they don't trust us, then the relationship has broken down and it's time for some civil unrest.

9 May 2010

Roll up to look at my pebbles – just £5 a ticket

As we know, European flights have been a bit tricky these past few weeks. Couple that to the dreary industrial action at British Airways, the lousy exchange rate and the complete shambles that is our economy, and it's certain that many people will be thinking about taking their holidays in Britain this year.

Indeed, I was in Cornwall last week and, even though it's only the middle of May, the beaches were already peppered with families, huddling behind windbreaks and peering at the horizon through their anorak hoods, fervently hoping for a triumph of optimism over meteorological fact.

This is the problem with holidaying in the British Isles. We have good weather, of course, but it's like an unreliable old friend. You never know when it will drop by to brighten your day. And it never stays long. It has other places to go. France, usually, or the Caribbean.

So let's think about that for a moment. This year there will be more holidaymakers at large in Britain than ever before. They will not be able to lie on a beach reading a book because the same northerly winds that brought the ash cloud are keeping temperatures down to the point where nitrogen freezes. So we have thousands and thousands of people, on holiday, bored and with all the money they didn't spend on flights burning a dirty great hole in their pockets. I sense a great business opportunity here.

While in Cornwall, I couldn't help noticing that there was a bee museum. Yes, that's right. A bee museum. The bees do not balance balls on their noses or juggle miniature chain-saws. You just pay cash money to watch some bees fly about, being bees. It was just down the road from a gnome reserve, where you can go and trundle around the garden of someone who has very poor taste.

So, there is money to be made from insects and plastic garden ornaments. But for some reason what the bored British holidaymaker likes best of all is stones. If the stones are fastened together in the shape of a church, or an old house where someone's wife used to live, then you are quids in. But don't worry if this isn't the case.

Fallen-over stones are still massively popular with the army of moochers. They will spend hours, and pay out God knows how much on booklets and postcards and ice creams, and all you have to offer them in return is some rubble that you can claim once used to be an abbey.

Amazingly, though, you can even make money if the stones are just stones.

Round where I live there are some stones in a field. If you pay a pound, or 50p for children, then you are allowed to go and look at them. How brilliant is that? You almost certainly couldn't design a new type of Apple iPod or an Aston Martin DB9. But don't worry. You don't have to.

To make a living you just have to charge people to look at some stones that someone, a long time ago and for unclear reasons, up-ended in your top paddock.

There are some enormous stones in a field in Wiltshire that are free if you look at them from the nearby road. But the druids, or whoever manages the site, will charge you a whopping £6.90 if you want to see them close up. That's a fantastic business. Especially when you throw in the sale of the guidebooks, all of which say the same thing: 'We don't have a clue why these stones are here.'

Mind you, the guardians of a stone I saw in Cornwall go one better. They have got hordes of people paying £3 to see a stone that may or may not mark the burial place of King Arthur. A king who didn't actually exist. How mental is that?

There are some stones by the stream on the farm I've just bought. I'm going to claim they mark the birthplace of James Bond, open a gift shop and charge people a fiver to come and stand near them for a few minutes. You should be thinking along the same lines. If you have any sort of geology in your garden, put up a leaflet in the local post office and Wallace Arnold will be bringing them round in droves for a gawp.

The capacity British holidaymakers have for finding uninteresting things so interesting that they will pay money to look at them beggars belief. They will pay to watch cows being born. They will pay to see needlework. They will pay to look at your flower beds. If you have a hobby, no matter how nerdy it may be, you can make money out of it from June to the end of September.

Unless your hobby is looking at pornography on the internet. You probably won't be able to make anything out of that. But don't despair.

Industry is an excellent draw, especially if it's closed down. There's a disused tin mine in Cornwall that charges adults eight quid and children a fiver. And what do they see? A hole in the ground that is no longer producing one of the most dreary commodities in the already not very exciting world of metallurgy.

Imagine the possibilities. You could charge people money to go and look round your branch of what used to be Woolworths. 'This is where people used to choose their sweets, and if you follow me we'll have a look at where the racks of DVDs used to be.'

What else are tourists going to do? They've seen some stones. They've looked round the gnome reserve and they've watched bees. It's still raining, the children are still bored, you have their attention and that means you have a direct line to their credit card.

I met a man last week who rents wetsuits to people who want to go swimming but can't in the costumes they've brought because it's always too cold. He will also rent you a slab of polystyrene on which you can play in the waves. He has a £100,000 supercar, and I'm guessing now but I'd like to bet that by milking the misery of the trapped British holiday-maker, he's able to take his holidays abroad.

16 May 2010

Madam Minister, your briefs are full of flirty, dirty talk

There seems to have been some sort of brouhaha about a shortage of women in the new Camerclegg cabinet, and I must say, it does seem to be a bit unbalanced. This, I fear, is very unhealthy. There is nothing that fills my heart with such dread as an all-male gathering. This is why I avoid stag nights and 'lads' nights out' with the same fervent determination as I avoid close encounters with nettles and rabid dogs. I do not understand business, cigars bore me, I have no interest in cricket and if anyone slaps me on the back, I am filled with a sometimes overwhelming need to respond with a punch to the face.

When men are not talking about business and cricket and slapping one another's backs, they talk nonsense, wondering, for instance, if it is possible to live upside down, or cross the Atlantic on a vacuum cleaner. This sort of thing is useless when you have been charged with running the country. You may start out with every intention of working out how the Department for Business, Innovation and Skills could be abolished. But pretty soon, after you've checked on the cricket scores, you're going to be wondering if it's possible to ingest ice cream through your nose.

Men need women in order to function properly, and the reason for this is simple: a conversation with an interesting man is just a conversation with an interesting man. Ultimately, it's going nowhere.

Whereas a conversation with an interesting woman, provided she isn't completely enormous, could go out of the door, up the stairs and into the bedroom. Or into the garden. Or to the back seat of the car. It could go anywhere.

This is why men are much funnier and cleverer when women are around. Because we flirt and women flirt back. And flirting is the oil that lubricates the engine of ingenuity and wit.

I cannot be arsed to think a single original thought when I'm surrounded by men. But throw a woman into the mix and usually I have developed a new world order by teatime. Unfortunately, I'm not sure the cabinet is the right place for such behaviour. Trying to make Theresa May understand the need for national service is one thing. Trying to make her understand while imagining what she would look like naked adds all sorts of complications that the country can well do without at the moment.

What's more, we are talking about people here who are separated by many miles from their families. They are cooped up in a room together and it is at times like this when flirting can lead to all sorts of other problems. If you are not careful, you could end up in the bath with Edwina Currie.

Right now, the government has no money at all to pay for the war in which we are engaged or even the medicines needed to put the soldiers back together again. And it's hard to think how this can be sorted out if Liam Fox is playing a secretive game of mental footsie with Caroline Spelman.

You may argue, if you wish, that grown men and women with big jobs do not flirt, but I disagree. Only the very dull and the very dead do not. When a person is tired of flirting, they are tired of life. And we don't want people like that in charge of anything.

So, you might imagine that the best solution is to be governed entirely by women. Thanks to her multitasking skills, a woman in government could look after defence in the morning, work and pensions in the afternoon and health while doing the ironing. You therefore wouldn't need twenty-eight seats round the table. Just four.

However, I'm not sure an all-woman government would work at all because have you ever heard women talking when they think no men can hear?

We imagine it's all schools and shopping and needlework. But it isn't. I've been in the position these past few days to eavesdrop on a group of girls. Bright girls with important jobs. And what they've talked about – non-stop – is sex.

Not romantic, swoony, Mr Darcy-in-a-lake sex, either. Real, hardcore, back-end-of-the-internet sex. Who's been sodomized by whom and where. Who's had surgery on their inner labia. What lesbianism would be like. At one point I thought they'd moved on to gardening because I thought they were talking about a nearby clematis. But I'd misheard. It was clitoris. And it seemed to occupy them for hours.

One girl explained last night, when she thought I was asleep, that she got her builders to do as she wished by stopping on the way home, taking off her bra and standing in the cold for a few minutes. But they were quickly back on labial surgery.

Often, invitations were extended for the others to have a look at an interesting piece of pubic topiary. I found this amazing. I have been a man for fifty years and I have never been invited by another man to look at his penis. Nor have I felt the need to ask a mate to check out my testicles to see if they are 'normal'. And certainly, I've never got my builder to do as he's told by coming home with my old chap hanging out.

The women I've been with aren't unusual, either. A few weeks ago I overheard two girlfriends chatting, and the subject – for several hours – was masturbation. Was the Bullet better than the Rabbit? What positions worked best? And what fantasies? It was extraordinary because, again, I cannot imagine men discussing onanism in the same terms. In fact, I cannot recall it being discussed at all.

When we understand all this, we can see perfectly well why committees don't work. There are too many distractions.

This is why companies and countries run by one person are so productive. Because they don't spend all day flirting or talking about sex or seeing how far they can lean back in their chair without falling over, they get things done. I therefore have a suggestion. Soon, we will be asked if we wish to change the voting system. I think we should seriously consider introducing a dictatorship.

23 May 2010

Sheep are the robbers' new bullion

Alarming news from the north. Last week someone broke into a field on the outskirts of Knutsford in Cheshire and stole a hundred mummy and baby sheeps. The farmer's wife is distraught as one of the stolen animals was a pet. And they took its new lamb as well. It's all just too heartbreaking for words. And it's by no means an isolated incident.

Just a few days earlier in Lancashire, a farmer in Ramsbottom – I'm afraid I'm not making that up – woke up one morning to find that someone had half-inched 271 of his flock.

Meanwhile, in Wales, 200 were nicked, a similar number went missing in the Borders, and in Cumbria alone fifteen farmers have been targeted. It seems, then, that up north, sheep are the new bullion.

It's not just sheep, though. In Tamworth, Staffordshire, someone has been nicking piglets; in Norfolk, Mrs Queen lost £15,000-worth of cows; and in Shropshire some chap rang the police the other day to say someone had stolen 800,000 of his bees. That's on top of the 500,000 bees that were stolen from Lothian last June. At this rate I may have to think about fitting a burglar alarm to my tortoise.

So what's going on here and, more importantly, why has no one yet been caught? I mean, how hard can it be to find someone who has stolen a million bees? Surely he'll be in a hospital, swollen beyond all recognition and moaning the low moan of deep, relentless agony.

I want to catch him, frankly, because stealing someone's

bees is a bit like stealing someone's eczema flakes. What exactly are you going to do with them?

Then there is this sheep-rustling business. To steal 271 sheep with no one hearing, you need to have several things: some experience of how sheep behave, a knowledge of the countryside, a fleet of dogs and a big lorry. Now I'm no detective but I reckon that if we examine this evidence, the culprit is almost certainly going to be a shepherd. Interestingly, however, police investigating the crimes are not looking for someone sitting on a fence, in a brand new smock. Instead, they seem to have decided that crime syndicates are at work here. Wow! The Wurzels with sawn-offs.

Actually, it's a bit more complicated than that. Apparently, stolen sheep and underground, unlicensed slaughterhouses aren't troubled with European Union hygiene regulations. Which means the market could soon be flooded with a surplus of dodgy joints. It sounds to me as though there could be a Mr Big at large in the hills. Pablo Esco-baa, perhaps.

Frankly, though, I can't imagine the profits are that large. Which is why I find myself wondering why we now have Ronnie and Reggie Gummidge from the Cosy Nostra rushing about in the uplands stealing sheep when they could be doing the traditional gangster thing: robbing banks.

I always wanted to be a bank robber when I grew up. As a career, it seemed ideal: short periods of glamorous and interesting work followed by lengthy spells of relaxation in Spain. All my heroes were bank robbers: Butch and Sundance; Jack Hawkins's League of Gentlemen; Bonnie and Clyde. Bank robbers were cool.

There was a time when a bank was robbed every other night. We became used to waking up in the morning to the sound of Dixon tearing past our house in his Austin Westminster, on the trail of some blagger in a stripy jersey and a Jag.

You'd imagine that today bank robbery would be even more popular.

We all know the police are mostly engaged in the lucrative business of apprehending motorists. And the few who are allowed to concentrate on proper crime are either back at the station, filling in forms, or on courses, learning how to climb over a garden wall. The chances of being caught, then, are almost zero.

Obviously, if you wander into your local branch of Barclays and, halfway through the robbery, you succumb to the drugs you've taken and fall asleep, then, yes, you're going to get nicked. But if you really concentrate on planning and get all the details just so, you'll be fine. The only problem would be the crowds of well-wishers showering you with rose petals as you ran for the getaway car.

And yet despite all this, the last really big bank job on UK soil was in 1994, when raiders made off with £26.5 million from the Northern Bank in Belfast. That's an astonishing sixteen years ago. So what's happened? Why have people stopped stealing wedge, which makes you popular and cool and rich, and started stealing honey bees, which makes you go to hospital?

I wouldn't mind, but the people behind the Belfast heist have never been caught. And most of the money has never been recovered. One night's work: £26.5 million. And no time in the slammer. That's got to beat traipsing around the freezing moors at night, whispering orders at Shep in the hope that you can flog a dodgy chop to Mrs Miggins at No. 22 for a couple of quid.

It's odd, but I think I have the answer. If you go to a hilltop farm, you will find a sheep. But if you go to a bank, you can be pretty certain you will not find any cash. Obviously, they've given most of it to the Greeks, but what about the rest? I think it's melted because I haven't seen or used any for years. So to be a bank robber in the twenty-first century you don't need to be able to crack safes – just computer codes. And I'm sorry, but fiddling about on HSBC's hard drive is a miserable pursuit. Certainly, it's way less cool than nicking the Queen's cows.

It gets worse. Modern cars are almost impregnable, modern art is worthless, half the world lives with a panic button and a can of Mace under its pillow, CCTV has made all city centres no-go areas and most of the police are tooled up with shooters.

This, then, is why there has been such a spate of animal thefts. Because these days, what else is there to nick?

30 May 2010

Please, carry on filming, I'm only burning to death

With the next series of *Top Gear* just weeks away, we are in a frantic race against time to finish off all the films. I won't say what they're about here, though, because obviously you already know. This is because every single thing we do is photographed and videoed by passers-by. And then either posted on the internet or sold to the newspapers. Now that everyone has a camera in their pocket all the time, everyone is a paparazzo, and that has changed my life completely. I'm not complaining because, obviously, life will be a lot more worrying when the attention stops. But, that said, could I please make a small request.

When you stop me in the street to ask for a photograph, have some clue about how your phone camera works. That way, when you ask a witless passer-by to take a photograph of us, he won't spend twenty minutes holding it the wrong way round and taking endless shots of his own nose.

There's another annoyance, too. Yesterday I was snapped walking up Holland Park Avenue, going into Tesco, buying eggs, driving up the M40 and relieving myself in Oxford services. I'm not joking. I turned round while I was having a pee to find a lorry driver filming me. Doubtless, this riveting scene is already on YouTube. Unless, of course, the chap wants it for some kind of bizarre private collection.

I feel fairly sure that if I were to catch fire, no one would try to beat out the flames or find an extinguisher. They'd simply record the event on their phones.

You think I'm being silly? Well, you may recall that in the

run-up to the election, the former UKIP leader Nigel Farage decided to tow a banner behind a plane, urging people to, I don't know, stamp on a bratwurst. Unfortunately, the banner got entangled in the plane's tail fin and it crashed.

I'm certain you recall the photographs of him in the wreckage, with blood pouring down his face, and of the pilot, seriously injured in the seat next to him.

Now here's the strange thing. Someone took those photographs. Someone raced to the scene, saw two injured men hanging upside down and thought: 'I know. I'll get my camera out and take a picture of this.'

Of course, it's possible that the person responsible was a professional photographer, in which case the boundaries are blurred. It is a professional photographer's job to record events, not shape them. But I think this mainly applies during periods of civil unrest and war.

However, it is also possible the person responsible was a bank manager or an accountant. And I don't know about you but I think if I were presented with a badly injured man in the wreckage of a plane – no matter how much I disagreed with his opinions – I'd think about neck braces and mouth-to-mouth and fuel leaks rather than exposures and angles and what some pictures might be worth.

We saw a similar problem recently with the sun-dried baby on the beach. Someone decided that the best way of helping the poor infant, who suffered 40 per cent burns, was to take some pictures of him.

And then you have those people – and for some reason they're almost always German – who think it's a good idea to climb over the security fences at zoos.

Maybe they think the leopard or the tiger looks cute but, of course, as soon as they're actually in there, they quickly realize that it wasn't such a good idea after all. Usually as the creature is eating their leg. What would you do if you saw someone being eaten in a zoo? Throw things at the animal? Try to find a rope so what's left of the person can climb out?

Yes. I'd do something like that, too. But most people, if the internet is anything to go by, whip out their cameras and make a grisly little film.

It's almost certain these days that if you got into trouble at sea, you would not be rescued.

The police, as we know, are not allowed to help. David Hasselhoff is gone. And onlookers would simply take out their phones. You'll get your fifteen minutes of fame, all right. But it will be the last fifteen minutes you ever have.

What the camera does, of course, is detach the onlooker from the events unfurling in front of them. There's a sense as you operate it that you are watching the scene unravel on television and that, as a result, you are unable to help. In short, cameras dehumanize humanity.

But there is an upside. Because in recent years I've noticed that 'news' is not what's happened. It's what's happened on camera.

If a herd of tigers runs amok in a remote Indian village, it's not news. If a gang of wide-eyed rebels slaughters the inhabitants of a faraway African village, it's not news. But if it's a bit windy in America, it is news. Because in America everything that happens is recorded.

I find myself wondering if last week's Israeli raid on a Turkish ship in a flotilla carrying aid to Gaza would have had the coverage it did if the battle hadn't been captured on film. And likewise the racing driver who broke a leg after crashing in the Indy 500. It only became a big deal because we could watch the accident from several angles in slow motion.

In recent months this phenomenon has even spread to the natural world. I mean it. When an animal does something normal, it's not news. But when it is 'caught on camera' doing something normal, then it's in the *Daily Mail*. These days, if you snap an owl catching a mouse, you are Robert Capa.

In the end, this can only be good for all of us. Figures out recently show that more people in India have access to a mobile phone than a lavatory. Soon, it will be the same story in China and Africa. And then, when all the world's being filmed, all of the time, we can go back to a time when news was something interesting rather than something we can simply see.

That way, I wouldn't have to spend half my morning looking at pictures of Twiggy going shopping. And an eagle eating a fish.

6 June 2010

Surgery to solve the deficit – cut off Scotland

As we know, the country is in a terrible mess, and as a result, the head of every government department has been told to go away and implement cuts.

This all sounds very sensible but because I'm a television presenter, I know it won't work.

Here's why. Every Thursday night, the producers of *Top Gear* stitch together the various elements of the show to create a finished product that is around seventy minutes long. Because this is eleven more than the time slot, we have to make cuts.

Or as Clive James used to say when he was making TV shows, we have to throw away our babies.

It's extremely annoying. You've edited a segment to be as good as possible, and now you have to start with the scissors, losing the odd fact here and the odd joke there. It takes an age, it hurts and the same thing always happens when you've finished. The programme is better, tighter and sharper. But it's still six minutes too long.

So it's back to the drawing board. And this time, you must lose links and explanations. You are no longer performing liposuction on fat. You're cutting away at bone and muscle. Important stuff. You are bringing it in on budget but the finished product won't stand up. Think of it, if you like, as a hospital with no electricity. It's still a hospital but it's not much use if the iron lungs don't work.

To prevent this happening on *Top Gear*, we try not to trim

muscle and bone. When we're desperate to cut time, we lose limbs.

You may have seen the Vietnam special we produced a couple of years ago. What you didn't see in that show, however, was a sequence involving the Stig's Vietnamese cousin. This had been tough to make. We'd located a local motorcycle stunt rider, we'd shipped a bike over from Japan, we'd done two recces and written several treatments, and twenty-five people had spent a whole day filming the scene under a sticky sky and watchful gaze of government officials who kept wanting to see the rushes.

The reason you didn't see it is because so many unforeseen things had happened on the trip, the finished programme was miles too long. And when we'd slashed and burned the fat, there was still twelve minutes to go. So instead of slashing and burning at the muscle and bone, we threw away a whole sequence. Better, we thought, to lose an arm than ruin every organ in the body.

And that brings me back to Britain's economy. Yes, the NHS can sack a few managers and the Department for Transport can shelve plans to widen the B3018. Little things such as this will save millions but there will still be millions to go, which is why David Cameron and Cleggy, the tea boy, must think long and hard about losing the Vietnamese Stig. They must think about chopping a whole department. Obviously, I would suggest the Department of Energy and Climate Change because it's silly, when times are tight, to have a whole ministry attempting to manage something over which humankind has no control. It'd be like having a Department of Jupiter.

But the climate change department is relatively small, and cutting that when you are a trillion in debt would be like trying to solve a £50,000 overdraft by not having your hair cut any more. No, Cameron and the shoeshine boy need to lose something big and I believe I have the answer: Scotland.

Let us examine the benefits of this. In the last election the Scottish National Party, which wants independence from England, took nearly 20 per cent of the vote in Scotland. Add this lot to the non-voters who also want to go their own way and you realize there is significant support north of the border for Hadrian's Wall to be rebuilt.

Economically, the SNP thinks Scotland would be fine. I don't know why, since Scottish public spending is 33 per cent higher per head than it is in the south-east of England.

But on its website, the party says that Ireland is independent and is the 'fourth most prosperous country in the world' (really?) and that Iceland, another small independent state, is the 'sixth most prosperous country in the world'. (Apart from being totally bankrupt, obviously.)

Let's not get bogged down, though. The upsides go on and on. Without Scotland on the electoral map, Cameron would have a majority in the House of Commons, so he could lose the Cleggawallah, we'd never again have a Scottish prime minister and Scotland would become abroad – which would make it an exotic holiday location.

I think we could take this further. Why not draw the boundary between England and Scotland at York? This way, the SNP would feel that William Wallace's sacrifice hadn't been in vain and, better still, all the northern English constituencies could be governed by the sort of left-wing, wetland-habitat, save-the-bat and build-a-wind-farm government they seem to like so much.

So what, you might be thinking, is in it for those who remain – the Welsh and those in the south of England? Well, there's no doubt that letting Scotland go would be very painful, especially after 300 years of friendship. But what are the alternatives? The NHS? The Ministry of Defence?

No. I'm afraid it has to be Scotland. It costs the UK £5 billion a year and saving that, on top of the £6 billion in cuts from the fat elsewhere, would go a long way towards solving our debt crisis.

Oil? Well, obviously the Scottish oil companies such as, er, whatever they're called, will continue to pump the black gold into Aberdeen while the others, such as BP and Shell, could simply divert their pipelines to Kent. That's fair. Oh, and we'd have to move the Trident submarine fleet as well.

I want to make it plain to my Scottish readers that I do not want to throw you on to the cutting-room floor. I shall miss you with your funny skirts and your ginger hair. The SAS will miss you, too, since over the years 75 per cent of its soldiers are said to have been from north of the border. But we simply cannot afford to stay together any more. Goodbye, then, and good luck.

13 June 2010

Give to my new charity – Britain's Got Trouble

Oh, dear. I think I've been a bit naive again. Because I sort of assumed that in the run-up to the general election, all three political leaders had made it pretty clear that cuts would be necessary, and that as a result, all of us had reconciled ourselves to a few years of eating less and buying fewer electrical gadgets.

I figured also that after we'd finished laughing uproariously at the plight of the Greeks, we'd realized that we, too, would be in for a similar period of austerity. But I was wrong, because so far as I can see, no one is prepared to change their lifestyle one iota.

Let us examine the case of Nottinghamshire. The Tory-controlled county council and the Labour-run Nottingham council propose to shave a total of about £100 million from their spending and lose 2,000 jobs in the process. Have those affected reacted with a shrug of inevitability? Not a bit of it. They're all working to rule, and their union is making Churchillian noises about going to war.

It's not just council staff, either. You've also got a lot of middle-aged ladies jumping up and down on village greens protesting about plans to close their local library and not listening when anyone tries to explain it's all on the internet anyway.

Elsewhere, tax workers were outside the Treasury because their office-opening hours have been cut and students in Glasgow were to be found waving banners over plans to lose eighteen staff from the university's biomedical and life sciences department.

Doubtless, the druids will be similarly angry after Danny Alexander told the Commons that a £25-million visitor centre at Stonehenge will not now be built. I don't know how druids express anger but if Alexander turns up for work with a lot of warts on his face, I guess we'll know.

Whatever, the point is that no one seems to recognize the need for cuts in spending, and if they do, they don't think they should be involved. So what's to be done?

One chap called the *Jeremy Vine* radio show last week to discuss the problem with David Cameron. In a thick Birmingham accent, he pointed out that if you took all the money from the richest 100 people in Britain, all of our problems would be addressed and the other sixty million people could carry on as before.

Amazingly, Cameron didn't think this was a very good idea, so the man from Birmingham came up with another one. The prime minister should work for nothing. And therein lies the problem. It's impossible, really, to get people to accept the cuts when so many of them are bonkers.

And because they're bonkers, there can be no doubt that when the cuts do start to bite, there will be much wailing and gnashing of teeth, along with a selection of petrol bombs and much police brutality. We are, it seems, on our way back to 1979.

Last week I suggested a way of averting this would be to cut off Scotland. But no one in power seems to be taking that idea seriously. So I have come up with another rather brilliant wheeze: register Britain as a charity.

The last time I looked, British people were giving more than £10 billion every year to help those less fortunate than themselves. That works out at more than £200 for everyone over the age of sixteen.

We put money in the slot to cure cancer, buy swimming

pools for wounded soldiers, build orphanages in Romania, help keep drug addicts off smack, improve living conditions in Gaza: the list is endless. We give so much to charities for the blind that there are now more guide dogs than there are people for them to guide.

In recent months, I've bought pictures to provide music lessons for kids with learning difficulties, signed several rugby balls, supplied a boot full of dung to help keep my local town's lido open and then I spent a night with Louis Walsh to raise cash for Palestine. I even bought the chef Richard Corrigan at one party and I'm damned if I can remember why.

Then there's *The Big Issue*. I don't like it. I think it's boring. But it is the only magazine that I get every week. Sometimes I buy the same issue three times. Why? When I read *Private Eye*, which I enjoy hugely, I don't think, 'Ooh. That was brilliant. I'm going to buy it again.'

The reason is simple. We enjoy giving our money away. It makes us feel all warm and gooey. Which is why we almost always give whenever we are asked. No, really. I reckon that if I knocked on your door this afternoon, explaining that I was doing a sponsored drive to London, in a comfortable car, to raise money for the Amazonian tree warbler, you'd give me a tenner.

And think about what you're doing when you roll a 10p-piece into the lifeboat on the bar of your local pub. You are paying to rescue some drunken idiot from Surrey who's had too many gin and tonics and fallen off his yacht in the Solent, that's what. But it doesn't stop you giving, does it?

Of course, when you are really passionate about a charity's aims, we are no longer talking about the odd 10p. People are prepared to move mountains, or at the very least climb them, to raise thousands. Tens of thousands, even. And that's where my scheme comes in, because we are all passionate about the state of our nation.

I'm proposing, then, that your local MP comes round to your house every week with a collecting tin and that instead of organizing strikes and what have you, unions organize sponsored bike rides to Germany. We can all get behind this, eating as many pork pies in a minute and jumping out of aeroplanes, and then we can appear in our local newspapers, in fancy dress, handing over massively outsized cheques for huge amounts to the exchequer.

Other charities may react in horror to this but they shouldn't, because when the cuts come, they will suffer just like everyone else. If we adopt my scheme, the cuts won't come at all.

20 June 2010

No prison for you – just lick my cesspit clean

For reasons that are not entirely clear, the question of prison reform seems to have cropped up again. Good. It's very important we reform the system so that prisons become disgusting and unhinged. No electricity. No light. No heat. And full to overflowing with inmates who are allowed to eat only what they can catch, or grow in window boxes. Window boxes that they must make from their own fingernail clippings.

Unfortunately, other people think that prisons should be about rehabilitation rather than punishment. That they should be places for quiet reflection, whale song and afternoon poetry by interesting lesbians. Dostoevsky thought this. And so, to a certain extent, did Winston Churchill.

There is even a charity that exists to campaign for the rights of inmates and their families. And I'm sorry, but isn't that a bit weird? Because when you decide to help those less fortunate than yourself, there are so many worthy candidates. People with no homes, no arms and no chance. People with hideous diseases. People with their heads on back to front. And that's before we get to the heart-melting question of children and animals. So why, I wonder, did someone wake up one day and think, 'I know who I'll help. The man who stole my bicycle'?

It actually happened, though, and as a result we now have the Prison Reform Trust, which apparently believes that a prison sentence should be used only for the likes of Peter Sutcliffe. And, even then, that he should be treated with tenderness and a lot of crisp Egyptian cotton.

Well, let me make something quite plain to the lily-livered eco-hippie vicars who think this way. If you come round to my house this evening, asking if I'd like to buy the man who stole my television a gift, I shall say, 'Yes. But only if I can shove it up his bottom.'

It gets worse. Only last week one of the peace 'n' love brigade tried to claim that Britain's judiciary was in love with custodial sentences. Really? Because recently a furore erupted over a case in which Cherie Booth QC told a man found guilty of breaking another man's jaw that he would not go to prison because he was a religious person.

On that basis, the devout Osama bin Laden can hand himself in, knowing Cherie will simply fine him fifty quid. And the Archbishop of Canterbury now has carte blanche to kill as many badgers, and children, as he likes.

Strangely, however, the Haight-Ashbury views of the trust are shared by the outgoing head of the prison service. Yup. Mr Mackay wants fewer people sent to jail as well. And so, too, do the Prison Governors Association and Napo, the probation officers' union.

Such is the weight of opinion behind the call for more community-based punishments, I decided to do a spot of research. And I uncovered some interesting statistics. Last year 55,333 people were jailed for six months or less, at a cost of £350 million. And, apparently, as much as £300 million could be saved if they were given community jobs to do instead. That's a powerful argument, now that an ice cream costs £700.

And consider this. It seems that only 34 per cent of criminals given community punishments reoffend, compared with 74 per cent of those sent to a nice warm prison.

It's easy to see why this might be so. At present, criminals tend to mix with other criminals. I, for instance, do not know any smugglers or murderers, and in all probability you don't either. That's because these people live in a society where their crimes are considered the norm. At my old school, the worse the misdemeanour, the greater the so-called 'lad values' that encouraged us all to be more and more badly behaved. And I dare say it's much the same story in Wandsworth nick.

Before you think I've gone all soft, consider this. If we take them out of their cells, dress them in orange jumpsuits, shackle their legs together and get them to hoe the municipal roundabouts in our local towns and villages, then they will no longer be among their own. They will be among us.

As a result, we will be able to tell them things. And after they've spent six months on a roundabout, being told things, quite loudly, they may start to understand that their life is not normal and there is nothing particularly brilliant about shoving a pint pot into another man's face.

How brilliant is that? The hippie vicars are happy because the crims are out in the open air, getting fit and doing something useful. And we're happy, too – especially if we are allowed to throw things at them as we drive by. Tomatoes. Eggs. Bricks. And so on.

I'm starting to like this community punishment idea very much. And already I'm thinking of jobs around my house that need doing. Painting. Decorating. Licking the cesspit clean. Think. The offender would be able to see how a normal family lives and I would be allowed to call him names and hit him over the head with a stick.

Criminals could be made to retrieve shopping trolleys from Britain's most disgusting canals. They could be made to perform dangerous stunts at theme parks with killer whales and lions. And put the cones out on motorways. Imagine Boy George being made to put his head up a cow's bottom to see if its calf is the right way round while you call him names and pelt his backside with veg.

It gets better. Because if lags are made to pick up litter and weed central reservations, we'll need fewer expensive prisons, it will save local authorities a fortune and, what's more, the decent people currently employed by councils to do menial jobs would become free to earn a proper living in the private sector – inventing wireless routers that work, for example.

I can see now that my views on prison have always been naive. And I can see why prison officers are so in favour of community punishment instead. Because, to put it simply, everyone wins.

27 June 2010

Move along, officer, it's just a spot of dogging

The last government was so enthusiastically bossy that in thirteen years it introduced 4,300 exciting ways for us to break the law. It even made it illegal to detonate a nuclear device. But there's nothing new in this, really. All governments like to think up new rules. It's natural.

That's why I smelt a rat the moment Nick Clegg emerged from behind his urn and asked 'the people' to say which laws they wanted repealing. The deputy prime minister? Of Britain? Asking us if we want fewer laws? Nah. Plainly there was dirty work afoot.

And so it turned out, because on the very same day, a senior police officer was explaining that proposed government cuts meant there would be an inevitable drop in the number of officers. 'Aha. So that's it,' I thought. 'They have to cut the number of rules because they simply don't have the money to police them.'

This all sounds very brilliant, and you may be thinking that soon it will be all right to smoke in the pub and drive in the outside lane of the M4 and even, perhaps, use your dogs to scare off the fox that's eating your children. But don't get your hopes up because I'm willing to bet that in the next five years the number of laws that do actually get repealed is roughly none.

So therefore we must turn our attention to the police force and wonder what might be done to save money there. Many may suggest that, instead of cutting officers, those in charge might like instead to cut the number of courses constables are obliged to attend before being allowed to climb a ladder, or ride a bicycle, or dive into a lake to save a drowning child.

This, however, is probably fatuous, so I propose that we turn for inspiration to the Dutch. I realize, of course, that the Dutch police do not have the best reputation. Harry Enfield and Paul Whitehouse once did a marvellous sketch – 'I'm sitting here with my partner and, I'm alsho happy to shay, my lover, Ronald' – that reinforced a commonly held view that Dutch policing is one part crime-fighting to ninety-nine parts homosexuality.

More recently, we were told that in an effort to combat anti-Semitic crime in Amsterdam, Dutch policemanists were using 'decoy Jews'. The whole idea was ludicrous, even before we get to the question of: why not use real ones? Because, let's be honest, Rutger Hauer in a skullcap isn't going to fool anyone.

I first experienced the Dutch police back in 1975 when a group of Indonesian Christians from the South Moluccas hijacked a train outside the Hollish town of Assen to complain about . . . actually, I can't quite remember.

Anyway, this was on the news a lot at the time and what I do remember is being staggered by the Netherlandic forces of law and order that turned up at the scene. In Britain at this time policemen were all Dixon of Dock Green, but over there they all looked like a cross between Jesus and Jerry Garcia. The main spokesman was wearing loon pants and a bandanna and had hair so long, I felt sure he would trip over it should an attack on the train be deemed necessary.

But here's the thing. I bet you can't remember what the Moluccans wanted, either. Nor, I'm sure, can you remember how the stand-off ended. All we know is that a terrorist organization was formed, it struck . . . and then it simply vanished.

In Britain, it took our smart, clean-cut, well-turned-out officers thirty years to deal with the IRA. And the way things are going, it'll be even longer before they get to grips with Johnny Taliban.

So you have to wonder. What do the Dutch have that we don't? And if they do have something, could it work over here, now our police force is made up of two constables, one stapling machine and an elderly dog called Sam?

I posed this question to a Dutch friend recently, and while I may have been drunk – or he may have been stoned – he said, 'Yes. We are different from you. We can play football, for a kick-off.' He went on to explain about how law enforcement works. Here, if you put one wheel into a bus lane, you can expect to go to prison for several thousand years. But there, if there is a sensible reason and no bus was present at the time, the police will get back to their tender lovemaking and leave you alone.

Fancy some sex in the park? Try it here and you'll still be struggling out of your underpants when Plod turns up. In a main park in Amsterdam, officers are advised to turn a blind eye, provided the coupling is fairly discreet. Want a joint while walking through Amsterdam? Well, you can't. It's illegal. But provided you don't bother anyone else, the police won't bother you.

We have a word for that here, too. Well, two, if we're honest. Common sense. And I wonder what would happen if it were applied; if you could make a phone call in a car if you were in a traffic jam at the time, or you could smoke indoors if everyone else wanted to smoke as well, or if you could read poetry at a summer festival without having to buy a licence.

Imagine it. The police could worry about crime that does matter and ignore crime that doesn't. The savings would be huge and the increase in efficiency dramatic.

Of course, this would require some discretion from the policeman at the scene. And that could be a problem. I know plenty of Plod I'd trust with the job but, equally, my life in Fulham in the 1980s was ruined by an overzealous constable who really would have done me for 'walking on the cracks in the pavement' if he'd thought he could get away with it.

So here's what I propose. We adopt the Dutch system – if such a system exists outside the football-addled mind of my friend – only we give it a little tweak. If the case is brought to court and the magistrate deems it to be a waste of his or her time, then the arresting officer is made to pay – out of his children's piggy bank if necessary – the cost of getting it there.

4 July 2010

Burial? Cremation? Boil-in-the-bag?

As we know, death is a great leveller; communism in its purest form.

Your family may choose to remember you with a giant pyramid on the outskirts of Cairo, or they may choose to mark your passing with a bunch of petrol-station chrysanthemums, crudely tied to the railings on a suburban dual carriageway. But you're still dead.

It's much the same story with the bodies of those brave First World War soldiers that were recently exhumed from their mass grave in France and buried with more dignity elsewhere.

Now, their families can pay their respects in quiet reverence, which is very nice. But the soldiers themselves? Still dead, I'm afraid. I write about death a lot. It bothers me. I don't like the uncertainty of not knowing how or when it will come. Will it be tomorrow and spectacular or will it be many years from now with a tube up my nose? And what happens afterwards? That bothers me, too.

In my heart of hearts, I know that nothing happens. But of course I could be wrong. We may come back as mosquitoes – in which case I will find Piers Morgan's house and bite him on the nose just before he becomes Larry King. Or we may come back as lions. In which case . . . I'll do pretty much the same sort of thing.

Or there may be a heaven. If there is, I shall remind St Peter that Christianity is based on forgiveness, say sorry for not going to church, ever, and demand that I'm allowed in. And that – that is really what bothers me most of all about dying.

They say that we leave our body behind when we're dead, but what if we don't? What if there is a next life and we go into it in the same carcass that's transported us through this one? It's why I don't carry a donor card. Because I shall be awfully hacked off if I am gifted an eternity of milk and honey but I keep bumping into things because some bastard back on earth has my eyes.

It is for this reason that I have made it plain that, when I go, I wish to be buried and not cremated. Because you're not going to have any fun at all with the angels if you arrive at the Pearly Gates looking like the contents of a Hoover bag.

I'm bringing all this up because last week some Belgian undertakers announced that they will soon be offering the dead a 'third way'. A burial? A cremation? Or would sir like to be dissolved in caustic potash and then flushed away down the sewers? No, sir bloody wouldn't.

The process is called resomation and it works like this: you are placed in a silk bag with some water and some potassium hydroxide and then you are boiled until you become a greeny-brown paste.

Hmmm. Even if we leave aside the question of how you might manage in the afterlife as a paste, we must also address the question of reverence for the deceased. Many people may wish to urinate on John Prescott's grave, but chances are, when there is such a thing, no one actually will.

Think about it. Churchyards are rarely vandalized and no one plays ball games in them. Ships that go down with hands still on board are designated as graves and may not be investigated by diving teams. The ashes of those who've been cremated are scattered in places of great beauty. Not chucked in a dustbin lorry. This is because we have a respect for the dead.

And I'm sorry, but where's the respect in turning grandad into a paste and flushing him down the lavatory?

Yes. You are given some powdered bones after the reso-mation is complete, but every day you know that the paste is out there, too. It'll haunt you. Wondering if you've just caught a fish that ate it. Or whether you stepped in it on the way to work.

Needless to say, the engine behind the concept comes from the murky and dirty world of environmentalism. The Scottish company responsible says that cremating a body creates 573lb of carbon dioxide and that with its new system this is cut to virtually zero. What's more, the company says that if we dissolve the dead, there will be less pressure on space in graveyards.

This is like arguing that Prozac upsets the ecosystem and, once in the water, causes all fish to turn right. It may well be true but it's better than having the streets full of middle-aged women sobbing because they've got a parking ticket. And shampoo. Washing your hair in 'peace soap' made from mung beans may well ensure Johnny Polar Bear has a home for many years to come but you will have a dirty beard.

It's the same story with this caustic potash business. Melt-ing the dead may be practical but it is also absolutely horrific. Because let's be honest here; let's cut to the chase. We are talking here about boil-in-the-bag, aren't we? And that's just not on.

Boil-in-the-bag works – just about – for parsley sauce. But not for your mum. She breastfed you. She raised you. She was only ever as happy as you were. And you are going to boil her in a bag and make her into paste. To save a polar bear. It's the worst thing I've ever heard of.

If all we're bothered about is the environment and to hell with the dignity, why do we not throw our dead into the sea or into landfill? Or why do we not simply feed them to our dogs? This makes perfect sense, if you think about it. There are no eco-implications at all. No grave is required. The dog gets a tasty midday snack. Everybody's happy.

Except, of course, we're not happy, are we? Because you cannot feed your nearest and dearest to Fido. It's bad enough clearing up the dog eggs on a normal day. But clearing them up when you know they are Uncle Ernie? It's just a no, isn't it?

So's resomation, and I can't believe the Belgians will actually go for it. Because if they do, and my fears about death are correct, all they'll have to look forward to after a life in Belgium is being used by God for all of eternity to stick his wallpaper to the wall.

11 July 2010

Don't misread the whiff of Cameron's armpits

Have you ever watched a vast swarm of starlings reel around the sky in Africa? Or a million-strong herd of wildebeest? If so, I'm sure you've marvelled at their ability to communicate without actually appearing to do so. But you know what? I think humans can do exactly the same thing. Back in the 1980s the Comedy Store in London would allow a queue of wannabe comedians each to have ten minutes on the stage after the main performers had finished. By this time of night, most of the audience was either hopelessly drunk, extremely chatty or at home in bed.

So it was a tough crowd, even for a seasoned campaigner. For a bag-of-nerves newbie, hoping to get noticed, it must have been a nightmare.

And for one particular girl, on a night when I was there, it must have been even worse. She came on to the stage, picked up the microphone and delivered what we had to assume was her best line. You always deliver your best line first. That way, you have the audience on your side from the get-go. So she delivered her best line and she was greeted with absolute silence.

It was a fairly funny line but – as one – a couple of hundred people in varying degrees of inebriation decided not to make a sound. If someone had heckled, then she'd at least have had a well-rehearsed put-down to fire off. A heckle could have saved her. But none came. You could have heard a pin drop; well, you could have done were it not for the deafening sound of a poor girl dying from the inside out.

I've always been fascinated by that moment. Because how did all those people suddenly decide, without communicating, to behave in exactly the same way?

Clive James, the veteran broadcaster, wit and raconteur, always maintained that you will get a bad audience if you have a bad script. And that, conversely, if you are good, the crowd will be good, too. But I've now proved this to be incorrect. Two weeks ago, while recording the *Top Gear* show, James May, Richard Hammond and I talked for a few minutes about the new Nissan Micra, and there was the sort of quietness normally associated with church services. As a result, the whole scene was edited out of the programme.

However, as a test, we did exactly the same story again last week. The same people saying the same words on the same day of the week in the same place. And the audience laughed until their buttocks fell off. I found that very, very strange, so I did some research.

Back in the early 1970s, an American woman called Martha McClintock, from Wellesley College, Massachusetts, asked 135 college girls living in dorms to record their period start dates. To her amazement she found that, as the academic year wore on, the dates became closer and closer together. The girls were getting in sync.

How was this possible? Well, it seems that plants and insects – even cows – communicate with one another using pheromones. And some scientists believe that humans emit pheromones, too, through their armpits. Could it be that back at the Comedy Store in the 1980s we could smell the comedian's fear radiating out from her pits, and responded to it?

Is that possible? Could it be that the stock market goes haywire from time to time, not because there is anything fundamentally wrong with the system but because of hidden messages in someone's body odour? If so, we should all be a little bit terrified. Because what if reason tells us to do one thing but we are then compelled by our noses to do something else?

I do not want to buy Peter Mandelson's new book. I don't see why he should have any more of my money. But I'm frightened to death that I may soon be standing next to someone in a bookshop and, as a result of their whiffy pits, feel compelled to buy it. Likewise, reason dictates that if I see Mandelson crossing the road in front of me, I should press the accelerator as hard as I can and try to run him down. But what if, at the last moment, I get a hint of Mando juice and decide to hit the brake pedal instead?

It gets worse. Right now, all of us are in agreement that the country is broke. The human part of our brains is telling us we have more debt in relation to gross domestic product than almost any other country in the world and that savage cuts, along with tax rises, are the only answer. Of course, there are murmurings about the abandonment of free swimming lessons for the elderly, and arty people were running around last week moaning about a proposed Arts Council budget cut. But as a collective whole we are all agreed that something has to be done.

Unfortunately there is no doubt that, at some point in the not-too-distant-future, we will all decide – as one – that the cuts are not necessary and that the price we're paying is far too high. We shall simply wake up one morning and decide that David Cameron is a stupid idiot and that we must have a Labour government back in power as soon as possible. It is inevitable.

We see this all the time. Everyone has a Nokia phone. Then everyone has a BlackBerry. Everyone believes in global warming. Then everyone thinks it's rubbish. Everyone loves Jonathan Ross. Then everyone doesn't any more.

I've never understood what causes this to happen. But now it's clear: the cow/starling part of our brain is responding to messages in the ether. Like bulls, we are being led around by our noses. Someone, somewhere in the world turns left, so we must all turn left. This is not a sound platform on which to build an economy. Let alone a species.

I can only suggest that, in the coming months, Cameron focuses very carefully on personal hygiene. He can make the speech of his life, but unless he delivers it from behind an impenetrable wall of Right Guard, it won't make the slightest bit of difference. Deodorant. It's the only way we can survive.

18 July 2010

A few song lyrics could have done for Piers

For the past few years, many millions of people in this country have been scared to pop to their local shop or petrol station in case they bump into Piers Morgan. Well, I have good news. He's been given a new job hosting a television show in America, which means you can go to the bakery for bread knowing he can't possibly be in there.

Doubtless he will have received a Google alert about this mention and even as we speak will be scribbling furiously in his little diary about how I haven't been offered a job on television in the States because my teeth are too beige and I have a fat stomach.

Well, sorry, Piers, but I was in fact asked to meet with all the main American networks a few years ago. I even went over there for some meetings and it was all very grown-up. But in the hotel bar one night I did some maths and uncovered a problem.

They sign you up to do a pilot – quite why I had to make a pilot of a car show I have no idea – and if they like it, you are required to make six shows. If they go well, the run extends to twenty-five shows, and if those get high ratings, they demand a hundred more.

So you go over there to make one pilot and, whether you like it or not, you could still be there five years later. Now, of course, I realize this isn't an issue for Morgan but I have friends in Britain and after five years I'd be missing them terribly. I'd almost certainly become a mental, launching into anti-Semitic tirades at policemen and hurling telephones at hotel receptionists.

Aha, you may think, but what about the money? Well, for sure, if your television programme is a big hit on an American network, then yes, you will be very rich. So you'd be there in your Jacuzzi, with two Las Vegas showgirls, eating some swan, and your children would be 5,000 miles away thinking that, perhaps, you loved cash more than you loved them. I don't think that would be very healthy.

Besides, lots of people move to a new job for money and it rarely works out. Morecambe and Wise. Trinny and Susannah. Barry and Norman. You take the corporate shilling and your career will be over in a jiffy. I don't, by the way, include poor old Jonathan Ross in this. He is an extremely nice and kind man whose move to ITV was thrust upon him by people with an agenda. I'm sorry to say this here, but I think the whole episode was disgraceful.

Anyway, I had a problem. I was in America and due to meet all the big networks for a job I really didn't want. I therefore made a plan with my producers. Upon entering each meeting, we would take it in turns to name a band. And then each of us would have to get as many of their lyrics as possible into the conversation.

This is why, at one network, we were asked what made *Top Gear* so appealing, and my producer, Andy Wilman, answered: 'It's the karma karma karma karma karma chameleon.' It's also why, at the next meeting, I said it was 'art for art's sake' and that 'life is a minestrone'. I was so pleased with that one, I then said, 'served up with parmesan cheese'. Which may have been a mistake. Certainly no job offers were forthcoming afterwards.

I cannot tell you how much fun this is. You're being asked about back ends and put options by some of the brightest, sharpest people in television, and you're sitting there wondering how 'The Logical Song' went and if any of its lyrics have anything at all to do with anything anyone is saying.

Of course, you will argue that this is all fair enough if you don't really care about the outcome of a meeting. But sitting there running through Don Henley's back catalogue in your head would be stupid if you did. Really? Because I put it to you that all meetings are a waste of time and that you would achieve more if you simply sat on your hands and whistled Dixie. So you may as well play song-lyric bingo.

Think about it. If you have a meeting to agree a deal, then both sides will have to compromise, and that means everyone leaves feeling a bit disappointed. If you decide not to compromise, then what's the point of going? So, there can be no such thing as a 'good' meeting. It's either disappointing or useless. There is no other way.

As evidence, I give you the Copenhagen summit. Last year 115 world leaders flew to Denmark to discuss what might be done should global temperatures rise. After eight draft texts and an all-day get-together, involving thousands of people, everyone agreed they couldn't agree on anything.

It was always thus. As a cub reporter on a local newspaper I sat through thousands of council meetings that achieved absolutely nothing. I remember one in which the members spent an hour discussing whether they should have a glass or a plastic water jug at future meetings. And they ended by suggesting they discuss the issue in more detail next time they met.

G7? You may remember that after much pressure from Bonio and St Bob, Gordon Brown and co decided to discuss the possibility of cutting Third World debt to zero. So they talked for ages and discovered they all disagreed with one another.

Now stop and wonder how many meetings have been held between Israel and various other Middle Eastern states over the past fifty years. Anything achieved there? Well, a bloody great wall, but that's about it. They'd have achieved more if Binyamin Netanyahu had greeted President Bashar al-Assad last time they met by saying, 'Rudy's on a train to nowhere.' Why not? Nothing else has ever worked. And who knows, maybe Syria's president is a Supertramp fan. Maybe that's the key that would sort out the West Bank.

Let me finish on one final piece of evidence that all meetings are a waste of time. Someone in America recently called one to discuss who should replace the CNN chat-show host Larry King. And they decided that, of the six billion or so people on earth, the answer was Piers Morgan. My case rests.

25 July 2010

England's fate is in your hands, Ambassador

Britain has just sent a new ambassador to Finland. He is called Matthew Lodge and he will be living in a historically important house that was thoroughly modernized back in the 1980s using Finnish stone. I'm sure he will be very happy there. But how, exactly, will he fill his days? If you are the British ambassador in Washington, or Berlin, then obviously there is much to be done. There will be cocktail parties to attend, and UK citizens will lose their passports and need new ones. But Helsinki? The Foreign and Commonwealth Office says that Lodge will be responsible for relations between Britain and Finland.

What relations? We get on with the Finns in the same way that I get on with my neighbours. I know they exist. The end.

I realize, of course, that Britain and Finland are the only two democracies in human history ever to declare war on one another but it seems highly unlikely that this will ever happen again. So what are the ambassador's weekly reports going to say? How many different ways can he find to say, 'Relations between Finland and Britain remain cordial'? They've been that way since 1945.

We're told that Lodge will also be responsible for the well-being of British nationals living in Finland. Right. I see. And how many of those are there? Two? Seven? Nobody lives in Finland. Not even Finns. It's almost completely empty. You may as well be the British ambassador to Mars.

And I'd like at this point to apologize to Lodge for singling him out because, of course, it's pretty much the same story for our man in Denmark, Norway and indeed right across Scandinavia. The globe, too. I mean, what does the British ambassador to Slovakia do? No, really. What?

I should imagine he spends the first half of his year planning the annual cocktail party and the second half clearing up the Ferrero Rocher wrappers.

All of this conjecture brings me on to a breakfast invitation I once received from the German ambassador in London. There were just the two of us, in a huge room, and we had cold meats until, after an hour or so, a butlery sort of chap came in and coughed discreetly, signalling that my time was up. So I left, and as I did so I wondered: what on earth was that all about?

The only possible reason for the invitation was that, having had some cold meats in a very agreeable room overlooking Belgrave Square with an absolutely charming man, I would feel better disposed towards the Hun. And you know what? It worked. He gave me some ham. I bought a Mercedes-Benz.

This is why I am delighted to hear David Cameron telling British embassy staff all over the world that the days of croquet and gin slings are over; that they must now push hard to support British business. And it's also why I'm thrilled to see he's gone to India.

For too long Britain has concentrated its efforts on America in the vague hope of keeping the special relationship alive. But, truth be told, there is no special relationship. The idiots in the middle bit have never heard of us and the rest still hate us for shooting up the White House or pulling their forefathers' toenails out.

We helped them become part of an 'international' force in Iraq and Afghanistan. We helped them secure their need for oil. And what did British business get in return? A bollocking for spilling a bit of it on one of their beaches. How many US construction companies buy JCB diggers? How many Eurofighters are there in the US Air Force? Quite.

But if our giddiness with America was bad, then our attitude to the rest of the world was even worse. We either ignored it or dispatched John Prescott to tell them that they couldn't have cars and power stations because of the environment.

Tony Blair and Gordon Brown, meanwhile, maintained an ethical foreign policy that meant we just told foreigners in dresses and hats they had to stop whatever it was they were doing and behave like us.

All that has to change. We have to stop lecturing the men in dresses and beg them to think British. And the best person to do that is not Prince Andrew. No, it's the people who live there. And the people who live there are our ambassadors.

We must therefore pull them from whatever secretary happens to be filling their afternoons these days and set them to work, as salesmen. Our man in Delhi gives a local dignitary a cup of tea and a cucumber sandwich and, in return, he buys a Eurofighter. Well, it worked for me.

The big problem is, of course, what else will they sell? Tesco's home delivery service? A mobile dog-grooming service? Britain is a nation now of people who go to work, send emails and come home again. If you look at the business leaders who accompanied Cameron on his trip to India, few of them run companies that make anything.

And that – that – has to be the starting point. Because it's no good forging a special relationship with India or Finland or anywhere else if we have nothing to offer. It's no good giving our ambassador to Slovakia a Ford Mondeo to travel the country as a salesman if he has no samples to put in the boot.

Now is the time to turn this around. People will lose their

jobs over the coming months and years. They should be encouraged to go into their sheds and make something. Because now you won't need to worry about marketing. You have the ambassadors to do that for you. And you don't need to worry about a shop front, either. Because it's the British embassy in just about every capital city in the world.

The days of Brown and Blair are over. The days of patronizing, hectoring, ethical nonsense are gone. Britain is now back in business. We just have to work out what that business is going to be.

1 August 2010

Concussion is what holidays are all about

It's funny, isn't it? At home, you make sure your children wear cycling helmets when they go for a bike ride, you wear a high-visibility jacket when you are on a building site and you treat your fuse box like it may explode at any moment.

However, as soon as you go on holiday, you are quite happy to jump off a cliff and eat stuff that you know full well has spent its entire miserable life living on a diet of nothing but sewage.

We heard recently about a man who fell 150ft to his death while parasailing on the Turkish coast.

He looked like a normal sort of bloke who would take care when crossing the road and so on, so why did he suddenly think it was a good idea to be tied to the back of a speedboat, by a young chap, using a sun-ravaged harness, and then hoisted into the heavens?

You may think it was a freak occurrence. But if you type 'parasailing accident' into Google, you will quickly get the impression that no one has ever returned to earth at anything less than 180mph. Parasailing, it seems, is more dangerous than smearing yourself in Chum and swimming with some crocodiles. But will that knowledge keep me from the big blue yonder when I go on holiday later this month? No.

It gets worse. At home, I make sure my children are kept out of harm's way as much as possible, but on holiday I once watched them being attached to some parasailing equipment by a man who actually had to put down his spliff so he could tie the knots. Well, when I say knots . . . Then, later, I put my boy in an inner tube and towed him around the Caribbean at such enormous speeds that he fell out and was knocked unconscious. What was I thinking of? He is my son. He means everything to me. So why did I think it would be 'fun' to tow him across the sea, at 40mph, on his face?

Then we get to the question of vehicular transport when you're on holiday. At home, you have your car serviced regularly and put through an MOT without complaint. You like to know it's safe and that the brakes work.

But on holiday you are quite happy to rent something from a man called Stavros who makes you sign all sorts of forms you can neither read nor understand before you belch away in a cloud of burning fluids. Or you rent an amusing scooter that you ride much too quickly in shorts and a pair of flip-flops.

Would you let your eleven-year-old daughter ride about at high speed on such a thing? Of course not. It would be foolish, because if she fell off, she'd be peeled. Right, so why do you let her go on a jet ski? I do.

My youngest daughter and I have spent hours seeing how high we can jump over the waves and who can go the fastest while chasing the flying fish. And get this. When we've finished, I let her go snorkelling, knowing full well that the jet skis we've just climbed off are now in the hands of other father-and-daughter speed combos who really won't notice a little girl's head bobbing about in the waves.

The sea is an almost endless source of death and despair. Earlier this year, I plunged into it with a mate and spent several carefree minutes being bashed about by waves that were even taller than me. Then my friend was knocked over with such force that his arm was wrenched completely out of its socket. But did I get out of the water? Again, no. I'd seen what the water could do to a man . . . and I liked it.

Then we have the banana boat. You let your eldest daughter go in the speedboat while you climb on to the big inflatable penis with the rest of the family and then you sit there, trying to pretend it's exciting while simultaneously pretending not to notice that the rapist who's driving the towboat is playing tonsil hockey with your daughter.

And you think: 'This is harmless. Boring even.' And it is, but have you ever fallen off a banana? That's not boring at all, because usually, just before you hit the water, you get your wife's knee in your face; so now you're drowning in a sea of stars and bewilderment, wondering if she did it on purpose.

Eating? At home, you wash your vegetables and cook your chicken until it's technically coal. But on holiday? Well, after the swarthy waiter has stopped staring at your daughter's breasts and explained that tonight's special is a 'local delicacy', you're perfectly happy to put it in your mouth. Despite the fact that it's obviously a wasp that's plainly been cooked in a bucket of blubber, in a bag bearing the label 'Best before the Boer War'.

Then there's the wine. You like it not because it's cheap or tasty but because the hideous little oik in the apron has told you it's made by his brother. You know he means his brother works at the chemical plant that produces a wine-based substitute as a sideline but you feel that because there's a family connection, it's authentic and earthy, and so you drink lots of it, and then you climb into the deathtrap that has three brakes and wobble home in a blurred tunnel of double vision and stomach cramps.

Of course, you know drink-driving is stupid. Except when you have a sunburnt nose and you've spent the day on the beach. Then it's okay.

What is it then, I wonder, that makes us become so very different as soon as the Ryanair jet touches down in some dusty sun-baked tourist trap? Why do we suddenly think that it's a good idea to jump off a 100ft cliff into a puddle and let our children climb around on outboard motors that are still running? Why do we take leave of our senses?

Strangely, I think we don't. I think that on holiday we become what we're designed to be: thrill-seeking, fun-filled, risk-taking, happy-go-lucky wonder beings. And that when we go home, to the drudgery of everyday life, we are obliged to become something we're not: frightened and ever so slightly dull.

8 August 2010

I've sprayed wasps with glue, now what?

There seems to be some talk that the retirement age will soon have to rise to ninety-eight for men and one hundred and fourteen for women. And that since the country can no longer afford to pay a state pension, everyone will be expected to finish their last shift by getting a carriage clock and then jumping into one of the machines at the factory. This is excellent news. And I'm speaking from some experience because on Monday I jacked everything in. I retired.

Top Gear is a monster and feeding it takes up all the conventional hours – and a few that haven't been invented yet.

And to make matters worse, we decided that while we were filming the last series, it would be a good plan to make a few items for the next one as well.

I'd film all day, then write until the wee small hours, waking up in hotels and spending the first fifteen minutes of the day wondering where the hell I was. Occasionally, I'd get calls from the family saying they were in Mallorca, or Devon, or Cornwall, and having a lovely time, and I was consumed with a jealous rage. Why wasn't I there, too? Kids, you know; they don't grow up twice.

By June I was absolutely knackered. By July I think I was starting to go a bit doolally, and by last week, after three months without a break, I'd had enough. So I made my mind up. I would go home from the last shoot on Sunday and I would retire.

I began to long for it; dream about what I'd do. And what I would do, mostly, is absolutely nothing at all. It became all-consuming, to the point that I was counting the hours until it was all over – something I hadn't done since double physics with Dr Jones back in 1975.

And then the day came. I woke at seven and went downstairs, without shaving, and I read the papers until about eight, when I had a good stretch and made another cup of coffee. Then I was bored.

I decided to look in the fridge but it was empty, so with absolutely nothing to do, I read the business section of the papers, even though I had no idea what any of it meant. By ten, I was so desperate that I was reading the *Daily Mail* and trying to understand why it had published a picture of Kelly Brook. I failed, so I went to look in the fridge again. Then I looked out of the window.

As the clock ticked round to midday, I thought it would be nice to meet friends for lunch. But they were either away on business or on holiday. My children? That was a no, too. They were all too busy with 600 of their closest personal friends.

I thought then that I'd have a wander round the garden to see if anything needed doing. And I found a tree that needed planting. 'Excellent,' I thought. 'That will keep me busy for ages.' And I was right.

It took me a full fifteen minutes to find the gardener and another six to explain what I wanted. Then I had another look in the fridge to see if perhaps there was a cold sausage that I'd missed earlier.

There wasn't, so I went for a walk to see how things were getting along on my farm. I noticed immediately that the barley was ripe, or medium rare, or whatever it is when barley's ready for harvesting. So I rang the farmer and asked him to fire up the combine. Then I went home again and, because no cold chicken had hatched in my fridge, I tuned in to a programme hosted by a man with a bright orange face in which people tried to sell stuff they'd found in their attic. Apparently, many retired people watch this, and after half an hour most determine that it's better to be dead, so they have a stroke. I didn't want a stroke, so I decided immediately to start a hobby.

But what? I dislike golfers, I am to DIY what Nicholas Witchell is to cage fighting, and I happen to know you can't put a ship in a bottle using the only tool that I can wield with any confidence – a hammer.

Undaunted, though, I came up with the best pastime in the history of man. What you do is find an aerosol tin of spray adhesive, such as you would use to stick posters to a wall. You then lie in wait and when a wasp flies by, you leap out and give it a squirt. Bingo. One minute it's flying; the next it's tumbling silently out of the sky with a confused look on its stupid little face.

I realize that these days you get into terrible trouble if you say you've shot a baboon in the lung but this is different. Because there are not millions of baboons flying around in your garden, ruining any attempt to sit outside and have lunch. Baboons don't sting you for fun, either. And anyway, gluing a wasp together in mid-air requires patience and skill and gives the creature a sporting chance.

Plus, putting a paralysed wasp in the bin while shouting, 'Ha. Now what are you going to do, you little bastard?' is much less cruel than enticing it into a jam jar and letting it suffocate in a pile of its mates' corpses.

In fact, I shouldn't be surprised if the RSPCA doesn't give me a medal or a certificate of some kind.

The only downside to my new game is that you will miss more often than you hit. And this means a great deal of glue ends up on your furniture and your computer. But trust me. The satisfaction of seeing a wasp suddenly stop flying? It's worth ruining your house for that.

Unfortunately, this is a seasonal pastime and soon the wasps will be gone. Then what? No, really. What do you do to fill your days when you are old and there are no insects and no work? You die, really, because having tried it for a whole day, I've decided that thinking of things to do is far more exhausting than getting up and doing them.

15 August 2010

Naughty bits & melons – I learnt it all in Albania

Every year, I tell my children, with a serious, Dickensian face, that they may have a fun holiday at Easter but in the summer we must go somewhere that will expand their minds. Cambodia. Alaska. Bolivia. These are the places I always have in mind. Unfortunately, I'm always too busy to enforce these rules, which is why, this year, we ended up in Kassiopi in Corfu. And all you can learn there is how not to catch chlamydia.

And so it was on the third day I decided that the kids must put down their vodka shots and their new Italian scooter friends and come with me on an expedition to Albania. We would go to the ruins at Butrint. And we would learn about how the Romans invented mortar.

Sadly, though, the ferry to Albania is almost certainly the slowest moving vessel in history. It does half a mile an hour and I couldn't help noticing it had a funnel made from cardboard and gaffer tape. It was the *Herald of Not So Free Enterprise*.

I therefore decided, in a strident way, that we would charter a boat, and so it was, after a complicated exchange with Greek customs, during which there was much blowing of whistles, we pulled into the Albanian port of Saranda in a 68ft Ferretti motor yacht. There was nowhere to park it, so we tied it to the coastguard's boat, which had sunk – in about 1956 – and went to have our passports checked in what appeared to be a Russian public swimming baths, only with more smoking.

We then hired a guide called Fatso and he was delighted. 'British. Very good comedy,' he said. 'Norman Wisdom. Mr Bean. And number one funny show: *Top Gear*. In Albanian, word for man organ is pronounced "car". You make show about cocks,' he said, poking me in the chest and roaring with laughter.

It wasn't quite the education I'd had in mind, but no matter. Off we set through what looked like a cross between Odessa, Miami South Beach and Benidorm in 1969. If you can imagine such a place.

All guides who grew up with communism like to give you facts and figures that prove their country is better than yours. This was a point picked up deliciously by Sacha Baron Cohen, who famously pointed out that Kazakhstan is the 'world's number one exporter of potassium'.

Fatso, however, made Borat look like an amateur. After explaining that there were now two roads to the ruins – two! – and how much each of them had cost, and how Saranda is the sunniest place in all of Europe, he suggested we stop off at a nearby spring. 'Albania has more water than any other country after Norway,' he explained, before revealing how much water, exactly, is produced by the spring in question. 'It's 375 cubic metres every second,' he said, thumping the steering wheel of his van with joy. 'That is 1.35 million cubic metres every hour. And that is 32.4 million cubic metres a day. Albanian water, too. Best water in world.' He was nowhere near finished. 'In this region we produce 45,000 tons of watermelons every year. Second best region for watermelons in all of Albania,' he added, grabbing his heart and blinking to stop himself crying with pride.

My son, annoyingly, wasn't interested in these remarkable statistics and asked if there was a shop where he could buy an Albanian football shirt. Fatso was overcome with rage:

'Albania football team number one in world, but every match, referee is biased,' he thundered. 'One time, John Terry cut off Albania striker's head and Albania striker was sent off. In a match against Dutch peoples, we scored nine goals, all disallowed by referee.'

By this stage, I was eating the inside of my face in an effort to stop myself laughing. And that was before we got to Albania's crime rate. 'None,' he said, bouncing up and down in his seat. 'There is no crime of any sort. And Christians live side by side with Muslims in perfect harmony.'

We turned to Albania's recent past. 'In communists' time, there were some things good. Some things bad. Bad things? One man say to government spy that he had no spoon for his sugar and got seventeen years in jail. Another man ask why Corfu harbour have a light when we have no light. He got twenty-five years.' So what were the good things? 'Everyone have job and supply of water under control.'

At this point, we arrived at Butrint. This, it's said, is where Hector's missus and a few mates set up shop after the fall of Troy. It was very hot, and the guide there was keen to show us every building and how we could tell which bits had been built by the Greeks, which bits by the Romans and which by the Venetians. It's exactly what children should do on a summer holiday, this. Learn stuff. Not just drink vodka and snog.

But I wanted to get back in the van with Fatso and learn more about the glorious nation of Albania. He was waiting in the car park with an Albanian beer. 'Best in world,' he said. And it was. But then beer always is when you're hot and it's not.

On the way back to Saranda, I noticed that a sizeable percentage of all the cars had British plates. 'How come?' I asked. 'Ah,' said Fatso, 'many Albanians go to England, get job, buy car and come here with it on holiday.' I see. Another thing I noticed is that most of the houses had been knocked over. 'Why's that?' I asked. 'Earthquake,' he said with an impish smile. 'Government earthquake. You build house with no permission, special forces come with bulldozers and knock it down.'

And so there you are. We'd gone to Albania to learn about cement but we'd come away with minds enriched by so much more. We knew how much water is produced every hour by the spring. We knew how many watermelons are produced each year. We knew about planning regulations in Saranda and the Albanian word for 'cock'.

That's the thing about going on holiday with me. It's so much more fun. I should be a tour operator.

5 September 2010

Beware – Arabella won't stop at hay rustling

Sinister news from the shires.

After a summer that was too dry and then too wet, the hay harvest has been hopeless, and as a result, the price has reached £6 a bale. That's more than double the price last year and so it's now more expensive than marijuana. Yup. Grass will now cost you more than, er, grass. And that's if you can get hold of it at all.

One poor girl with a hungry horse rang me a while back to ask whether I was in a position to help since I'm now a farmer.

So I went to see the man I'd employed to cut my hay and he was perplexed. 'Let me just get this straight. You want a few bales for your friend?' he asked incredulously. It was as though I'd asked him if I could watch his wife take a shower. The answer was a big fat no.

As a result of all this, the nation's horse enthusiasts are in a state of blind panic. In the coming winter their precious animals may die of starvation, and consequently many have turned to crime. At night there are thousands of middle-aged ladies sneaking around the countryside, stealing bales of hay that have been left in the fields. Farmers all over the country have been targeted and are at a loss.

Hay can't be stored indoors, under lock and key, because it has a nasty habit of catching fire, and it's not possible to shoot the thieves because of various laws. One solution is to package the hay in bales so large they won't fit in the back of a Volvo but there's a danger, if you do this, that the enormous barrel could roll down a hill and kill one of the early members of the Electric Light Orchestra.

And so here we are. It's 2010. And such is the pressure on space that perfectly decent women called Arabella are stealing grass from farmers to feed their pets. What's it going to be like when it's not food for horses that becomes scarce but food for people?

As you may have heard, the harvests in Russia and Ukraine failed this year and now, with the biggest grain shortage for twenty-six years, the price of a ton of wheat has doubled to about £200. A bit of wonky weather in a couple of countries and suddenly a loaf of bread costs about the same as a pound of myrrh.

Without wishing to sound like an A-level politics student, it's easy to see what's gone wrong. There is simply not enough space on earth to grow food for the planet's ever-increasing population. And the consequences of this will be dire. Because if a woman with clipped vowels and a hairdo is prepared to become a thief to feed her horse, how low will she stoop when she needs to feed her child? For sure, there will be hair-pulling at the bakery. Maybe even some biting.

It's hard to know what to do. Even if we manage to inject some family-planning sense into the Roman Catholic Church, the population will continue to grow and this means that, one day, people are going to start to get hungry. And then they are going to start to starve. And then many will die. It's a fact. Genetically modified crops may delay the moment but it's coming. It's a mathematical certainty.

Unless, of course, we can find more land on which to grow stuff. You may think this is unlikely. We've been to the moon and it seems entirely unsuitable. Mars appears to be a dead loss as well, which means we have to look closer to home. And guess what. I've found some. Lots of it.

Mile upon mile of juicy soil, ready and able to produce millions of tons of delicious food for all the world. It's called the English countryside.

Last year I bought a farm in Oxfordshire and was delighted to discover that the government would pay me to grow nothing at all on about 400 acres. I can also get money to keep stubble in the ground for a bit longer than is sensible and for planting hedgerows. That's right. You work all day. Pay your tax. And the government then gives it to me so I can plant a nice hedge.

This is because of the skylark. Or the lapwing. Or some other whistling, chirruping airborne rat that doesn't matter. I like a bird. I'm even a member of the RSPB. But the notion that more than half my farm is a government-subsidized sanctuary for linnets while the world goes hungry is just stupid.

Especially as there's plenty of evidence to suggest it doesn't work. Examination of the latest environmental stewardship programme suggests that the only birds to benefit are the starling and lapwing. Which means the government is proposing to spend £2.9 billion on a programme, at a time of hardship and hunger, even though it knows one of the few beneficiaries is the starling – a bird that can knock down buildings with its urine and eat a whole tree in one go.

Now it may well be that this bird business is just a cover story to mask an undeniable truth – that, left to its own devices, farming would cease to be a viable industry. I must say I'm staggered by the smallness of the returns you get. You'd be better off spending your money on a powerboat.

However, I find it morally reprehensible that the previous government stated that it wanted 70 per cent of Britain's utilizable agricultural land to be in an environmental stewardship scheme by 2011. Did it not have calculators? Could it not see there's going to be a global food shortage soon and that setting aside nearly three-quarters of Britain for the benefit of a sparrow is moronic?

Of course, I'm not a farmer. I don't understand the complexities of the industry. But I am a human being and, while it's nice to walk through my fields, listening to the starlings eating my trees, I do think that giving me money to leave land for the birds is madness.

I therefore have an idea. Instead of giving farmers vital subsidies not to grow food, how about this? Give them subsidies to grow some.

14 September 2010

One dose of this and you could turn into a werewolf

This morning, all being well, my wife should be on her way back home from a charity bike ride to Arnhem in Holland. This involved cycling eighty miles a day, every day, for a week, and of course a great deal of effort and sweat was needed to get ready.

As a result, she spent much of the year in a gym, picking things up and putting them down again, very quickly, while listening to music such as Basement Jaxx and N-Dubz. Until – disaster. Just two weeks before the start date, *ping* – something important snapped in her neck.

I tried explaining that my neck was fine because I spent the year sitting in a chair watching television but this went down badly, so she went to the doctor, who suggested a muscle relaxant and painkiller called Voltarol. A packet of pills that, I kid you not, comes with an instruction manual.

Now, as we know, any man who consults an instruction manual must consider himself a failure. Instruction manuals are for the weak and the indecisive. They are for people who happily accept that someone, somewhere, knows better than they do. 'Grunts': that's what they're called in the American infantry. However, I couldn't work out why a packet of non-prescription pills should require instructions, so I had a read. And it was amazing.

First of all, you are told how to take the pills. You swallow them with a glass of water. Unless, I presume, you are French, in which case you push them up your bottom. The French ingest everything up their back passages. I'm surprised they don't eat this way as well. I'm also surprised they manage to have children.

Anyway. Back to the Voltarol and, specifically, the section on 'common' side effects. These include diarrhoea, nausea, vomiting, headaches, dizziness, vertigo, a rash and a change in liver function.

Now, call me a party pooper if you like, but on balance I think I'd rather have a sore neck than run the risk of cycling to Holland with diarrhoea running down my legs, vomit exploding over the handlebars and a liver that thinks it's a piece of Lego.

It gets worse. Less common side effects include chest pains, yellowing of the eyes, collapse, swelling of the tongue and a propensity to vomit blood. In other words, if you take one of these pills to make your neck feel a bit better, there's a 1 in 1,000 chance you'll become a werewolf.

Sadly, though, it could be even worse. Because there's almost a 1 in 10,000 chance you could suffer blistering eyes, bleeding, blurred vision and confusion. In other words, you become a zombie.

So far, I have singled out Voltarol, but a trawl through the big wide world of medicine reveals that nearly all household pills 'n' potions can have dramatic side effects. Nurofen, for instance, can increase the risk of old people becoming deathly white and having a heart attack. Imodium can make your intestine paralytic, while a pill I was once prescribed for a slipped disc could, it seems, cause my gums to disintegrate and my teeth to fall out.

Boots, meanwhile, will happily sell you a hay fever relief that could cause your face to swell up, while it seems Sudafed is basically a magic mushroom. It can cause you to have nightmares and run about the garden imagining you are being chased by Jesus.

Then, of course, there's the big daddy. Viagra. This will cause your penis to stiffen, enabling you to have penetrative sexual intercourse – but with whom? That's the question. Because, according to the instruction manual, it will need to be someone who's turned on by a man who might be bleeding from his eyes and his nose. Still interested? Well, beware, because other potential side effects include nausea and 'sudden death'.

So, there you are. You start out with a bit of rumpy-pumpy and wind up covered in sick and blood, with a dead man on top of you.

Of course, this is all nonsense. We are all well aware that all drugs are subjected to rigorous tests before they are allowed on to the market and that if Voltarol really did turn patients into flesh-eating zombies with altered livers and blistered eyes, someone would have noticed during clinical trials.

You may recall, several years ago, six healthy men were given a new anti-leukaemia drug called TGN1412 to see if there were any unpleasant side effects. After a short while, apparently, they began to run about the surgery, tearing off their shirts and complaining they were going to explode; heads swelled up to three times the normal size, toes and fingers began to fall off and immune systems collapsed. As a result, TGN1412 is now not on the market.

Its maker didn't say: 'Well, there you are. A complete success. It cures leukaemia and all we need do is pop a little instruction manual in the box saying that there's a chance the patient might turn into the Elephant Man and explode.'

That's the point of clinical trials. You test the drug on animals. Then you test it on people. And if it all goes horribly wrong, you can't put it on the shelves. We know this. We know the drugs we can buy are safe. Why, then, do we have these stupid leaflets saying we may suffer from sudden death?

Well, it's the same reason my quad bike is festooned with stickers telling me that if I get on and ride it for even a short while, my head will be severed and I will catch fire. It's why the sun visor in my car is smothered in ugly notices telling me that a possible side effect of the airbag is that it will kill me. It's why police community support officers aren't allowed to help children cross the road.

It's because when there's a chance of something bad happening, there's always a lawyer in the background who can argue that the person concerned should have been warned. And that brings me back to a small point I made earlier.

I suggested the French habit of putting everything up their bottoms dramatically reduced their chances of having children. But I was forgetting something. Sex this way is how you end up with a lawyer.

19 September 2010

But I've killed Baz already, Mr Safety Instructor

Like all right-minded people, I rejoiced when David Cameron announced last week that he would drive a bulldozer through the health and safety rules that have paralysed industry, killed millions and removed all sense of personal responsibility from absolutely everyone in the land.

Sadly, however, his announcement came too late for me because just a day later I was due to attend my first health and safety course. It's now compulsory for any BBC employee who travels to parts of the world that aren't Stow-on-the-Wold or Fulham.

I was seething with rage because it would be unpaid and it would last from eight in the morning until seven in the evening for an entire working week. So when was I going to write my newspaper columns? Or prepare scripts? Or do any actual work? This is the problem with health and safety people. They simply don't understand that we have work to do and that there's just no time for their high-visibility, no-job's-worth-dying-for nonsense.

Because you know what? As a journalist, I reckon some jobs are worth dying for. If a journalist had got advance word of the massacre in Rwanda, then maybe it could have been stopped. Would that have been worth a life? Damn right it would. And the life I'd have taken is that of the stupid health and safety officer who thinks you should be on a how-to-use-a-ladder course rather than the front line.

And anyway, how, in six days, could they possibly hope to cover all of the hazards a programme such as *Top Gear* might face on its travels? Altitude sickness, what to do if you get a fish in your penis, extreme cold, road accidents, how to be beheaded with dignity and what to do while being shelled in Mogadishu. The suggestion was that we'd emerge after a week as a cross between Dr Christiaan Barnard and James Bond.

The first morning suggested this wouldn't be so. We were taken into the gardens of the conference centre in Bracknell in Berkshire, where, among the rhododendrons, two firemen called Baz and Tel were staging a mock battle using a mock gun. Then Baz fell to the ground with mock blood spurting from a mock prosthetic wound in his arm. Apparently, we were supposed to have heard a shot but, sadly, Tel's mock gun had jammed.

It was like watching the Wokingham Amateur Dramatic Society stage a version of *Apocalypse Now*, and I thought: 'Holy shit. I've got six days of this.'

Afterwards, we were taken to a classroom for a lecture on how to deal with the sort of bullet wound we'd seen but I couldn't really concentrate because I was dying for a cigarette and it was two hours until break. The morning passed in a blur of acronyms, none of which I can even remember now. DRAB. Or is it BARD? And what do the letters stand for? All I do remember is that, thanks to the Labour government, we must now refer to an RTA (road traffic accident) as an RTC (road traffic collision) because accidents imply no one was to blame whereas collisions don't.

And blame? That's another whole industry filling a million more crap hotels in Berkshire with their courses and their fat women in trouser suits.

Then, the lecturer's radio crackled. There'd been an accident in the grounds: Baz had fallen out of a tree. So off we rushed to see what could be done. And there was more fake blood pumping out of yet another fake wound. This is how it went on. Lecture. Baz had a horrible accident. Lecture. Baz had a horrible accident. Lecture. Baz fell out of trees, trod on landmines, crashed his car, got shot, got blown up. Baz was the unluckiest fireman in history.

And, to make everything a bit more weird, a funeral was held at our hotel on Thursday. Now, I hope and pray that the deceased did not die in a hail of gunfire because during the post-crematorium 'do', we were running around outside, learning how to take cover in a gunfight.

And, to make everything worse, when one of the mourners approached to ask for our autographs, James May shot her in the face with a water pistol.

I was learning very many things and what I was learning is this: it is impossible to see a tripwire in a wood, it is disgusting to stick your fingers in an open wound, Serbian checkpoint guards cannot be reasoned with and unexploded ordnance has an acronym but I'm damned if I can remember what it is. Oh, and if you have a beard and you have a heart attack on the street, you are 40 per cent less likely to survive . . . because passers-by are unwilling to give the kiss of life to someone with facial hair.

Later, I learnt that men with spinal injuries get a hard-on and that it's impossible to work out where gunfire is coming from. Which is why, when the shooting started, Richard Hammond hid in front of a bush. And was killed.

On Thursday afternoon Baz fell out of another tree and needed to be moved because the Wokingham Amateur Dramatic Society was threatening to cut our heads off. We rolled him on to a blanket in the correct fashion but we couldn't move him because none of us had been on the BBC's manual labour course. I wish I was joking about that but I'm not. Baz died, I'm afraid. Again.

At this stage you probably imagine I'm going to sign off by saying it was all a complete waste of time and that in six weeks' time almost all of what I learnt will have been forgotten. But here's the thing. On day one, Tel told us about a twelve-year-old girl who had been hit by a car.

She rolled on to the bonnet, with a broken leg, and then slid down on to the road, where she banged her head and fell unconscious. A crowd gathered and everyone agreed that she should not be moved because she might have a spinal injury. She died. And she died because her tongue was blocking her airway.

I now know what to do in that situation. And was that one single retainable fact worth a week of my time? Honestly? Yes.

26 September 2010

This tired old bird deserves another chance

Last week we were told, for the umpteenth time, that unless eleventy million pounds is raised by next Tuesday, the last airworthy Vulcan bomber will be mothballed in a shed, where it will be eaten by rats and used by birds as a lavatory.

You're probably fed up with these stories. We're always being told by those who rescued this plane from oblivion that they've spent the £100 you gave them last year and that now they will dangle from your heartstrings until you give them some more.

There are many worthy organizations that want your money.

Sick kiddies. Landmine amputees. Our Brave Boys. So why give it to a lot of people with adenoidal problems and cheap shoes just so they can indulge their passion for a plane that was used only once in anger in its entire twenty-four-year service life? You may remember. It flew all the way to the Falkland Islands to bomb the runway at Port Stanley. And mostly missed.

I understand your cynicism but if we take this argument to its logical conclusion, then there is no point in paying millions of pounds every year to keep the Tower of London upright. It, too, served no useful purpose when it was new and is now nothing more than a glorified safe, guarded by thirty-seven pensioners in silly dresses. Let's pull it down and sell the land to Wimpey.

Stonehenge is also a waste of time and money since nobody knows what it was for then, and now it's just a magnet for lunatics. And why should I give Bill Oddie any of my hard-earned cash just so he can sit in a box, counting ospreys? Screw 'em. What have they ever done for me?

Happily, in this country, we are extremely good at preserving things that we think matter. Many of our magnificent old houses are kept in tip-top order and those who sit on the summit of the *Sunday Times*'s Rich List donate millions each year to keep a few dabs of Constable's oil in air-conditioned comfort.

Recently, Rowan Atkinson announced that he wished to build a splendid modern house, designed by an esteemed architect, in the Oxfordshire village where he lives. But the neighbours went nuts, suggesting that it would look like a petrol station and would consequently ruin the olde worlde charm of their surroundings. Yup. They were prepared to stone a national treasure to death to keep things as they had been for 200 years.

I experienced similar problems with my house, albeit on a smaller scale. Planners allowed me to make many modifications using modern materials such as glass and steel. But they were absolutely insistent that the door between the hall and the kitchen must remain. 'It is a very important door,' said one expert.

It's not just doors, either. Beavers, stamps, hedgerows, bats, books, woodland, monuments, boats, pottery, sporting equipment, poetry, record players. Find something old and I'll find you a group of enthusiasts who are working round the clock to preserve it for future generations. I even know of one man who collects and restores vacuum cleaners.

However, we seem to have a very different attitude to machinery. After the war, for instance, most of the aircraft that had helped to keep Johnny Hun at bay were taken to fields in Wiltshire and Blackpool and chopped into tiny pieces. We didn't need them any more in the jet age so Wellingtons, Lancasters, Blenheims and Sunderlands were simply scrapped. That's why, today, there are only around fifty working Spitfires in the whole world.

It was much the same story with Brunel's steamship, the SS *Great Britain*, which now resides at the docks in Bristol. This was a massively important piece of engineering, the first ocean-going steel ship to have a propeller, and it was big, too. A hundred feet longer than anything that had gone before.

I'm delighted to say the lottery fund stumped up much of the cost of renovating Brunel's masterpiece. But it drew the line at the 1,000-horsepower engines. Even though these were really what set the ship apart and made it interesting, it would not cough up and, as a result, the motors that visitors see today are electrically powered fakes.

Then you have the Science Museum. Only a tiny fraction of its exhibits are on show in London. The rest – some 200,000 – are housed in a collection of dingy hangars near Swindon. And, of course, a recent application to the lottery to turn this site into a full-on museum where visitors could see the cars and the missiles and the planes that made Britain an economic powerhouse was rejected in favour of a cycleway or some such nonsense. 'Preserve a car?' To the Miliband boy and his mates, that would be like paying to preserve the bubonic plague.

Generally speaking, the job of maintaining Britain's mechanized past is the responsibility of wealthy individuals. Nearly all the working Spitfires, for example, are in the hands of rock stars and blue-bloods. It's the same story with most of our country's automotive history, and that's before we get to the traction engines that are maintained by a group of people who think Fred Dibnah was a god.

The idea of getting a grant or sponsorship to preserve a Type 42 destroyer or a Tornado is simply laughable. And that's why it is important we do whatever is possible to help the men in plastic shoes keep that Vulcan airworthy. Sure, it's not as glamorous as a Spitfire, which is why, when it flew low and slow over my house the other day, my children couldn't have been less interested. My dog thought it was noisy and wet itself. Nobody could really understand, therefore, why I was running about in the garden, pointing and grabbing my private parts.

It's true, of course, that this big, loud, delta-winged, retaliatory fist never did anything noteworthy. But since it was built, purely, to drop nuclear bombs on Russia, we should all thank God for that. And be grateful, when we hand over a hundred quid to keep it up there, that we still can.

3 October 2010

Just speak English, Johnny Europe

So far, David Cameron's cuts aren't too bad. A few middle-class babies will have to suckle on their mother's breast milk until they are fourteen, George Osborne has decided to use his own money to buy a Christmas tree for No. 11 and various workers on the tubular railway have been told to get out of their cosy ticket offices – that no one uses any more – and do a spot of work.

However, we all know worse is to come. Free swimming lessons for the elderly will end, greasy women in the north will have their flatscreen televisions confiscated and the navy could lose an aircraft carrier.

That's why I've spent the week racking my brains for a big cut that won't affect anyone. And I think I have an idea.

We must tell people who work for the European Union to stop pretending they can't speak English.

Let me explain. There are twenty-three recognized languages in the EU, which means there are 506 possible bilateral combinations. And because of the impossibility of finding someone who can translate Danish into Estonian, the EU now has to use a chain of translators, which, I'd imagine, massively adds to the chance of a misunderstanding.

Certainly, I know if I was sitting in one of those booths, translating a dreary treatise on fiscal stability from Welsh into Hungarian, I'd never be able to resist changing what had actually been said just a little bit. Maybe dropping in the word 'nipples' occasionally. Or 'testes'.

But worse than the complexity and opportunity for

tomfoolery is the astronomical cost. It's around €1 billion (£875 million) a year and, thanks to various lunatic Basques, things could get worse. The cost isn't just borne by taxpayers, either. If you invent a new type of nasal hair-remover and wish to patent it in all fifty American states, the cost will be £1,600. If you want to patent it across half of the EU, the cost will be £17,500 – thanks to a £12,250 bill for translation services.

For all we know, a Greek bloke invented the Apple iPad back in 1958 but he's still waiting for someone to translate his idea from Hungarian into Portuguese.

Plainly, something must be done, not only to save all the member states money, but also to make our industry more competitive. And it's obvious, isn't it? Those translators have got to go.

The raw data suggest this will not be too much of a hardship, even in Britain, a country famed for its blinkered attitudes to the noises other people use to communicate. According to official figures, 23 per cent of the population here can speak, read and understand French.

Unfortunately, these figures are nonsense. You may claim that you can speak French, by which you mean you can order a loaf of bread and ask for the pen of your aunt. But do you know the French for jump leads? Or Scart lead? Or collywobbles?

The acid test is to imagine yourself in bed with a French girl who can speak no English. Do you have enough to get by? Really? Because, trust me on this, if you say, 'Et maintenant, comme le chien,' she is going to be very angry. And point out that it is, of course, 'la chienne'.

That's the trouble with French. You may know the word for railway station but do you know if it's male or female? Of course you don't, which is why you would come a cropper if you were asked to speak to Monsieur Nicolas Sarkozy about the possibility of sharing nuclear submarines. You'd probably end up giving him your mother's recipe for toad-in-the-hole.

No, when they tell us that 9 per cent of people in Britain can speak German, what they mean is that 9 per cent of people in Britain either have an O level in the subject or once went to Cologne on a business trip. They do not mean that 9 per cent of the British population could hold important talks with Angela Merkel on Chinese trade tariffs.

The fact of the matter is this: thanks to our absurd school league tables, only 5 per cent of A-level students sat an exam in a modern language last year. And even those that passed can hardly claim they were fluent.

So, without translators, almost everyone in Britain is sunk. But that is emphatically not the case with Johnny Foreigner, because contrary to what he may claim when you ask for directions, he does speak English.

English is the mandatory first foreign language for school children in thirteen EU member states. Couple that to the fact that most kids in Europe would rather watch Bruce Willis than some French idiot in black and white smoking a cigarette while pondering the meaning of his ham sandwich, and would rather listen to Lady Gaga than whatever it is the Italians call pop music, and you end up with a government statistic that does appear to be true. Around 90 per cent of European kids can speak English better than many people in Newcastle.

Things are less clear-cut with the older generation, but I'm sorry: if you can't speak English, then you are simply not intelligent enough to represent your region in the European parliament. Your neighbours may as well elect a table or a horse.

The time has come, therefore, for the whole continent to stop communicating with its silly grunts and noises, and take up English. We can explain to the French and the Germans that they may speak in their oh-la-la Gott-im-Himmel language when they go home at night but, to save money, it has to be English at work.

Who knows, we could roll this out all over the world, which would save the United Nations and the G20 a fortune as well. And we should, because it's ridiculous that taxpayers have to cough up simply because some halfwit from Zimbabwe thinks he's making a statement by speaking in ticks and clicks at important meetings.

Nobody really understands how language has evolved but we must understand that today, in a world of fast communications and global consequences for the smallest of things, it's time we waved it goodbye.

10 October 2010

Turkey joining the EU? Over my dead dog's body

Back in the summer, Mr Cameron made an impassioned plea for Turkey to be allowed to join the European Union.

He pointed out that for many years this great bridge between the world of Christianistas and Muslimism has been a NATO missile launch pad and that you can't expect someone to guard the camp and not be allowed inside the tent.

I'm sure that up and down Britain people called Nigel and Annabel nodded sagely at these kind words.

Many middle-class couples take boating holidays off Turkey's idyllic coast and come home with ornate birdcages and lovely rugs. Apart from the boatman who slept with their daughter, they like Johnny Turk very much.

How, they wonder, can the EU possibly turn its back on Turkey, with its lovely 'for you my friend special price' traders and excellent restaurants, while granting membership to the revolting Bulgarians? And the Romanians, with their silly pork-pie hats and donkeys? It's ridiculous.

In the past, Turkey's applications were denied because they liked to cut off people's heads, and such a move would have infuriated the Greeks. Today those excuses no longer hold water. Turkey has abolished capital punishment, and infuriating the Greeks is now seen, especially by the Germans, as a good thing.

Turkey has even managed to sort out its prison system. In the past, you were beaten on the soles of your feet for no particular reason and male rape was encouraged. We know this because we've seen *Midnight Express*. Now, torture is discouraged and the homosexuality is apparently quite tender.

It all sounds fine, then. But I've just spent a bit of time in Turkey and I don't think it's fine at all. And not just because the barmaid at my hotel had only one word of English, which was 'no'. This made ordering a beer extremely complicated.

First of all, I didn't go to Istanbul or one of those turquoise coves you see in the brochures, because that would be like judging Britain on a brief trip to London and Padstow in Cornwall. No, I went to the eastern part. The region the Foreign Office advises us to avoid. Turkey's Lancashire. And I'm sorry, but the only thing I want less in the EU is rabies. It was absolutely awful.

In my view, a country must have certain standards before it can become a member of the EU, and my No. 1 line in the sand is: dead dogs at the side of the road. Of course, you occasionally see a rotting mongrel in Portugal and it's very sad. But in Turkey they lie there like the forest of single shoes we see by the A1. Thousands of them. Maybe they are used as handy direction pointers when one is having friends over for dinner: 'Left at the Labrador. Right by the Dalmatian's head, and if you see the sausage dog, you've gone too far.'

The EU is supposed to be a group of civilized countries working as one. And I'm sorry again, but accepting a country that can't be bothered to clear up its dead dogs would be like Boodle's private members' club accepting a man who thinks it acceptable to masturbate in public.

Sadly, though, there are other issues that must be addressed. Petrol, for example. I realize, of course, that if you water it down a bit, you can increase profits dramatically. Furthermore, when your customer breaks down with a ruined engine, he will be many miles away, with no means of coming back to your place of business with a pickaxe handle. But it's not on. Even the Spanish have cottoned on to this.

It's the same story with plumbing. The idea is that when you pull the chain on a lavatory, the contents of the bowl are taken far away from your nose; not fanned directly into the air-conditioning system, which itself is made from decaying dogs. This sort of thing may be acceptable in Mexico, but not in what should be seen as the world's boutique.

We must also address the violence. Yes, we have road rage in Britain and it's not particularly edifying, but in Turkey it seems that if someone carves you up in traffic, you are legally entitled to leap from your car and beat him to death.

And then there is the transport infrastructure. A road is a complicated piece of engineering. Foundations must be dug. Many different types of stone and gravel must be laid and compressed and hardened before a top coat of asphalt is laid. Filling a crop-dusting aircraft with grey paint and flying over the desert may be cheap, but you end up with something so bumpy that your eyes stop working properly and you fail to see the next military checkpoint.

Of course, we cannot deny Turkey's membership of the EU because it has military checkpoints. We have such things at Heathrow from time to time. And Northern Ireland. But when the soldiers point their automatic weapons directly at your head through slits in sandbag walls and there are tanks, it all feels very far removed from, say, the Dordogne.

I like the diversity of Europe. I like that the Spanish kill cows as sport and northern Englanders race pigeons, a bird the French call 'lunch'. It's a wonderful melting pot, but some things would sit in the stew like a – well, like a dead dog, actually. And being asked for your papers by a man in a tank? That's one of them.

The problem is that Turkey simply doesn't feel European.

Poland does. Ireland does. Even Bradford does. But Turkey feels odd. It feels like part of the East. It's an interesting place and a nice spot for a holiday, I'm sure. There is economic growth, too, but having it in the EU would be as weird as having Israel in the Eurovision song contest. Oh, hang on a minute . . . No. It would be like having a branch of Primark on Sloane Street.

And there's the thing. Mr Cameron says it's not reasonable to expect someone to guard the camp and then not be allowed inside the tent. But that's not true, is it? My local policeman guards my house from vagabonds and thieves but that doesn't mean I want him to come and sit by the fire every night.

31 October 2010

No one needs to know their adze from their elbow

Last week a colleague of mine called James May claimed that any man who could not land an aeroplane and put up a shelf and defuse a bomb was nothing more than an organic bag for keeping sperm at the right temperature until it's needed by a lady.

Speaking to us from the pages of the *Radio Times*, he says traditional skills are disappearing from the curriculum and that there are now many men who think it's endearing and cute to be useless. It isn't, he says. 'It's boring and everyone's getting sick of it.'

I should explain at this point that Mr May is fanatical about the workings of things. For fun, he will take a motorcycle engine to pieces, and for relaxation, he will countersink a screw. At night, he takes penknives or model trains to bed so he can, as he puts it, 'look at them'.

Unfortunately, like all fanatics, he cannot understand the mindset of those who do not share his opinion or abilities. Me, for example. He is right because he draws outlines of all his tools on the wall so he can see at a glance when one is missing. I am wrong because I am confused by zips. He is right because he is organized and methodical and interested in the teachings of Michael Faraday and James Watt. I am wrong because I've got better things to do than read the instruction manual for a vacuum cleaner.

I drive him mad because I cannot see how things go together. Once, he spent fifteen minutes, in a state of increasing exasperation, watching me struggling to attach a strap to a pair of binoculars I'd bought. Eventually he could take no more, snatched the rat's nest that I'd made away and did the job for me. And that is the point. If you cannot do something, then get someone who can to do it for you.

Mr May says children should be taught basic woodworking and needlework skills at school. I disagree. I was taught for many years how to do long division. I even had extra lessons in the hope that the secret of this arithmetic witchcraft could be unlocked. But it was all to no avail. I am now fifty and I still don't understand it. So when I need to divide one number by another, I fire up Mr Samsung and get him to do it on my behalf.

It was the same story in the school woodwork centre. So far as I could tell, every single tool in there seemed to have been designed specifically to puncture my lungs. Telling me that I had to learn how to use a lathe was like telling me I had to learn how to use a tampon. It was pointless. And painful.

And again, that still holds true today. Whenever I attempt even the simplest job around the house, we need scaffolding for eight weeks to put the place in order again.

Every day, at least three white vans with ladders on the roof will come to my house and disgorge men in bobble hats who chew pencils, listen to Radio 1 and mend stuff that's gone wrong. Stuff, Mr May says, I should have been able to mend myself.

But I really and genuinely can't. I can't ever find the end on a roll of Sellotape. I don't understand clasps. Plumbing is a dark art. My lawnmower is a vindictive swine that wants to kill me. The only good news is that you have to pull on a rope to make it begin. And this has never once, ever, worked.

I am not unusual. History is littered with the corpses of people who thought they could save a few bob by doing a job themselves. Lord Finchley, for example, who attempted to mend an electric light – an endeavour that prompted the writer Hilaire Belloc to say: 'It is the business of a wealthy man/To give employment to the artisan.'

Like Finchley, I am not wired up to understand engineering, which is why my respect for those who are is boundless. I can cook an egg, so I don't really have much admiration for Gordon Ramsay. I can write a sentence, so I don't fawn over Sebastian Faulks. But I cannot drill a hole in a wall without knocking it down. Which is why I go all weak-kneed over Isambard Kingdom Brunel.

And, to a certain extent, James May.

He's boring and pedantic and methodical to the point where you want to cut his head off. But we need people like him who can weld, in the same way as he needs people like me who can . . . er . . . I'll get back to you on that.

When he buys a gun, for example, he takes it into his workshop and inspects every detail of its design and construction. When I buy a gun, I take it outside and shoot the sky near where a pheasant had been moments earlier. And when the gun goes wrong, usually because I haven't cleaned it, I take it to the gun shop, where a man – who Mr May would put out of work – charges me a small amount to put it right again.

But back to Mr May's claim that basic woodwork and needlecraft skills should be taught in school. There are two problems with this. First, there's no point trying to teach someone like me how to make a bookcase. I can't. And second, we are no longer living in 1953.

Teaching someone how to rivet is like teaching someone how to do cave paintings – it's simply not relevant today. Woodworking is fine only as a hobby, and you should never trust a man who has a hobby. Hobbies are for people who were caught masturbating by their mums.

'Stop that and go and do something useful.'

Today the only engineering a child needs to understand is electrical. How to mend a wireless broadband router. How to align a satellite dish. How to transfer iTunes from one computer to another.

And permit me at this point to let a little secret out of the bag. James May can do none of those things. He doesn't like electricity. He doesn't trust it. He even told me once that he doesn't believe it exists. So, when his router goes wrong, like you and me, he spends all day on the phone to a man in India.

7 November 2010

Use Jordan and Jemima to sell Britain

Last week Mr David Cameron breezed into China – where hardly anyone has heard of either him or the country he represents – and explained that it really is no good having a one-party state with censorship of the internet. I don't think this was a very good idea.

I realize, of course, that he has to make some noises about human rights, or the bleeding-heart liberals back at home get all angsty. But really. How would you like it if a complete stranger barged into your kitchen one day and explained that you are not bringing up your children properly?

Quite. Well, that's undoubtedly what the Chinese thought of Mr Cameron's lecture. Who are you? Shut up. And would you like to buy some training shoes?

The purpose of Mr Cameron's visit is to make the Chinese aware of British business in the hope that after we've bought 25 billion pairs of their nasty shoes, they would perhaps like to buy a packet of Prince Charles's Duchy of Cornwall biscuits.

So why begin with a spot of light criticism? When you walk into a boardroom, hoping to sell the assembled buyers your wares, your opening gambit should not be 'I don't like your carpet very much'. It's for this reason my local green-grocer does not collar me as I walk past his shop with the words, 'Oi, fatso, do you want to buy some potatoes?'

Let's gloss over this mistake, though, and move on. By 2015 Mr Cameron hopes to have almost tripled Britain's exports to China from £7.7 billion a year to a whopping

£18.5 billion. God knows how. The Chinese have already said they are not interested in our telecom, insurance, banking or media. So, what's left? I assume that's why George Weston, boss of British Associated Foods, was there, too. Because if Mr Cameron wants to do that much trade, the prince's biscuits on their own will not cut it. He must be planning to sell some Ovaltine as well.

I like this about Mr Cameron. He seems to understand that doing business around the world will make everything a bit better at home. But, again, I sense a mistake. He was accompanied by three big-hitters from the cabinet and a selection of business leaders. There was the aforementioned Mr Weston, with his malty mug, and more than forty others.

But, foolishly, he did not take the pin-ups from his newly created pool of commercial ambassadors – Anya Hindmarch, who makes a living selling handbags to my daughter, and Tamara Mellon.

The *Daily Mail* printed a picture of the latter naked last week, and pointed out her dad was once linked to Diana Dors and she used to dabble with drugs. This may or may not be true but, either way, it's irrelevant. What is relevant is that she started the successful Jimmy Choo shoe business and is, how can I put this, easy on the eye.

Johnny Chinaman may not care much for Mr Cameron – especially when he was probably expecting Winston Churchill – but I can assure you he would have listened to what Ms Mellon had to say. And Ms Hindmarch, who has beautiful eyes.

There was some debate last week about the television programme *Countryfile*. It seems that when the show moved to a primetime slot, four presenters were relieved of their duties because, it is claimed, they weren't pretty enough.

This, from their point of view, is very sad and I hope they

do well in their new careers. On the radio. But the fact is this: most people prefer to be spoken to by someone who is attractive, and so, given the choice of two equally qualified TV presenters, it makes sense to employ Julia Bradbury. Especially on a chilly day.

And so it goes in the world of business. If an ugly man comes to my office trying to sell stapling machines, I will probably not listen to a word he says. But if the same company sends a pretty girl, I will probably buy half a million. Please, do not hold that against me. I can't help it. I was born with a scrotum and it messes with your head.

Of course, I'm not suggesting Mr Cameron should have gone to China with a selection of girls from the pages of *Razzle*, but I do think that when British business is being sold on the world stage, it is important we hold our hosts' attention.

President Nicolas Sarkozy can rock up with his lovely and clever wife, Carla Bruni, who can help keep everyone awake when the speeches have gone on a bit, and Silvio Berlusconi usually has a tribe of weathergirls in tow. This has been a problem for British prime ministers in the past. Without wishing to be mean, Audrey Callaghan was not exactly Michelle Obama. And Cherie Blair, by all accounts, could be awfully bossy. Samantha Cameron would appear to be the perfect combination, except that she's not really interested in going to China and selling Prince Charles's biscuits. Which is where Jordan comes in.

Jordan, or Katie Price, is best known for having massive breasts and too much make-up. But peel all that away and you are left with a surprisingly pretty girl who is extremely clever. She must be. She has amassed a small fortune by simply not getting into cars very carefully.

Then you have Victoria Beckham, who's bright enough to

have stayed famous by simply not eating very much. She'd be a tremendous trade envoy because she's sharp and pretty and can talk about football.

Britain, in fact, is awash with women who could sell the nation's biscuits. There's Alice Temperley, who is a dress designer; Helena Bonham Carter, who is an actress; and Jemima Khan, whom the papers call a 'socialite'. Sprinkle a bit of Helen Mirren into the mix, garnish with a generous portion of Konnie Huq, and you have a world-class sales team. Send that lot in to bat and the people of Poundbury would be in employment for a thousand years. I bet they could even flog Rolls-Royce jet engines to the Australians.

14 November 2010

Foraging – an old country word for violent death

Like many people, I enjoy settling down on a Sunday evening to watch *Countryfile*. It's so peaceful and right. No badger ever has tuberculosis. No one ever rips their face off on barbed wire. And all the presenters are so attractive. There are no old boilers messing up the lovely pastoral views, apart from John Craven, obviously. But mostly he's marooned back at base these days, flogging calendars with deer on them to old ladies. In last week's show, after they'd introduced us to the man who invented walking in Ireland and shown us a boat that went on a river, they presented an item on foraging.

It was great. Lots of extremely attractive middle-aged women went into the countryside with wicker baskets where they picked leaves and weeds and kelp. And then they all gathered in an agreeable barn to cook and eat what they'd found.

It looked fantastic. And it sounds idyllic, doesn't it, taking your family out on a crisp, frosty morning to forage for breakfast? Indeed, a few days earlier a group of Londoners had decided to descend on Hampstead Heath to pick wild mushrooms. Unfortunately, that expedition made it into the news because it infuriated local environmentalists.

Jeremy Wright, who does something green and worthy at a college in London, was quoted as saying he'd seen one person stuffing a hessian sack with fungi. And then said that if everyone picked wild mushrooms on the heath, there would be none left. Plainly, he would rather our mushrooms were flown into Tesco every morning from Israel.

I had a similar problem recently while out picking samphire at my holiday cottage. Even though it was in my garden, a local eco-ist informed me sternly that I was killing tigers or bears or some such nonsense and that I must stop immediately. Which I did . . . n't.

Now, obviously, anything that enrages the green movement is a good and worthwhile thing, but before we all sally forth, it is important to make a couple of points on the mushroom front. Because we live in a police state, it is illegal under the Theft Act of 1968 to pick fungi for commercial gain. And later in the day you will almost certainly suffer an agonizing death. Either that, or you will suddenly find your toaster hysterically funny.

The problem is that there are thousands of varieties of mushroom – there are 340 on Hampstead Heath alone – and many are either hallucinogenic or fatal. The parents of Daniel Gabriel Fahrenheit went west after eating mushrooms they'd foraged. And he must have been mentally affected, too, otherwise why would he decide that the freezing point of water is 32 degrees? And the boiling point 212?

It is impossible here to tell you what danger signs to look out for. There are simply too many. But I can tell you when you'll be safe.

If the mushrooms are a pale, er, mushroom colour and come ready-cleaned in cellophane in a big shop with fluorescent lighting, all will be well.

On a foraging expedition, however, the message is simple: beware. So what else is there?

Well, on *Countryfile*, they were uprooting just about everything, as though the whole of England is one giant snack. But trust me on this – it really isn't.

According to the Safe Gardening website, you will die badly and in great pain if you eat the berries from Boston ivy,

English ivy, lantana, Virginia creeper, yew, privet, the castor oil plant, mistletoe, holly and – weird one this – potatoes.

Now, I know what a potato looks like, but all the others? Haven't a clue. Only today, I was out walking with my dogs when I encountered a bush laden down with what I thought were sloes. And since I'm partial to a pint or two of fruit-infused gin before bed, I thought I'd pick some. But were they sloes? Or were they berries from deadly night-shade, which, apparently, are the same colour? I shan't know until I'm hunched over the lavatory one night, vomiting my own spleen out of my nose.

What about apples, then? Well, in the olden days, foraging for these used to be called 'scrumping' and would earn you, at worst, a clip round the ear from the local bobby. In my garden, though, it's called 'theft' and the lead poisoning you will receive from my Beretta will do you no good at all. The same goes for my crab apples and raspberries.

So. Not mushrooms, then, and not fruit. Which leaves us with what? Well, according to our man on *Countryfile*, you can pick pennywort, which he says is great in salad. Do you know what pennywort looks like? Nope? Me neither. And the same goes for sorrel and all the other things he plunged into his basket. So far as I'm concerned, it's all just wide grass.

There's another problem with foraging.

A problem that became blindingly obvious on *Countryfile* when the yummy mummies served up all the food they'd picked and cooked. The assembled throng did their best to look like they were dining on peach and peacock but it is impossible, even if you are Robert De Niro, to pretend that something tastes delicious when, in fact, it's a nettle gar-nished with seaweed.

Oh, they made all the right noises about nature's larder and the bountiful green and pleasant land but each time they spooned what they'd found into their mouth, they really did look like a bunch of bulldogs chewing on wasps.

So, there we are. While foraging may appeal to the thrifty, nature lovers and people who just want to enjoy the simple things in life, you must know before you set off with your trug and your rosy-faced children that, at worst, you will not survive the day and, at best, what you come home with will taste absolutely disgusting.

Happily, though, there is a way round this. It's called Waitrose.

28 November 2010

WikiLeaks – I dare you to face Roger Sensible

Guests who stay in our spare room imagine that having climbed a rickety back staircase in an adjoining barn, they are far away from the main bedrooms. But they are not. They are right next to where I sleep and I can hear every word they say.

This often makes for a frosty mood around the breakfast table the next morning. They sit there, not understanding why I am slamming their coffee cups down and telling them that if they think my culinary endeavours are so terrible, they can bloody well cook their own bacon and eggs.

Over the years, I've heard every conceivable complaint. My fireplace is hideous. My dog has a crotch fixation. And how I must surely be making enough money to provide a bit of central heating. It's jolly hurtful. But I can usually fight back by advising them that they'll never have children if they continue to make love like they did the night before.

Can you even begin to imagine how many friends you'd have left if they had been able to eavesdrop on your post-mortem analysis of their parties? Precisely. The world cannot function without secrets. And that's why I'm so disappointed by this WikiLeaks nonsense.

It is important that America's embassies around the world can provide candid reports to the power brokers back home about the sex life of French ministers, the temper of Gordon Brown and exactly what sort of parties Silvio Berlusconi is hosting. But if the sender knows his reports will be read by the person he is writing about, his observations will be next to useless. Obama Barack would be sailing along, imagining

Vladimir Putin is kind to animals and that George Osborne has a deep and booming voice with much gravitas and depth.

It goes deeper, too, because if everyone thought everything they said would be broadcast to the entire world, no one would say anything at all. It's hard to be a trade envoy to the Middle East if all you can do is smile and nod.

Silence can work in certain diplomatic situations – when a couple split up, for instance, it's always tempting to say, 'I never liked her anyway. She was a witch and her bottom was massive,' but prudence requires that you pull benign faces and mumble platitudes because you know there's always a chance that two weeks later they'll be back together again.

However, when you are the British prime minister and you are asked by the American ambassador for your government's stance on Pakistan, mumbling just won't work. He needs to know the truth. And you need to tell him. And you need to be able to do so, safe in the knowledge that the Pakistanis will not find out what you said.

Those who believe that everyone has a right to know everything say that cables from US embassies around the world should be reproduced on the internet. Well, if that's true, why does the founder of WikiLeaks not simply post his location on Google Earth? If he thinks we should know everything about everybody, why – at the time of writing – is he in hiding?

Apparently, it's hard to see what law has been broken. The Americans are saying that if there is a loophole, then they must work fast to close it. But this is fraught with difficulty because you are rummaging around in the foundations of a democracy. Pretty soon, newspapers would be unable to run stories about footballers who've been sending inappropriate pictures of themselves to two-year-olds.

You need to be careful that by shutting the door on disgruntled government employees whose stupidity could cause all sorts of international incidents, you are not also shutting the door on a journalist's remit to get to the truth. Which is why, once again, we must visit my idea for an all-powerful Ministry of Common Sense.

It was first mooted many years ago when a chap called Peter Wright planned to write a book about his time in MI5. There was much debate at the time about whether this should be allowed and, legally, both sides seemed to have a point. So, I decided what we needed was not an expensive recourse to law but to a government-appointed bloke in a jumper who would realize that, morally, it made no sense to publish the book and put a stop to it.

Since then, there have been many occasions when councils and health and safety zealots have acted within the framework of the law but outside the parameters of common sense. Again, victims should have been able to appeal to the minister. I like to think he'd be called Roger. In my experience, people called Roger are usually quite level-headed.

Roger's job, then, would be to sit in an office, listening to both sides of an argument before deciding what would be best. This week, for instance, he'd be asked whether Ann Widdecombe should be allowed to stay in the dancing programme. Some would say it's her right and that, obviously, the sort of people who can be arsed to vote wish her to remain in place. Others would say she's ruining the competition for people who can do hopping with one leg over their shoulder. And he'd decide that she should go.

Then he'd have to deal with Ray Wilkins, the Chelsea assistant manager sacked by Roman Abramovich last month. 'Yes, of course you should have your job back.' And then he could turn his attention to the students who are keeping warm on these chilly days by kicking police cars. And then you'd pop in to say you'd been caught doing 33mph, in the middle of the night, when no one was around, and he'd let you off.

In my life, I've been to court twice, and on both occasions I've been on the moral high ground. But, technically, I've been wrong and have lost as a result. This is why we need a minister of common sense. Because immediately he'd get to the bottom of this WikiWee business. What it is doing is in the public interest and probably legal. But what it is doing is also wrong.

5 December 2010

Stop all the clocks for British No Time

Earlier this year, various people – including David Cameron – started to wonder out loud if it would be a good idea to stick with British Summer Time all year round. It seems a fairly harmless suggestion but it met with considerable hostility.

Those who rise early say that, in fact, we would be much better off sticking with Greenwich Mean Time all year round.

And then you have those who say that we should have British Summer Time in the winter and then double British Summer Time in the summer. This is what happened during the war.

But this argument seems to find little favour with Europhobes. 'No. We can't have the clocks going even further forward than they do now because then we'd be in the same time zone as the Hun and the bally Frogs.'

You even have Cornish people saying that, under the present system, they have midday when it's still only 10.30 in the morning. And that any change would cause noon to fall between their bacon and their eggs. And in Scotland, of course, where it's permanent daylight in the summer and constantly dark in the winter, it makes more sense to dispense with time altogether and become a hedgehog.

Naturally, road-safety organizations are particularly vocal on the issue. They say that year-round lighter evenings would make it safer for 'kiddies' coming home from school – and this is probably true. But on the downside, it would surely increase the number killed while fumbling their way to lessons in the pitch-black mornings.

I know this probably hasn't occurred to the Royal Society for the Prevention of Accidents – an organization that endeavours to prevent an incident that, by its very nature, cannot be foreseen – but if I've got to be hit by a bus, I don't really care whether it's in the morning or the afternoon. I do, however, care about the question of time. My life has become so hectic in recent years that I did not even have time yesterday to go to the lavatory. And the day before, I was so busy I missed the office party.

I'm sitting here now with a dull ache in my groin. This has nothing to do with the picture I've just seen of Gwyneth Paltrow in her amazing new dress. It's been throbbing for weeks. I suspect it's a hernia. But I do not know for sure because I have not had a moment even to telephone the doctor for an appointment.

I suspect I'm not alone, either. I bet thousands of people die every year because they simply didn't have the time to get better.

We're all in the same boat. It used to be easy to meet friends for a drink or dinner. Not any more. Now, they are always chained to their laptops or stuck in a meeting. And woe betide the man who suggests 'one for the road' at the end of the evening. Because everyone has to be up at five to fly to New York.

Never mind British Summer Time. Hosts now need flexible British Party Time to accommodate those who are popping in after work because they need to be up early and those who have been in the office till gone midnight. You are just finishing serving one lot with coffee and mints when the next batch arrive and want a prawn cocktail. This means you can go next door and get jet lag.

I don't understand why this is happening. I have exactly the same job now that I had five years ago. All my friends have exactly the same jobs, too. And, thanks to electronic communication, those jobs should be easier. Even allowing for the fact that we must set aside two hours of the day to root about in a cupboard, trying to read the serial number of the Wi-Fi router so it can be fixed by a man in Mumbai, we can still deal with stuff far faster than we could in the days of ink and stamps.

There's more. In the past, we needed to go into a town and park if we wanted to do some Christmas shopping. Now, we can do it all online. Cooking? No need. I just move the mouse around a bit and in a matter of moments a motorcycling Pole is at my door with a steaming pile of pad thai.

In my kitchen there is a tap that delivers boiling water from what feels like the centre of the earth, so that I don't have to stand around waiting for a kettle to boil. Coffee comes instantly from the wall. The air is conditioned so I don't need to step outside for a breather.

All of these things should mean I now have several free hours in the day to ruminate on John Prescott and write thank-you letters and do stuff with the kids. And yet. My son broke up from school six days ago and I have not seen him once. Not even fleetingly. Because I'm so busy, I'm getting up just as he's thinking about maybe going to bed.

My mother says often that I should slow down. I bet yours does, too. But this is not possible. If I had chosen to spend the past few hours making daisy chains, this column would not have been written. Which would have made me very sacked. This, therefore, is the problem we need to be addressing. Instead of listening to a few racist Corns and Jock McSheep-Fan, we need a whole new strategy.

At present, it's a nuisance changing all the clocks in your house twice a year, so here's what I propose. For eleven months of the year, we have British Work Time, when we do our jobs and mend our routers and have heart attacks.

And then, every August, we have British No Time, when the speaking clock is turned off and Big Ben is covered with a tarpaulin. You get up when you feel like it, sit in the garden until it's too chilly and go to bed when you are tired. They have a similar system in France. It's one of the reasons they all live to be 147.

There's another, too. They understand that time is useful only if you're doing something useful with it.

19 December 2010

The small society built on jam and dung

Poor old David Cameron seems to be struggling to explain what he means by the 'big society'.

And I'm not surprised because, in the five seconds allocated to politicians on the evening news, it's difficult to outline a seismic shift in the way we all think and behave and live.

To most people, the big society means that if you cut your leg off in some farm machinery, instead of expecting to be saved by a government-funded ambulance driver, you should sew it back on yourself. Many find this idea unappealing.

What's more, Margaret Thatcher once said there was no such thing as society. So now the Conservative party is telling us it wants a big version of something it used not to believe existed at all. Which means that, all of a sudden, the atheist wants to build a cathedral.

To try to get a handle on the subject, I took the trouble of reading a big society speech Mr Cameron made last week and I'm afraid I'm none the wiser. He seems to be saying that we have to expect less from the government – which is what Mrs Thatcher said – and that if we are not happy with our local school we should simply get together with our neighbours and build a new one. Which is broadly what everyone on the corner of Haight and Ashbury was saying in 1967.

I'm not sure I'd know how to go about building a school. And I'm not sure my neighbours would be much help, either, because last week one of them died. And the other one's a bit busy because he's the prime minister. So, all on my own, I'd need to find some teachers and make sure they weren't kiddie fiddlers, which is likely to be more complicated in future. And then I'd need loads of bricks and cement. I think it would be easier – and cheaper, frankly – to hoick my kids out of the school I didn't like and send them to Eton.

The trouble is, however, I like the smell of Mr Cameron's idea. I don't understand the details and I don't like anything with the word 'big' in it – it sounds like a promotion at a sofa shop. But I can catch a whiff of what he's on about and, in short, it's this: 'Ask not what your country can do for you but what you can do for yourselves.' And that brings me on to the Oxfordshire town where both Mr Cameron and I live, Chipping Norton.

In 1932 the people of this hilly outpost got together and bought themselves a fire engine. And then, after the war, they sold it to the newly established, government-run fire brigade. The money raised from the sale was used to pay for a football pitch, a cricket field and some tennis courts.

Plainly, this sense of independence was still going strong in 1963 when the townspeople came together once more to raise money for a swimming pool. This lido was subsequently built, and eventually the cost of running it was taken over by the West Oxfordshire district council.

However, in 2002, the council announced that it could no longer afford to run a heated outdoor pool, especially as it had just opened a new leisure centre, and that, as a result, it would be closed down. Nothing unusual in that. The *Jeremy Vine Show* is rammed with people saying they now have to swim in puddles and skips. Swimming pools are closing faster than pubs.

However, in the fine town of Chipping Norton a handful of locals decided that instead of ringing the *Jeremy Vine Show* and moaning, they'd form an action committee to keep the pool open.

And pretty soon this committee decided to hold a fund-raising auction.

I remember it well. The old town hall was stuffed to the gunwales with people who'd donated prizes. There were hundreds of them. I know because I was the auctioneer and it went on for hours. 'A jar of home-made jam, sold to you, sir, at the back. Two bags of dung. Who'll give me a tenner?'

It was a fantastic evening.

There was lots of hub and tons of bub, and at the back there were shifty-looking people from the council thinking, 'Oh no, we're going to lose our seats,' and that spurred us on.

It was like a scene from an Enid Blyton book. The butcher bid. The baker bid. The candlestick maker bid.

My daughter, who was only seven at the time, couldn't quite understand why we were there. 'Why do we need to save the town's pool?' she said. 'We have our own.' But even this budding Thatcher soon got into the swing of things and helped her dad by bidding for things that wouldn't sell. We went home with a puncture repair kit and six signed copies of my own book.

From memory, the evening raised £12,000, which was — with a bit of help from the town council — enough to keep the pool open for a year. So, twelve months later, we were back to do it again. And we've been back every year since.

The result? Well, the pool is still open, providing local people with a nice place to go on a summer's day. But, more than that, the fundraising evening means the man from the pub who donates a free dinner with wine gets to meet the man from the bookshop, and the woman from the florist gets to meet the kids from the local school band. When I pop into the town now to buy a packet of fags, the people I see are no longer strangers, and that makes it a happier place to live.

I intensely dislike the word 'community' because it is constantly misused in news reporting. What is the Muslim
community? The very idea that every single Muslim in the
country has exactly the same opinion about everything makes
me feel queasy.

There's no such thing as the Chipping Norton community,
either. It's a town full of different people who think differently about many things. But now, thanks to the swimming
pool and the fundraising efforts needed to keep it open, there
is a community spirit.

It's not a big society. It's better than that. It's a small society, and I urge you all to give it a bash where you live.

20 February 2011

Proud to sponsor this police shootout

While appearing on television recently, I questioned the wisdom of car companies sponsoring football teams. Because while those hideous Audi-branded seats at Old Trafford do much to endear the German motor manufacturer to Manchester United's million-strong army of fans, they have the reverse effect on the billion or so people who support a different team.

Audi is therefore paying hard-earned cash to ensure that my son will never ever buy one of its products. He couldn't bear the thought that some of his money would be going to Sir Alex Ferguson, who he thinks might actually be the devil.

Sponsoring a football team is a bit like sponsoring a religion: 'Tesco. Proud to be the official supplier of fine foods to Britain's synagogues.' You can see that there would be problems with this. It'd be like Apple sponsoring abortion clinics in the Bible Belt. Or a man I know who once tried to get his company, a well-known cigarette brand, to sponsor public executions in West Africa.

If I were running a large company and I wanted to put its name in front of millions of people, I'd sponsor a hospital. Because there are only two possible outcomes for those who pass through the portals. They either die, in which case nothing is lost, or they are repaired, in which case they will be forever in your debt.

On the face of it, sponsored vets look like a good idea, too. If they perform a successful operation on your dog, they could shave Audi's logo into its fur and few would complain.

Especially as the sponsorship deal would make the operation less expensive.

But I see a downside to this. If the vet who fired a bolt gun into the back of my donkey's head had been wearing a Sony jacket, I'd have emerged from the experience feeling less well disposed to the idea of buying a Vaio laptop any time soon.

You might imagine that it's a good idea to sponsor a television programme since it's safe to assume that everyone watching is doing so on purpose and will like what they see. But today, with Sky+ and online availability, most people will zoom through your carefully constructed messages. Or if they are watching live, they will dislike you for wasting their time. Certainly, I made a solemn vow in series three of 24 never to buy a Nissan. I had tuned in to see Jack Bauer shooting swarthy-looking men in the knee, not some dizzy bint driving about the place in an off-road car.

Sponsorship, then, is a tricky business. You need to ensure that many people will see your company's name, that all of them are happy with the positioning you've chosen and that no one's donkey is killed. Which brings me on to proposals to sponsor the police.

This isn't a joke. The Hertfordshire force now has so many faith advisers on its chaplaincy team – including humanists – that it is extremely short of money. And, as a result, a senior officer has written to local businesses asking them to sponsor ten vehicles used by special constables.

In return for cash, the businesses would get their name on the cars, which, says the letter, will provide the 'benefit of being associated with the constabulary brand'. Did you know the constabulary was a 'brand'? Me neither. I thought it was just a lot of people in plastic shoes pretending to be Nigel Mansell. However, despite the upbeat nature of the letter, I'm not sure it's a good idea to let Currys or DFS or Asda sponsor the police force. Or service. Or whatever silly name the government halfwits have dreamt up now.

First, and this is a serious point, if a policeman in, say, a PC World jacket turned up in a car with PC World written down the side to investigate some wrongdoings at the company's headquarters, many people, myself included, would assume he would emerge after a short while to say that everything was in order. In other words, there'd be a perception that fat cat bosses, as we must call them these days, are simply buying immunity from prosecution.

There are other problems, though. A lot of people do not much care for the police. Some of these people are burglars and robbers, and a company might decide it's not too bothered about alienating them by visibly supporting the force. But what about when the police run radar traps and fine you for driving a bit too fast? Certainly, if I were to be apprehended by a sergeant in a Burger King hat, I'd ensure that from that moment on I never ate another Whopper.

My biggest problem with this sponsorship idea, though, is dignity. There was a time when British policemen looked good with their tall hats and shiny buttons. Today, they either look like everyone else with their silly high-visibility jackets or they look like cartoon characters from shoot-'em-up video games with their black overalls and their sub-machine guns.

Neither outfit lends itself to sponsorship logos. I mean, seriously, can you imagine how the world would react should there be a televised gunfight in the middle of Hitchin and all the goodies were running about in jackets promoting a local garden centre? We'd be a laughing stock and rightly so.

Plus, one of the less savoury jobs performed by officers is informing families that someone dear to them has been killed in some awful way. I don't think they'd be able to achieve the right level of gravitas if they were dressed up as the Michelin man.

We know that, as a rule, the government is completely useless at running anything and that Richard Branson and Sir Sugar will always do a better job. If I were in No. 10, I'd hand over pretty much everything to the private sector – starting with the forests – but even I would be forced to conclude that some aspects of government work must be run by public servants using public money. The armed forces are one of these things. GCHQ is another. And so are police.

Besides. I pay half what I earn in tax.

And it's nice to think I'm getting at least something in return.

27 February 2011

Hello, reception. I've actually used my bed, please don't be angry

For the past few weeks I've been travelling the world, and once again I'm filled with a sense that no one knows how to run a hotel properly. For example, when you are staying at the top of a thirty-storey skyscraper, four lifts are not enough. Because at eight in the morning, when everyone is going downstairs for breakfast, you can be waiting until lunchtime for a car to arrive.

And it's even worse when you get back at night and you are busting for a pee and one of your colleagues, who's staying on the fourth floor, decides it would be amusing to press all the buttons as he gets out.

Mind you, the vertical nature of a hotel is nothing compared with those that are laid out horizontally. Because it can often take several days to get from the reception area to your room, where inevitably your electronic key card does not work so you must go back to the front desk and start all over again.

At some hotels these days it's best to book another room on the way to the actual suite you've been given so that you can store basic emergency supplies: pants, soap and some high-energy chocolate bars.

Then we have the problems of learning how your room works. I realize, of course, that many hotels send a porter to explain everything when you arrive but you never listen because you are too busy rummaging surreptitiously through your wallet to find a suitable tip, and then doing mental exchange-rate maths to work out whether you are about to give him £2,000. Or, worse, 2p.

The upshot is that, later on, when you want to turn out the lights, you have absolutely no clue how this might be achieved. And when you finally manage it, by hitting the light fittings with your shoe, you realize the air-con is still on and you must find the control panel in the dark.

Then you wake up at two a.m. with jet lag and decide to watch television. Well, in every single modern hotel this is not possible because the remote-control device has 112 buttons, all of which are the size of a match head, and you can't locate the switch to turn the light back on to find your glasses.

So you stab away at what looks promising and all you get are messages from the Japanese engineer who designed the set to the man whose job it is to install it. Why can't hotel managers understand that almost all of their guests need just three things: a button for volume, a button for news and a button for porn? I don't want to adjust the contrast or the aspect ratio. I just want to find out what's going on in Japan and see some ladies.

Oh, and when I'm taking a shower, I am not wearing my spectacles, which means I cannot read the labels on all the little bottles in there. I'm therefore fed up with washing my hair with body lotion.

The worst aspect of staying in a hotel, though, is trying to do your laundry. It shouldn't be that difficult. You just bung it all in a bag and give it to someone at the reception desk.

But no. There's always a form on which you must say precisely what you are handing over. The form lists every possible item of clothing that anyone anywhere might want cleaning. Ball gowns. Scuba suits. Fencing masks. Ruffs. Doublet and hose. Army uniforms. G-trousers. All of this is intended to demonstrate what a wide and interesting clientele comes to the hotel but it's a bit annoying when all you want is some clean underwear.

You search and you scan for the right box to tick but it's never there because, in hotel management-speak, 'knickers' is a rude word. Eventually, between ostrich feather hat and quilted smoking jacket, you find the word 'pants'. But this, you then realize, means 'trousers'.

So the search begins again until eventually you work out that, in business land, shreddies are known as undershorts. With a sense of triumph you fill in the box called 'guest count', saying you have eight pairs you'd like to be cleaned – but wait, what's this? It's another column called 'hotel count'. In other words, it's a form in which you give the hotel your opinion on how many pairs of dirty pants you have and then it is given the opportunity to disagree.

This says it all. In essence, the hotel guest these days is nothing more than a robber and a cheat. A person who has checked in to drink the gin and fill the empties with water, claim for underwear they don't own and check out without paying. At best, we are a nuisance.

Certainly, I felt that way while staying at the Palazzo Versace hotel on Australia's Gold Coast. This is the place where contestants from ITV's *I'm Not a Celebrity* come to vomit up the bugs they've eaten while living in 'the jungle'. And I can see why. It is very Peter Andre. Here, I was not made to feel like a thief but I was made to feel very ugly. The corridors were full of pictures of beautiful, famous people in varying degrees of undress. None had a pot belly and a suitcase full of dirty shreddies. Downstairs there was a salon offering 'eye couture', and in the room a booklet 'suggests' what guests might like to wear at any given time of day. Jeans and a T-shirt didn't get a mention.

It's also very clean. And to keep it that way, guests are constantly made to lift up their feet so that a tribe of former boat people can mop up bits of imaginary food that have been dropped on the floor. Then, at night, an army of yet more cleaners patrol the open spaces with factories on their backs, fumigating and vacuuming and desperately trying to rid the building of any evidence that it might have people in it.

But the best bit came one morning when the manageress came over to our table to announce that she'd reviewed the film from the previous day's CCTV cameras and had noticed two of our party playing the piano in the reception area. It's hard to think what else one might do with a piano but she was most insistent. It mustn't happen again. Behind her, I couldn't help noticing, there were two fully-grown men snogging.

27 March 2011

This kingdom needs a dose of Norse sense

Every so often an organization with a bit too much time on its hands does a survey and concludes that Norway is the best country in the world. We're told that no one has ever been murdered, the cod is superb and there are many dew-fresh meadows full of extremely tall blonde girls who have nothing to do all day except knit exciting underwear.

Economically, we're told, they are also better off. Thanks to all the oil, Norway is the second-wealthiest and most stable country in the world and has the second-highest GDP per capita, after the statistical anomaly that is Luxembourg.

And, of course, we mock. We explain that it's all very well living in a crime-free gated community where everyone seems to be out of a commercial for Ski yoghurt, but unless you occasionally step on a discarded hypodermic needle and catch AIDS, you aren't really living life to the full.

If none of your buses is full of sick, you become one-dimensional and boring. This is why so many Norwegians commit suicide. It's also why, in all of human history, Norway has produced only a handful of people who've made it big on the international stage. One painted a figure screaming. One walked to the South Pole. And the other made a name for himself by suggesting that the sun only shines on TV. Which suggests that he only ever watches *Teletubbies*.

And that, it seems, is what Norway's all about. Designed by Playmobil and run along the lines of Camberwick Green, it's the set for a children's television show, with lots of rosy cheeks and a *Midsomer Murders* attitude to immigration.

Lovely, but so far as the rest of the world's concerned, there's not much of a there, there.

Well, for reasons that are not entirely clear, I've been to Norway quite a lot just recently and I'm sorry, but I can't quite see what's wrong with it. I suppose the speed limits are a bit low, and the only way you can enjoy a cigarette and a glass of wine at the same time is to buy a house. Also, it's a bit chilly, but that just gives you an excuse to put on an excellent Kirk Douglas *Heroes of Telemark* jumper and some splendid woolly mittens.

Let me give you one small example of why I like it there. When a British person asks for my autograph, the request always comes with a back-handed compliment: 'I dislike your programme very much and I hate you on a cellular level but my son is a fan, so sign this or I'll ring the *Daily Mail* and explain that you ruined a small boy's life.'

Russians explain that if you don't stand still until they've gone back to their hotel room for a camera, they will kill you. Aussies slap you on the back a bit too hard and Americans get massively carried away. But in Norway, you get a 'please' and an 'if it's not too much trouble' and a 'thank you'. One man became so excited that I'd posed for his picture, he took out his penis and began to masturbate. I've never experienced gratitude like that anywhere.

Then there's the spirit of *janteloven*. It's a tall-poppy thing that dictates you really mustn't be a show-off, no matter how much money you have. Delightfully, there's no such thing as Cheshire in Norway. It's why 19 per cent of Norwegians who win the country's lottery buy a Toyota. Only one has ever bought a Porsche.

Politically, Norway is sort of communism-lite. Thirty per cent of the population are employed by the state, 22 per cent are on welfare, 13 per cent are too disabled to work and, as parents are given twelve months' combined paid leave when they have a baby, the rest of the population is at home changing nappies. This is probably why there is absolutely nothing in your house bearing the mark 'Made in Norway'.

Interestingly, and contrary to what you'd expect, there is crime. An American was pickpocketed in 2008. And there are beggars. Mostly, though, they are from Romania and that does raise a question: why Norway? Why leave the warmth of your homeland and settle in a country where a glass of beer is £40 and if you sleep on the streets, you wake up with your face stuck to the pavement?

Well, I asked, and the answer was surprising: 'Because in Norway when you ask someone for money, they give it to you.'

Can you see anything wrong with any of this? Kind hearted souls in excellent jumpers giving away their money to those less fortunate than themselves. No Premier League footballers bombing about in Ferraris. No bankers smoking cigars the size of giant redwoods. No grime. No graffiti. And a range of first-class shops that aren't full of anarchists weeing on the Axminster.

And now we must ask ourselves: how could we achieve such a level of harmony here? We are northern European, just like the Nors. We like a drink, just like they do, and we like to have a fight afterwards. Which they do as well. I'm tall and have blue eyes so, probably, my great-great-grandad was a Viking. Just like yours. So why is Britain such a mess when Norway is the living embodiment of civilization?

Some might say that Norway excels because almost no one there goes to church. They are the least religious people on earth. But we aren't a nation of Bible-bashers, either. So it must be something else. Others say it's the oil. But Norway has had one of the highest standards of living since the seventeenth century. So that's not it either.

No, I reckon the reason Norway is so nice is that the population is tiny. And countries with a small number of people in them – Iceland, Estonia and, er, the Vatican – work better than those that are filled to the gunwales.

I'm afraid, then, the only way of getting the UK to match the Scandinavian model is to abolish the UK. Norway separated from Sweden in 1905, and we should follow suit by severing the knots that bind together the wildly disparate bits of Britain. In short, I think the sovereign state of Chipping Norton would work rather well.

3 April 2011

Big smile – and check me down below for ticks

I wonder. Have we lost the ability in this country to rejoice in the good fortune of others? To be happy for someone else? Buy a big house and 'it's all right for some'. Have the big house taken away and 'it serves you right'.

Let us take the case of Kate Middleton's mum. Her daughter is marrying a prince and so we should be happy for her. But we keep being told that she's a social mountaineer who has been engineering this marriage since the days when Kate was a foetus. And that she used to be an air hostess. A bloody trolley dolly. Pushy cow.

We saw the same sort of thing when Judith Keppel became the first person to scoop the big prize on *Who Wants to Be a Millionaire?* Because she lived in Fulham and said 'bath' properly, we were invited to despise her on a cellular level. Lucky cow.

And woe betide the celebrity who dares to take a stroll on the beach while on holiday. Look at her! She may have fame, success, money and a pretty face but her swimsuit is disgusting and she has cellulite and we hope that very soon she catches cancer and dies a screaming, agonizing death.

Have you ever looked at the comments left by readers on a newspaper's website? They're just a torrent of bile and vitriol. Protected by the anonymity of the internet and freed from the social niceties of physical contact, people go berserk. Lottery winners are particularly vulnerable, it seems. And Nigella Lawson? Fat cow.

No one can earn more than the prime minister, no one can

be better looking than Ena Sharples, and good luck to anyone who dares to appear on the television talking like Brian Sewell. Did your parents go to university? Well, you've had all the chances that life can afford, so you can clear off.

This unwillingness to be happy for others is now so acute that we don't even seem to be able to be happy for ourselves. I realize, of course, that people in Birmingham have suffered from this for centuries. Joy is not a Brummie thing. Everything, even if you've made it yourself, is rubbish. There is no word in the West Midlands for 'wow'.

Now we're all in the same boat, a point that was proved exquisitely on the BBC local news programme that was transmitted in my area on Tuesday evening. It had been an absolutely beautiful day: cloudless, warm and awash with the scent of blossom. The sort of day that made you glad to be alive.

In the olden days, a local news programme would have shown us spring lambs frolicking about on their rickety legs and small children dribbling ice cream in the park. Not any more. Now you could see the news team desperately trying to persuade the water company that the good weather would mean a hosepipe ban very soon. And then when that failed, calling the local hospital to see if anyone had been admitted suffering from sunstroke. 'Well, what about a malignant melanoma, then?'

Doubtless they will have scanned the *Daily Mail* to see if there is a link between warm spring sunshine and the arrival of more immigrants, or a catastrophic fall in house prices. And then the *Guardian* to see if it was yet more conclusive proof of global warming and that soon we would all perish in terrible heathland fires.

The news editor must have been tearing his hair out: 'We can't tell people that it's been a lovely warm spring day. There must be some danger. Some terror. Some death. Get me some misery.' And boy, oh boy, did one of the reporters come up trumps.

We were told that the warm weather may appear to be lovely but that there is a hidden menace out there: the tick. A perfectly healthy-looking woman was brought in front of the cameras to explain that she had been bitten by a tick two years ago and her life had been ruined as a result. Then a professor was wheeled out to say that the long warm spell followed by a late Easter would cause many more people to be out and about in the countryside and that we were facing a . . . please say 'perfect storm'. She didn't. She said it was a 'high-risk situation'.

It turns out that we've just had a Tick Bite Prevention Week – I'm surprised you missed it – during which people were advised what to do if they discover they are being bitten by a tick. First, you must not under any circumstances try to remove it, as this may cause part of the mouth to remain in your skin, spreading Lyme disease. Nor must you swat it with a rolled-up newspaper, as this may cause the arachnid to vomit into the bite wound.

There is, it seems, only one safe way to remove a tick that's in the process of gorging on your blood, and that's with a specialized tick removal tool. If you are one of the few people not to have such a thing handy when disaster strikes, a small pair of tweezers can be employed, if you know what you're doing. Which, let's be honest, you don't.

The best solution, however, is not to get bitten in the first place. Experts suggest wearing light-coloured clothing and recommend that, after you've showered in insect repellent, you tuck your trousers into your socks.

And here's the best bit. After you've been for a walk, you should thoroughly examine your entire body and get someone else to 'inspect the areas that are hard to see'. I am not making this up. These mongers of doom are suggesting that after you've been for a stroll in the wood, you should get naked and insist that your wife has a good ferret around in your undercarriage for evidence of tick infestation.

See what I mean? It's a lovely day. You fancy a nice walk. But there's misery out there not just for you but also for your nearest and dearest, who must spend the rest of the day snouting around in your dingleberries.

Still, in the spirit of what Britain has become, I'd like to finish off by saying this: last year, about 60 million people did not contract Lyme disease from a tick bite, whereas 3,000 came a cropper. And that, of course, serves them right for being ramblers.

24 April 2011

Cancel the breast op and buy an iron lung

The National Trust announced last week that the public will soon be allowed to look round the Oxfordshire house of William Morris. It will, says the Trust, be a marvellous trip down Memory Lane, since none of the contents has been touched since the motor industry magnate's death in 1963.

It will also be a trip into the soul of a truly great man. Because although Morris was Britain's richest self-made man, visitors will note that the carpets in his bedroom were offcuts from his factory in Cowley.

Closer examination of the wardrobe will reveal a collection of Phillips Stick-a-Soles, suggesting he liked to repair his shoes rather than buy a new pair.

Morris, then, did not spend much money on himself. But, my God, he lavished a fortune on others. He gave away more than £30 million of his fortune to worthy causes – that's equivalent to about £700 million today. He funded Nuffield College, Oxford, and during the polio epidemic of the 1940s and 1950s he paid for 5,000 iron lungs to be distributed around the Commonwealth.

My great-grandfather was similarly generous. While researching my family tree for the BBC's *Who Do You Think You Are?* TV programme I was amazed – and a bit distressed – to discover that he gave millions of pounds to the Methodist church. If you worship today in a chapel up north, be aware that the windows, pews and roof . . . well, to be blunt, they're mine.

Of course, a lot of people today ask what happened to the

spirit of philanthropy. There was even an editorial in Her Majesty's *Daily Telegraph* lamenting the fact that the attractive combination of personal prudence and public generosity seems to have gone out of fashion.

There's a very good reason for this, I think. It's because in the days of Morris and my great-grandad there really wasn't much you could actually buy. In the 1930s there were no Sunseeker yachts or Ferraris or time-share opportunities in Portugal.

We were told last week that Kate Middleton's brother is on course to make 'serious money' from his upmarket cake business. Upmarket cakes? There's another drain on the resources of today's rich. Another temptation that was not placed in the path of Morris.

He was able to buy all those iron lungs because his wife was not sitting at home thumbing through OK! magazine and wondering if she should have a new pair of Christian Louboutins because Amanda Holden's got some. Nor would he have been invited to spend £750 on a haircut.

When you make a few quid today you are inundated by a horde of oily Uriah Heeps who arrive in your inbox, genuflecting like seaweed and offering you a service that can provide a dozen black orchids at three in the morning anywhere in the world. Would my great-grandad have been so generous if he'd been tempted by the private-aircraft salesman from NetJets? And if Morris had been shown a watch with a button that summons International Rescue should he be in distress, would he, perhaps, have provided only 4,999 iron lungs?

The other day, at a swanky London restaurant, I ordered a pot of tea for four and the bill was £78. I have framed the receipt and it sits on my office desk as a constant reminder that the world has definitely gone mad.

Then there was a friend who said to me: 'I tried to buy

some cheese at Daylesford this morning. But I only had £162 on me.' Ridiculous? Perhaps. But at the Gloucestershire greengrocer it seems £162 barely gets you a beetroot.

Last week I needed a coffee table, so I went to a coffee table shop and discovered that prices started at £600. Of course, it's always been possible to spend a vast fortune on furniture but very few people actually did. Now, though, the coffee table shop is rammed full of women with £500 Nicky Clarke hair and £200 sunglasses spending four grand on a chair. To go in a room they don't use, in a house where they don't live.

There's no space for philanthropy in a world where the path of the righteous man is beset on all sides by the iniquities of the selfish and the tyranny of greedy men. Men who think: 'Yes, I could let that silly woman spend her money wisely but instead I'll get her to think that she ought to buy a coffee table for £600.'

In many ways I am one of those silly women. I recently bought a farm. I didn't need a farm and I don't know anything about farming, a point made very clear by the vast swathes of red ink in the accounts book. The only pleasure I get from it is walking through the big wood, thinking: 'This is my tree.' I really am a tragic, pitiable waste of blood and organs. And so are you if you've got an iPad. Or a whirlpool bath. Or anything you don't really need. Which is pretty much everything you own.

The problem is, of course, that we think everything is necessary. We've got it into our heads that the eggs from a chicken won't do and that they must come from a gull or a quail. We think people will laugh if our phone is a year old. We know that we need a holiday cottage. And we think the wanton excess is okay if we turn up at a charity fundraiser once a year and buy a signed rugby ball in the auction.

Look around your house this morning. Look at your coffee machine and your fridge with the ice-making machine in the door. How much pleasure do you get from these things, compared with the pleasure you would have got if you'd spent the money instead on an iron lung for someone else?

I know a man of fairly modest means who funds two schools in Africa and the Philippines. Then there's the footballer Didier Drogba, who, it seems, runs what's left of Ivory Coast's education department single-handedly. They are philanthropists, and I would suggest that ultimately their investment is going to make them a damn sight happier than the man who spent his cash on a new pair of breasts for his wife.

1 May 2011

A man's ego hangs in his downstairs loo

If you were to be awarded the Nobel prize in literature, you'd be very proud and, consequently, you'd want to hang the certificate somewhere prominent. But not so prominent that it looks like you're showing off. Not on the outside of your front door, for instance: that would be poor form.

People face a similar problem when they are photographed meeting Mrs Queen. They want everyone to know that this has happened, but hanging the picture in the hall? No. That's too soon. It's the same as saying: 'Do come in. Would you like a drink? Oh and did you know I once met Her Maj?'

There is only one room, in fact, where it is possible to place evidence of your accolades and achievements. And that's the downstairs lavatory. I was at a friend's house last weekend and you simply wouldn't know from anything about him, his family or the main rooms in his house, that he used to be pretty famous. But pay a visit to the bog and, holy cow: every word that's ever been written about him, every glowing review, every gong. They're all there, strutting their stuff in front of what, let's face it, is a captive audience.

He's not alone, either. There's a well-known British comedian – you know who you are – whose whole demeanour says, 'I'm just an ordinary bloke doing an ordinary job. Nothing to see here.' But go for a pee in his house and all of a sudden it's, 'I'm GQ's Man of the Year!'

Check this out. Next time you are at someone's house, excuse yourself from the dinner table, go into the hall, past the black-and-white pictures of the kids when they were blonde and lovely, turn left at the skiing montage and have a look in the bog. It'll be crammed with letters from Henry Kissinger and faded reviews from the *New Musical Express*. It's entirely possible you may even have to move a Bafta to close the door.

People may argue that they put all this stuff in the bog precisely because they don't want it to be seen by visitors. But if that's the case, why not put it in the attic, or the laundry cupboard? Or even your own bathroom? You know full well that at some point everyone who comes to your house will go for a pee. Which means you know full well they are going to learn that back in the Seventies, before you became an accountant, you were in a band that Julie Burchill quite liked.

I bet that this weekend hundreds of couples are sitting around their breakfast tables thinking: 'Where on earth do we put this picture of us going into Westminster Abbey for the royal wedding?' And all of them will come to the same conclusion: 'Let's take down the unfunny Victorian shooting cartoon from above the cistern and put this up instead.' They can convince themselves that no one will see it there while basking in the warm glow of satisfaction that, in fact, everyone will.

However, there's another issue here. I have a photograph of me being hugged by Cameron Diaz and, obviously, that goes behind the bog itself, because it's a picture I want men to see while standing there, with their old chap in their hand.

But if I'd been at the royal wedding? That's different. That would need to go on the wall facing the bog so it could be seen by girls while they were sitting down.

You in earnest conversation with Lord Carrington? Behind the bog. You sharing a joke with George Clooney? Facing wall. You out for dinner with Kate Moss? Hmmm. Top of the loo seat, probably.

Downstairs bogs are a portal to a man's ego. I know a man

whose khazi walls played host to a £5-million Degas. Where's
he going with that? What's he saying? Frankly, you don't need
to be a head doctor to work it out. He's saying: 'Oh, that old
thing.' Which is what people say when they turn up at your
house in a Rolls-Royce Silver Ghost.

People were speculating all last week about whether or
not Obama Barack should release the pictures of Osama bin
Laden's body, to prove to a sceptical world that he really is
dead.

I still can't quite believe we've arrived at a time when the
president of the United States goes on television to say the
world's biggest terrorist has been killed and we all think:
'Yeah, right.' But that's by the by.

It was eventually decided that the pictures could not be
released for fear they would be used as a rallying point for
the disaffected and the daft. So what will become of them?
Obviously Obama cannot place them on top of his piano or
on a worktop in the kitchen. Putting framed pictures of a
Muslim who's been shot in the face among the holiday snaps
would look a bit weird. But neither can he simply put them
in a drawer in his office. When he's old, he wants people to
say: 'Oh my God, were you in charge when they shot bin
Laden? Tell me more about how you succeeded where Bush
and Clinton failed, oh mighty one.' He wants them to be seen
by people, but only if the people in question think they were
not meant to be seen. It's definitely the bog, then.

Or is it? Because Obama – as we now know for sure – is
an American. And I'm not sure Americans are very concerned with the bothersome business of modesty. You can
rest assured that Margaret Thatcher has the *Sun*'s 'Gotcha!'
headline from the Falklands war hidden away in the smallest
room, whereas if she were an American it would be projected each night on to the front of her house.

You walk into a British doctor's surgery and you may well spot a small certificate on the far wall, behind some cupboards, saying that he's qualified. In America it'll be in a huge gilt frame on his desk.

I bet you any money, too, that nearly every Oscar ever awarded to an American lives in their sitting room, with its own spotlight. But where do you suppose Colin Firth put his? Next to the bog brush, I should imagine. Whereas the picture of him coming out of the lake? Facing wall. Definitely.

8 May 2011

We didn't have an affair – and that's all you need to be told

The press should not be free to screw up the lives of my children. That's why I'm pro-injunction.

It had been a fairly normal day. Woke up, rowed with the kids, spoke to my mother about yet another operation she needs, made breakfast for a ten-year-old Japanese girl who's come to stay. In the afternoon I faced up to the fact that *Top Gear* is being sued for libel and malicious falsehood, dealt with the fallout from recent tabloid allegations that I'd fed a pretty blonde some lettuce and at around midnight settled down to write some newspaper columns. Then my phone exploded.

Someone on Twitter had claimed that Jemima Khan had taken out a super-injunction to prevent intimate photographs of us being published. Jeremy and Jemima? Presumably the claimant has some kind of *Chitty Chitty Bang Bang* fixation.

Now if you are going to be romantically linked with anyone, then I'd rather it was Jemima Khan than, say, Huw Edwards. But, even though I hate doing this, I'm duty-bound to say that the claim is incorrect. Although I know Jemima quite well – my wife and I had been round for dinner with her the night before – we have never been alone together. There are no intimate photographs. The end.

Naturally, Jemima was very upset. Rather too upset, I thought. She tweeted to say she was 'in a bloody nightmare'. She found the very notion of being intimate with me 'upsetting'. After a while I began to think, 'All right, love. Steady on.' I know I'm a bit fat and my hair's pubic and I have teeth the colour of plywood. But there's no need to tell the world you're feeling sick at the mere thought of being intimate with me.

At work, it got worse. My producer said the idea was comical. At this stage I began to get quite upset. If we look at Jemima's previous loves – Imran Khan and Hugh Grant – I fit right in there.

Slap bang between the two. In my mind.

And in the mind of the *Daily Telegraph*, too, because the next day it ran big pictures of us on its front page, saying that we hadn't had a fling. Which is the same as saying, 'They bloody have, you know.'

The *Daily Star* went further. '*Top Gear* Jezza in sex pics fury' screamed the front-page headline. It then said in tiny letters that the allegations were 'false' and, in an editorial on page six, that 'it's all rubbish'.

You don't see an editorial, though, when you're walking past a newsagent. My kids simply saw a story saying that I was caught up in a sex-picture tangle. As their friends saw it too, they had a bad day.

So. Had I known about this story before midnight, would I have taken out an injunction to stop it appearing? To protect my children? Yes. In a heartbeat.

And that's a point everyone seems to be missing in the big debate about press freedom. Yes, we want a free press but we don't want a press that's free to wantonly screw up the lives of my children, or Jemima's, or yours.

I realize, of course, that injunctions, allied to Max Mosley's drive to make the papers reveal stories to victims in advance, will pretty much put the tabloid press out of business. They'd be reduced to printing pictures of a shark leaping out of the sea. Which is what the *Mirror* did on Tuesday.

Deciding which of these injunctions should be granted is

tricky. What's personal and what's not? When does a private life stop and a public image begin?

According to Charlotte Harris, a media lawyer: 'There has been a terrible mis-characterization of the people involved.' Apparently, 80 per cent of injunctions go to the victims of blackmail, harassment and stalkers and those who suffer threats to their families. Only a tiny minority are given to footballers who have been in bed with a teenager.

So it's all very well saying that all injunctions should be overturned now, but if they were, it would be a charter for lunatics and blackmailers to do and say pretty well whatever took their fancy. Moira Stuart likes to smash up wheelchairs. The editor of the *Daily Telegraph* is at the centre of a paedophile ring. Just so long as the newspaper says the victim denies the allegations, it's all legal.

If newspapers were a bit more fair-minded, if people thought their side of the argument would be heard, instead of relegated to page ninety-four, there would be no need for so many injunctions.

I am not a saint. And as I'm in the pay of the BBC – a publicly funded body – it might seem reasonable for newspapers to question some of my lifestyle choices. But they wouldn't question them. They'd demand that I be sacked. They'd say I'd sparked fury and work themselves into a frothing rage. That would alarm my family and that's why I try to keep my private life private. It's why I'm pro-injunction.

It is said only the rich and famous can afford a gagging order. But only the rich and famous ever need one. Others say that everything anyone at the BBC does should be published. What? Sophie Raworth's sexual fantasies? Pictures of Jeremy Paxman on the lavatory? Where do you draw the line?

I suppose we could start by drawing it just above the point where someone says on Twitter that Jeremy Clarkson and Jemima Khan have had an affair. And even though everyone knows it to be rubbish, it somehow becomes front-page news for two days.

15 May 2011

Garçon! A hike in my flat's value, please

I've never quite understood this country's obsession with property prices. Because if the house you're trying to sell has fallen in value, it stands to reason the house you're trying to buy has fallen in value as well. So what does it matter?

However, it is possible to make your house shoot up in value while everyone else plummets into a world of negative equity, unpleasant letters from the bank, despondency, despair and, eventually, death. Simply open a really good restaurant at the end of the road.

Checklist: balsamic vinegar and olive oil on the tables; lots of weird bread items in a nice basket; some silly cheeses; and pretty waitresses in jeans. That's about it, really.

Let us examine the case of Padstow, a fishing village on the north coast of Cornwall. It's always been a popular holiday destination and, as a result, property prices in the area were always 20 per cent higher than anywhere else in the county. But then along came Rick Stein, who opened a jolly good restaurant, and now, as a direct result, Padstow property is 44 per cent more expensive than the Cornish average.

Then you have Bray, in Berkshire. For centuries you would want to live there only if you were keen on brass rubbing. But then up popped the Fat Duck and the Waterside Inn and now you can't even buy a can of pop in the village shop for less than £1 million.

I am similarly fortunate. Not that long ago a super-expensive farm shop and restaurant opened just a few miles from my house and, as a result, every metrosexual in London now wants a country retreat in the area. The result? Well, last weekend some *Daily Mail* reporters stood at the end of my drive for a while and decided my sorry little collection of ramshackle outbuildings was worth a whopping £2 million*.

I don't really understand why restaurants have this effect. But nothing else will transform an area quite so drastically. Last week, for instance, a £35-million modern art gallery opened in Wakefield. It looks a bit like the Guggenheim – if you stand very far away and squint – and it houses forty-four sculptures by Barbara Hepworth, who everyone has heard of. I imagine.

Feeling a need to move to Wakefield as a result? Of course not, because an art gallery, as we know, is just a building behind which children on school trips can go for a smoke.

Then, of course, just up the road in Doncaster there was the ill-fated Earth Centre. Built with millions of our money, it was a place where visitors could look at a yurt and watch their own excrement being disposed of in an eco-friendly way.

Doubtless the locals felt that such an attraction would cause the value of their houses to soar. They were to be disappointed.

As soon as it opened, property prices in the nearest village fell and didn't start to rise again properly until after someone realized that nobody wanted to look at their stools being mashed and the Earth Centre was closed.

Shopping centres don't work, either. They just mean more traffic in the area. And while public transport links are good, you can't exactly buy a house in the hope that someone will

* This number should be taken with a pinch of salt because they also valued my car at £70,000 – almost exactly twice what I paid for it two years ago.

come along soon and build a railway station in the back garden.

It's the same story with Richard Curtis. I could have bought a house in Notting Hill for about £2.50 before the film came along. Afterwards, the same house would have been worth £2.5 billion. Had we known in advance about that movie, we all could have made a fortune. But we didn't, and that's the problem: guessing which area is about to become hot. And that brings me back to the question of restaurants.

Next week a friend of mine who has had much success with clubs and bars all over the world is opening a pizza joint on Portobello Road in west London. You may scoff at this and claim the area is already so expensive that one new cafe can't possibly make a difference. However, what you don't know – I didn't – is that Portobello Road is the longest road in the world.

It starts in Notting Hill, and this is the bit we all know. Pretty art students selling fascinators from trestle tables and Paddington Bear wandering about looking for Mr Gruber. Then it goes all trendy and there are many people in bars, wearing extremely thin spectacles. And then it reaches the A40 flyover and you assume it stops. But it doesn't. It keeps right on going, plunging north through parts of London that have no name until, eventually, it gets to what looks like West Beirut. In one of the windows I could make out the bulky form of Terry Waite, chained to a radiator.

And as I sat there at a pre-opening dinner, drinking rosé with the trendiest people in all of London, local hoodie types emerged from nearby houses on those stupid small bicycles all people on council estates seem to have. They couldn't believe what they were seeing. They didn't realize that spectacles could be so thin. And many had very obviously never seen a real live homosexual before. There was much pointing.

Here's the thing. Soon, and I can guarantee this, they will all be gone. This one restaurant, all on its own, will cause the small bicycles to be replaced with Vespas. The shops currently selling taps and hens will be sold to bijou furniture designers who will fill the windows with driftwood coffee tables at £4,000 a pop.

And the flats in the area? You could probably part-exchange one today for a tin of boot polish. Whereas next year, when Jude Law is living there, and Sienna Miller's popping past your window to buy a granary loaf, a one-bedroom basement flat will fetch half a billion. You mark my words.

Oh, and before I go, here's another tip. I gather Curtis's next film is to be set in Hitchin. Or I might be making that up.

22 May 2011

A quake's nothing until it becomes a wobbly iDisaster

Last week Iceland exploded again. Against a backdrop of images that looked like an atomic bomb had gone off, weathermen were saying the resultant ash cloud was heading our way and that soon all Britain's airports would have to be closed.

This would have caused inconvenience to thousands of us, as we'd have been forced to spend the next few months listening to friends telling very improbable stories about how they got back from Prague. 'I had to crawl to Madrid and then I got someone in a rickshaw to take me to Toulon, where George Clooney offered me a piggyback.'

Weirdly, it seems only yesterday that Europe was shut down by the first cloud of Icelandic high-altitude dust and I was boring anyone who'd listen with the astonishing tale of how I got home from Warsaw. To précis: I drove.

And it's not just Iceland that has gone wonky recently. Who could have guessed after the 2004 Boxing Day earthquake and tsunami that, just over six years later, there'd be another double whammy off the coast of Japan? An event so massive we all forgot instantly that only days earlier a tectonic shiver had reduced the wonderful New Zealand city of Christchurch to a crumpled pile of broken sewage pipes, decapitated churches and shattered dreams.

In the twenty-first century alone, we've had Haiti. And Pakistan. And the floods in Queensland. And Hurricane Katrina. And a seemingly never-ending stream of tornados reducing America's Bible Belt to matchwood. And the French heatwave that killed almost 15,000. And swine flu.

When I was growing up in the 1960s the natural world seemed so stable and safe. I don't remember my parents ever feeling the need to hoard soup and paraffin. Sure, they'd occasionally make me send food I hadn't eaten to a place called Biafra, and while Aberfan was grisly, it was a) man-made and b) not really in the same league as the Asian tsunami.

In short, we used to be surprised when we woke in a morning to find that Mother Nature had girded her loins while we were asleep. Now it's the other way round. We're amazed when we wake to find the world is pretty much as we left it when we went to bed.

So what's going on? While eco-mentalists are examining the sky for telltale signs of impending doom, and NASA is scanning the heavens for the pinprick of light that will herald the dawn of our extinction, is some major Hollywood-style catastrophe unravelling in the upper mantle? Is the crust cracking up? Is the world falling to pieces? Or is it all down to the iPhone?

Iceland is always exploding; has been since a volcanic burp brought it into existence in the first place. As recently as 1963 there were no islands of any note off the south coast but then the planet decided to be sick and by 1967 the region's guillemot community had a whole playground. It's called Surtsey and it's a mile across.

Today the arrival of a new landmass would keep the rolling news channels going for years, but back then no one had a smartphone, which meant that, to all intents and purposes, the event never happened. If the recent Japanese earthquake had happened in 1970 it would have made a few paragraphs on page twenty-nine of *The Times* and that would have been that. Now, though, CNN needs to be fed, twenty-four hours a day. And it's not picky about what it eats. If it's on film, it's news. If it isn't, it isn't.

In many ways this is a good thing. In the past a tsunami was something that really only existed in schoolbooks and we in Britain had absolutely no idea what it might be like to be stuck in an earthquake.

Now, though, thanks to a Japanese office worker who filmed the shaking filing cabinets in his office, we do. And in case we forget, YouTube is on hand to remind us.

Floods? Well, in Britain they used to come up to the news reporter's ankles, and only then because he'd spent an hour before the broadcast looking for the deepest puddle in which to stand while delivering his report. Now, thanks to Apple and Nokia, we know what it's like when a flood picks up an articulated lorry and smashes it into a petrochemical refinery. We know that floods don't lap. They rage and boil and ruin rather more than your new button-back settee.

There's more. Without mobile phones, few of the uprisings in the Arab world this year would have had much traction. A few youths would have gone on the streets, thrown some stones and been shot. It wouldn't have been news here because we wouldn't have been able to watch it.

Remember Rodney King? He was a black man in America who was ordered out of his car after a police chase and beaten up. News? Not really. I imagine that sort of thing happens a lot. But because the beating was videoed, it was on the front pages.

So, yes, now that we all have them, the camera phone is a tool for justice, and for putting us closer to the action when the world springs a leak. However, there is a problem.

In April 1994 there were many pictures on the news of Kurt Cobain, a rock star who had apparently killed himself.

And then there was the televised death of the Formula One driver Roland Ratzenberger at an event in Italy. There was, however, little coverage of the unfilmed Rwandan genocide that saw about 800,000 people hacked to death in 100 days. Only when pictures of the aftermath started to roll in did it get noticed.

This is still going on today. Whenever Bangladesh is overrun by some terrible natural disaster, we never really know. This is because the only means most people over there have of recording it is with an easel and some oil paint. Whereas whenever it rains in America, we are treated to some grainy, wobble-vision mobile footage of a fat man sobbing and pointing at his upside-down Buick.

It used to be said that if it bleeds, it leads. Now, though, if you want it to stick, you need a pic.

29 May 2011

I'm going to cure dumb Britain

Normally, when a couple decide they need a nanny to look after their child, the list of requirements is quite small. Can you cook a sausage without blowing the house to smithereens? Do you have a rudimentary grasp of English? And are you able to walk past our fridge without eating every single thing inside it?

Actually, I'm being a silly. A mother is bothered about these things. A father tends to worry mostly about aesthetics. Well, I did. I wouldn't deliberately choose an ugly sofa or a hideous coffee table, so why would I want to clutter up the house with a nanny who looks like Robbie Coltrane?

Anyway, according to various reports last week, the actress Gwyneth Paltrow and her crooning husband, whose name has temporarily gone from my mind, have advertised for someone to look after their children, aged five and seven. And their list of requirements is enormous.

The successful applicant must be able to teach ancient Greek, Latin, French and either Japanese or Mandarin. He or she will also be proficient in painting, sailing, a martial art, chess and drama. So what they seem to want is a blend of Julie Andrews, Robin Knox-Johnston and Boris Spassky. Maybe Stephen Fry would do – except, perhaps, for the martial art – but I fear the salary of £62,100 plus expenses, and a free flat, might not be quite enough.

The story attracted much tut-tutting on the radio and in the newspapers. But there will be no scoffing from me because, if the story is true, I think the couple should be applauded for setting such high standards.

In the olden days, cleverness was celebrated. People would flock to exhibitions to see new machines and meet the men who'd invented them. Talks were popular. Authors were the rock 'n' rollers, and poets deities. Not that long ago, you could be an engineer and rich . . . at the same time. But then along came *Blind Date* and that changed everything. Because here was a show specifically designed for morons. Occasionally, for comedic effect, a clever person who could speak properly was invited into the pink and purple idiot chamber so that the host, Cilla Black, could make mocking 'oooh' noises on discovering that they had been to university.

Suddenly, it was uncool to be intelligent and well read. Cilla told us every single Saturday night that it was much better to be a hairdresser. And, as a result, the future wasn't bright. It was orange.

Blind Date was the master and originator of the 'all right for some' mentality that now pervades every part of our lives. Anyone good-looking, or rich, or lucky is perceived to have committed some kind of crime against the chip-eating masses. Today, this has reached such an absurd level that we are expected to weep at the loss of Jade Goody and are bombarded by the antics of minor-league non-celebrities who have pretty much the same genetic coding as a cauliflower and a bit less intelligence than a dishwasher.

I was told last week by someone who worked on *The Only Way Is Essex* – it's a TV show, apparently – that, when asked to name the prime minister, one of the stars said: 'What? The prime minister of Essex?' Upon being told that there is no such post, he thought for a while and then said: 'Gordon Ramsay.' Meanwhile, on the other channel, Andrew Marr was talking about the origins of cities. And no one was watching.

Clever people, today, are scary. Stephen Fry is bright enough to know this. It's why he does knob gags. Stupid people only really like to see other stupid people on the television because it makes them feel good about themselves.

They reckon that if someone with the IQ of a cylinder head gasket can get on the box, there is hope that they can too.

Obviously, if this continues, Britain will be sunk. If our children feel they must be gormless to fit in, we shall soon be a big, dark backwater full of fat people celebrating their idiocy with another bag of oven-ready E numbers. And so, obviously, it's important to turn things round. But how?

Earlier this year, a man with an IQ of 48 was barred by the High Court from having sex. It said that he was too stupid to understand the consequences and health risks. Yes. But what it also seemed to be saying is that he might produce a child that's just as daft as him.

There are those, I know, who think that the judge was correct and that all stupid people should be neutered. But I reckon it's better to undo the teachings of *Blind Date* and humiliate the nation's morons into changing their ways. I believe this is possible. When I worked in Rotherham, I met many people who could barely speak. If you'd asked them to write down every single fact they knew on a piece of paper, they'd have needed only a stamp. And yet, despite having less knowledge about the world than a tree, they could add up a darts score faster than a Cray supercomputer. This means people have the capacity to be bright and useful but that no one has worked out a way to make them realize it. Until now . . .

Tomorrow morning, I have a meeting scheduled with the controller of BBC1 and I'm going to suggest we make a new TV game show in which contestants are picked at random from the streets and told that, if they answer a selection of fairly simple questions correctly, they will be given sex with a supermodel, much money and a speedboat. However, if they get one of the questions wrong, the studio audience will be encouraged to howl with laughter at their stupidity. Maybe we could go further and put up signs outside their house saying: 'The person who lives here thought the capital of France was Southend.'

I think it would be a long-running smash. And I very much look forward to the day when the children of Gwyneth Paltrow appear and sail off into the sunset in a shiny new speedboat with a bag of cash.

5 June 2011

Advice for men – don't try to keep your hair on

I don't want to be unduly rude about Wayne Rooney, but it seems the irritating little brat, who plays annoyingly well for Manchester United and annoyingly badly for England, has had a hair transplant. And I'm sorry, but what on earth is the point of that?

He was a very ugly little troll with sticky-out ears and a bald head, and now he is a very ugly little troll with sticky-out ears. It's an improvement but only in the same way that Dawn French's recent diet is an improvement. The fact is, you'd still want her on your team in a sumo wrestling match.

I wonder about this hair transplant business. Did Silvio Berlusconi, for instance, think that if he emptied the sweep-up bag from the local Hair Port beauty salon on to his bonce, he could burst back on to the world stage looking like George Clooney? He doesn't. He just looks like an oily, perma-tanned buffoon with a hair transplant.

I have a hair-loss problem. It's all fallen out at the back. And I know that for several thousand pounds I could have it fixed. But what would be the point? I'd still look like a telegraph pole that had eaten a space hopper. Fixing my hair hole would be like trying to improve the overall appearance of the Elephant Man by cutting his fingernails.

There's no doubt that for some people cosmetic surgery is important. It can be used to boost self-confidence and it can certainly help if you've been trapped in the cockpit of a burning Hurricane. Plus, in the world of celebrity, where long lenses can pick out a spot of cellulite from half a mile away, it is handy, too.

My eldest daughter came into the world looking like the lion from *Daktari*. The poor little mite had to spend the first three years of her life staring at nothing but the ends of both her noses. So she had cosmetic surgery, the squint was corrected, and nobody would have denied her that.

For sure, I wouldn't want a doctor to fill my lips with collagen because it's made from the skin of a bison, but there's no doubt that the full Steve Tyler does make a girl prettier. And I'm sure Botox is useful if you need to look impassive at all times; in a game of poker, perhaps, or when you are being tortured.

I've sometimes looked down at the vast stomach that hangs over my trousers and thought: 'Well, I could get rid of that by skipping, not drinking anything more exciting than Ribena and eating like a mouse for a year.' But wouldn't it be easier to pop into a hospital and have all the fat hoovered out?

We are forever being told that we spend more in Britain on cosmetic surgery than we do on tea, and that this year more men will go into the vanity cabinet than will join the army.

So what? If you have a wart the size of a melon on your face, or a prolapsed bottom, or teeth that grow out of your forehead, then by all means have the problem sorted and feel not one jot of shame or guilt. These are sophisticated times and you should use whatever science has created to make yourself happy.

However, when it comes to hair, it's best to let nature take its course. I'm not talking about women now. Nobody wants to see what looks like half a pound of Old Holborn poking out of your bikini bottoms. And '99 Red Balloons' was a one-hit wonder for Nena because nobody wanted to see her back on *Top of the Pops* with what appeared to be two guinea pigs peeping out from her armpits. No. I'm talking about men, and specifically the head.

Some chaps think when they go bald that it would be a good idea to grow a beard. Why? It just looks like your face is on upside down.

Others go down the Rooney route and have a transplant, but in my, albeit limited, experience this doesn't work either. Because you end up with hair that grows like conifers on a Scottish hillside. In rows.

Worst of all, though, are chaps who believe they can hold off the ageing process with dye. This is a mind-blowing waste of time. We have been able to determine this by examining Paul McCartney.

By all accounts he is a fairly wealthy man, so we can presume he uses the very best hair-colouring products that Boots can provide. And yet he still looks like a man walking around with a dead red kite on his head.

It's much the same story with Mick Jagger. Does he really think as he flounces down the street with that luxuriant auburn barnet quivering slightly in the breeze that passers-by will mistake him for a seventeen-year-old? Crowning that wind-battered old face with that hair is like crowning York Minster with a heap of solar panels.

And, anyway, what's the point? The only reason a man might choose to cover up his greying temples is to make himself more attractive to the opposite sex. But when you are nudging seventy, I really don't see how this works. Because surely your hair will be writing cheques your gentleman sausage can't cash.

I have a general rule in life, which so far has stood me in reasonably good stead. Never do business with a man who cares about his hair. This is even more important than avoiding a man who goes to the gym or who has a Rolex watch.

Any evidence of layering or product suggests that he is vain and therefore not to be trusted. Certainly do not buy a house from someone who spends more than £25 on a haircut because I can pretty much guarantee it will smell of sewage every time it rains and fall down after six months.

Look at it this way. When England recently drew 2–2 with Switzerland in a lacklustre performance at Wembley, there was one notable absentee from the stands. Wayne Rooney. He didn't even bother to turn up and cheer his mates on, or his country, because he was across town, having his hair transplant.

12 June 2011

We demand our weekends back, Adolf Handlebar

Many thousands of people are not reading this today because they're driving around an unfamiliar village ten miles from where they live, desperately looking for a pair of wilting balloons tied to a gatepost. This will indicate that they've found the right house at which to drop their six-year-old for a party.

Afterwards, they'll have to drive at high speed to a railway station in the vague hope that their fifteen-year-old son has actually woken up on time and caught the train he said he'd catch.

Then, after discovering that he hasn't, and isn't answering his phone and is probably dead in a gutter somewhere, it'll be time to pick up a third child from her sleepover and head back to the unfamiliar little village only to find the balloons have vanished along with the house at which the six-year-old was dropped.

A report out last week said that by the time a child is eighteen, parents will have spent a full year of their lives ferrying it about. An endless round of school trips, social events and sporting fixtures means that you will have driven 23,500 miles. Which is about the same as driving round the fattest part of the world. And you know what? I don't believe it.

Taking my youngest child to and from school clocks up seventy-two miles a day. That's 13,824 miles a year. So that's more than 110,000 miles by the time she is thirteen. And that's before we get to the weekend, when my wife and I have to employ a team of women with long sticks in what we call the map room.

It's their job to vector us in on the postcodes of parties, and to work out which of us is nearer to whichever child has finished one thing and needs taking to something else. We have learnt much from watching the *Battle of Britain*. Some days, we need the Big Wing.

Of course, occasionally we are too hungover to provide this vital role, in which case the kids will be expected to use public transport. They're not very good at this. The eldest has developed an incredibly annoying tactic of volunteering to come home on the train but then ringing from far away to say her credit card is maxed out and that she can't. The boy, meanwhile, reckons that there's a bus stationed in our local town waiting for the rare moments when he has to use it. And he can't understand why sometimes it's not there. The youngest isn't exactly sure what a bus is.

And I don't want to sound like an old person, but it was never like this when I was a kid, because back then I didn't choose friends on the basis that I liked them; I chose them on the basis that they lived within cycling distance.

I had a bicycle at home, which I would ride for fun whenever there was nothing on television, which was – let's think now – almost constantly.

And I had a bicycle at school, which I would use for getting to and from the local girls' school. Which was seventeen miles away. My bicycle was my passport to adulthood. My bike was freedom.

Not any more, of course. A bicycle now is seen as a portal to the Pearly Gates. There's a sense that unless you are dressed up in a spinnaker of luminescence and your head is shrouded in what appear to be five cryogenic bananas, you will definitely be killed within seconds of climbing on board. This takes the fun out of riding.

But it's nonsense. Yes, a friend of mine peeled his face off the other day after falling off, but cycling-related deaths are down by a third since the mid-1990s, and it's probably fair to say there's never been a safer time to go for a ride.

Sadly, though, there's a problem. You see, cycling is seen now not as something that might be exhilarating or even useful but as a frontline propaganda weapon in the war on capitalism, banking, freedom, McDonald's, injustice, Swiss drug companies, rape and progress. Every morning London is chock-full of little individually wrapped Twiglets, their wizened faces contorted with hatred for all that they see. Fat people. Cars. Chain stores. It's all fascism. Fascism, d'you hear?

From what they see as the moral high ground, they sneer at pedestrians, howl at buses, bang on cars, scream at taxi drivers and charge through every convention that defines society with their walnutty bottoms in the air and their stupid legs going nineteen to the dozen.

This sort of thing frightens a child in much the same way that little Norwegian children were frightened when jack-booted Nazis marched through their towns and villages, shouting and generally being scary. Little Olaf, cowering in the cellar, never once thought, 'Ooh, I'd like to be like them when I grow up.'

To address this, we must wage a war on the militants. First, we must make it an offence, punishable by many years in jail, to ride a bicycle in anything other than what I like to call home clothes. Cycling shops selling gel for your bottom crack and outfits with padded gussets will be raided by the police and the owners prosecuted.

This way, cyclists will be stripped of their uniforms and made to look like human beings. They will also be forced to abandon their crash helmets. Nobody in their right mind believes that a bit of yellow polystyrene could possibly keep a head intact should it be run over by the rear wheels of an articulated lorry. So get rid of them.

With the Nazi clobber gone, we shall start to insist that cyclists develop some manners. They should take a leaf out of the horse rider's book, thanking other road users for slowing down rather than shaking their fists because they didn't slow down enough. We need them to recognize that Bob the builder and Roary the racing car have just as much of a right to be out and about as they do.

This way, children will grow up to think that cycling is fun. And as a result of that, parents will be freed at weekends to do what they want, safe in the knowledge that their thin, healthy children are getting the social lives they need without being a bloody nuisance in the process.

19 June 2011

Houston, our spaceships are ugly

Next month the space shuttle *Atlantis* will blast off for the final time, and when it returns, that will be that. America will no longer be capable of getting a man into space. So what, then, will become of the International Space Station (ISS)? For now, the crew in their polo shirts and slacks can be ferried back and forth by the Russians while the Europeans – not us, obviously, or the Greeks – can be relied upon to pop up every now and again to empty their bins.

This is done by what the European Space Agency calls its fleet of space freighters. They take washing-up liquid and other vital supplies into space and are then loaded up with all the rubbish for the journey back to earth. The idea is, of course, that they burn up on re-entry but not every part is destroyed. Indeed, only last week, sailors in the South Pacific were advised to stay in their cabins in case they were hit on the head by bits of just such a ship. Called the ATV *Johannes Kepler*, it did mostly burn up but still dumped various components into the ocean in what can only be described as an act of government-sponsored littering.

There are only three Euro space freighters left, and because the governments that fund the programme are now having to give all their spare cash to Stavros and Mr O'Flaherty to keep them in beer and skittles, there won't be any more.

That means the space station will have to be abandoned. And is that any great loss? We're told that many useful experiments are being conducted up there, but what are they exactly? All the crew seems to do is grow mustard and take pretty pictures of earth. And has anyone thought what will happen to the ISS when the binmen stop coming and the Russians realize they only have a space programme to stop their scientists skipping off to Iran?

Remember Skylab? NASA engineers decided that it could not be kept in orbit forever, so, with their slide rules and their side partings, they decided to bring it down into the sea off South Africa. Unfortunately, they got their sums a bit wrong and most of it crashed into Australia. That time, the American government was hit with a $400 fine for littering. Which it refused to pay.

Boffins, then, may well be reluctant to bring the ISS down in case there is a similar diplomatic incident. But it can't very well be left in space either because of what's called the Kessler syndrome.

At present, there are around 300 million bits of man-made debris orbiting earth at extremely high speed. Some are little flecks of paint or globules of unburnt rocket fuel. But there are also hammers and nuts and bolts. Should one of these things hit the abandoned space station at a closing speed of 35,000mph, there would be many more bits and pieces hurtling around up there, and what an egghead called Donald Kessler worked out is that each time one of these pieces hit another, more smaller bits would result until, eventually, earth would be surrounded by an impenetrable shield of rubbish. Trying to drive a spaceship through it would be like trying to drive a car through a thunderstorm without hitting any of the raindrops.

So here we are, trapped on our own planet by our own mess. We've filled space with junk and littered the oceans with broken-up space freighters and solid rocket boosters and the souls of many dead astronauts. We've spent trillions and all we have to show for it is a bit of useless moon rock and a profound understanding of how to grow mustard when there's no gravity.

What happened to the spirit of the 1960s when John F. Kennedy made his big speech about why we choose to go to the moon and do the other things – what were the other things, by the way? What happened to our dreams? And why am I, a committed fan of the shuttle and the whole nerdy business of space exploration, starting to feel so jaded?

The problem, I think, is aesthetics. Back in the 1950s, futurists would predict what sort of cars we'd be driving in the twenty-first century. But the cars we actually have are better than those that filled their wildest dreams. It's the same story with computers. They never saw the delicious iPad coming, did they? Or Concorde. Or the Gherkin.

But it was very different with space. The film director Stanley Kubrick dreamt up *Discovery One*, a gloriously slender craft with a ball on the front and six big engines at the back. Then we had *Thunderbird* 3. Orange. Jaggedy. Sexy. And the *Eagle* transporter from the television series *Space* 1999. It was very cool. And, while there are words you can use to describe the space shuttle, 'cool' isn't one of them.

Then there's the ISS, which a) is only as far away from earth as Preston is from London and b) looks like a skip full of discarded kitchen appliances.

Mind you, even that's a lot better than the space freighter. In your mind you can probably see a jet-black Mack truck with rockets on the back but I'm afraid in real life it isn't even slightly like that. In fact, it looks like a wheelie bin that's got tangled up in a teenager's crusty bed sheet.

Now, of course, I realize that when you are building a machine for use in space, you don't have to worry about aerodynamics or sleekness. But that's the problem. How many small boys dream of the day when they can go to space in a wheelie bin? How many people think that the freighter's interior, which looks like a *Blue Peter* project, is a worthwhile way of blowing all those taxpayer billions?

To keep the space programme alive, the boffins, and the accountants that fund them, must understand that we don't want practical, bare-minimum engineering. If you're going to call something a space freighter, make it look like the *Nostromo*; make it look impressive. Give it a bit of wow. Equip it with space guns and, most importantly of all, make sure it has a big red self-destruct button so that when you've finished with it, you can vaporize it before it crashes into the Galapagos Islands.

26 June 2011

Look what that little DVD pirate is really doing

In the olden days when we watched movies on video recorders, we could fast-forward through all the legal and commercial claptrap to the start of the actual film.

Not any more.

Now we are forced by electronic trickery to sit through the endless roll call of production companies, disclaimers and suchlike, until eventually we are presented with a reminder that if we copy the film, we are committing an act of piracy and we will be keelhauled.

I have a deal of sympathy with this argument. Foreign television companies pay a fortune for episodes of *Top Gear* and then transmit them with much trumpeting and brouhaha, only to find that most of the audience is elsewhere, having already watched everything on the internet. A couple of years ago *Top Gear* was the most illegally downloaded show in the world.

Things are even worse for the producers of Hollywood blockbusters. They spend £100 million making an all-action spectacular in which cars are driven at high speed into actual helicopters. And absolutely no one pays to watch the finished result.

Just last week various film companies told the High Court that file-sharing sites on the internet are costing them hundreds of millions a year and that firms such as BT and Virgin Media must take action to block them. It's all a total waste of judicial time, partly because if you close down one avenue of access, another will begin immediately somewhere else. But mainly because most of the people who steal films don't really think what they're doing is wrong.

Some argue that if you copy someone's car, it's not theft because the original is still with its rightful owner. But that's legal doublespeak. Most people – and when I say 'people', what I mean is 'teenagers' – have grown up with an internet where everything is free. Phone calls. Facts. Pornography. Nothing costs anything at all.

They go to one site, and a song they want is available for nothing. So why would they go to iTunes and pay 79p? In their silly little heads it makes no sense.

Of course, the idiotic hippie who wrote the song probably thinks it's fair enough, too. But one day, when he's older and wiser and millions of people are stealing his music, he will start to wonder how the concept of theft became so blurred. Perhaps it's always been so.

When I was growing up I would steal rhubarb from the nuns at the local convent. It was their rhubarb. They'd grown it. And they were doubtless looking forward to stewing it and having it for pudding one night with some double cream. I deprived them of that. And yet this was not considered to be burglary. It was called scrumping and, at worst, I could expect a clip round the ear from Constable Plod.

Later, when I was away at school, the council knew that whenever roadworks were necessary in the local village, it could expect to lose pretty well all the cones and most of the flashing amber beacons. Only when we helped ourselves to the temporary traffic lights did it finally come round and make a fuss.

We see similar problems in the workplace. Take a computer home and we all accept that this would be theft. But what about a pen? Nobody's going to mind about that – unless, of course, it's a Montblanc and you took it from the managing director's top pocket.

Hotels are a hotbed of legal fuzziness. I spoke last week to a chap who says his wardrobe at home is stuffed full of dressing gowns he has nicked from various suites around the world. Even though he works in the DVD business, he says that because he has paid many hundreds of pounds for the room he is entitled to take the robe home.

Really? Because on that basis he's also entitled to take the television and the sink. Worse. He can spend £300 on the weekly shop at Waitrose and after settling up he'd be within his rights to swipe half a dozen boxes of Black Magic chocolates.

Shoplifting is an interesting case in point, actually. Obviously, it would be poor form to nick a fridge freezer but a Bounty bar? A gentleman's magazine? I'm a fervent believer that Woolworths went west simply because nobody in the store's history ever actually paid for anything. Every branch was always full of schoolkids with fast hearts, wide eyes and bulging pockets.

And this, I think, is the issue we face with the internet. When a fourteen-year-old downloads the latest collection of noises from JLS it has a known value of 79p. It's a modern-day penny chew, a stalk of rhubarb from the nunnery. It's nothing.

It's the same story with a film. You're nicking something that'll soon be on Sky anyway. And yes, I know, some of you will have read this online, having bypassed the subscription fee. Why not? Rupert Murdoch won't miss a quid.

The trouble is that so long as we continue to believe that theft is only theft if the stolen item is bulky, tangible and expensive, the time will come when Bruce Willis will be forced to hang up his vest and every film made is a tuppence ha'penny slimmed-down version of *The Blair Witch Project*. And the only news you get will be from Twitter. And your book will have been written by someone who actually admits it's worthless.

And you'll have to wade through hours and hours of unimaginable tripe on the music scene before you find a song written by someone who knows what they're doing. A someone who'll eventually hang up their guitar and have to get a proper job so that they can actually get paid.

I don't think there's a damn thing that can be done to stop theft on the internet. It's uncontrollable. But I do think there is something that can be done to change people's perception of illegal downloads. Stop saying that if you nick a film, you are a thief or a pirate. Pirates are cool. Kids have pirate parties and everyone loves Jack Sparrow. Surely it would be better to say that if you nick a film, you are a mugger.

3 July 2011

Dear BBC, why d'ya think Dick Whittington gave Salford a miss?

And in other news last week, Chris Patten, who is chairman of the BBC Trust, said the corporation is too centred on Notting Hill, too bothered about chilli and lemon grass, too Peter Mandelson and completely out of touch with most licence-fee payers, who simply want pies with a splash of chlamydia. Doubtless this tub-thumping rallying call is all part of the BBC's strategy to move various shows and departments from London to a small town called Salford. Which I believe is the stupidest media decision since someone on a tabloid newspaper said: 'Hey, guys. I can listen to Prince William's voicemails.'

A lot of the arguments against the BBC's move have been centred on the expense, but I believe there's a more important problem than money. In short, Salford is up north.

I do not speak now as a trendy southern poof who misses Tony Blair and has angst about sending my kids to private school. A television show found that since 1740 every single person in my family tree was born, married and died within twelve miles of one Yorkshire village. I am therefore a pure-blood northerner, a man who makes Michael Parkinson look like Brian Sewell. Cut me in half and you'd find I run on coal and whippets.

But here's the thing. While I was being raised in the north, my parents would occasionally risk the highwaymen and take me to London on trips. There are photographs that show a six-year-old me looking at an elephant in London Zoo and pointing at a black man on Bayswater Road. I remember trying to make a soldier in a busby blink and gazing in open-mouthed wonderment at the sheer size of the Palace of Westminster. It all seemed so much more exciting somehow than anything I'd ever encountered oop north.

And now, thirty years after I escaped from Yorkshire, that still holds true. I still get a tinkle fizz when the motorway ends and I'm plunged into the labyrinth. I still get a kick out of the BT tower and from hailing a black cab. I absolutely love London. And I'm sorry, but if the BBC now said I had to move back up north, I'd resign in a heartbeat. Many others faced with the same problem have done exactly that.

We are told that too many BBC shows are made by Londoners in London, but that simply is not true. *Top Gear*, the show on which I work, is based in the capital but, so far as I know, every single one of the production team is originally from somewhere else. The producer is from Glossop, in Derbyshire. One of the researchers is from Loughborough, in Leicestershire. Until recently we even employed a Scot. Richard Hammond is from Birmingham. James May is from one of the moons of Jupiter. We are therefore as 'London' as the Chelsea football team . . . when John Terry is ill.

London is full of the cream. The bright. The sharp. The ambitious. People who had the gumption at some point to up sticks and leave the two-bit town in which they were raised and do a Dick Whittington.

You see it as you drive about: cafes rammed full of people reading big newspapers and talking about big things and drinking coffee that people in Salford have never heard of. It's where the shows are. It's where films premiere. It's the nation's Oxbridge. It's the best of the best of the best.

Salford? It's just Salford. A small suburb with a Starbucks and a canal with ducks on it. It's a box that has been ticked. A gentle tousle of the politicians' mop. According to Wikipedia, its only real claim to fame is that a man there was run over by Stephenson's *Rocket*. Oh, and someone once found a head in a bog.

This does not qualify it as a great place to make television shows. Indeed, it's a very bad place. Every week we have to try to entice a guest to our studios, which are in Guildford. Sometimes it's tricky. But it's nowhere near as tricky as it would be if we had to get them up to Manchester. Or as expensive. Every week I'd have to say: 'Ladies and gentlemen, please welcome ... Stuart Hall. Again.' That might become wearing.

And how could a news programme run from Salford? It's nowhere near any court that matters and nowhere near a single politician.

Furthermore, if we ran the show from Salford, we'd be employing people from Salford. People who were born there and thought, 'Yes. I like this. I see no reason to go anywhere else.' And in the world of television that could be a genuine handicap. Every year we'd end up making a Christmas special from the Dog and Duck or the nearest Arndale centre. A television show needs to be run by worldly people. Not people who are frightened to death of the next town.

And what would be the upside? Who cares where a show is made? Who cares whether the *Blue Peter* garden is in London or not? Who cares whether Simon Mayo is speaking to you from Portland Place or a glass-fronted tower up north? It makes not a jot of difference. At the end of a show now it often says BBC Wales or BBC Scotland. If at the end of *Top Gear* we put up an ident saying BBC England there'd be hell to pay internally. But why? Nobody who'd paid for the joke would give a damn.

The big problem here is that politicians – and they're behind this shift, be in no doubt about that – have got it into their heads that Britain is a big place. But it isn't, really. It's titchy. Moving half the BBC from London to Salford is the same as a parish council moving the table around which it meets from the village hall to the community centre.

Britain is a small place with a whopping great world-class city in its bottom right-hand corner. It therefore makes sense to me that every head office, every government department, every newspaper and, most of all, every television and radio show is based there.

10 July 2011

Okay, I'll come clean on Rebekah and the Chipping Norton plot

A recent piece in Her Majesty's *Daily Telegraph* suggested there is a turning point in the career of all prime ministers after which their place on the scraphcap of history becomes assured.

This is probably true. Tony Blair was doomed from the moment he said to George W.: 'Yes. Let's bomb Iraq.'

John Major had had it after Black Wednesday, and Gordon Brown became a spent force . . . well, when the nurse cut his umbilical cord.

According to Peter Oborne in the *Telegraph*, David Cameron's moment came when he chose to become involved with the Chipping Norton set – 'an incestuous collection of louche, affluent, power-hungry and amoral Londoners' who all have homes near one another in the Cotswolds.

I see. So this pretty little market town, whose most notable resident to date was the famously power-hungry and amoral Ronnie Barker, is actually a haven for the worst excesses of corruption. Behind the hanging baskets and the tea shoppes, the man in the hardware store is let off his VAT bill if he hands Cameron an under-the-counter tin of gloss paint.

It's all rubbish. The fact is that 99 per cent of the population of Chipping Norton are not in the Chipping Norton set, and that 99 per cent of the set don't actually live in Chipping Norton.

According to every single report I've read, Matthew Freud, the PR man who is married to Elisabeth Murdoch, is a leading light and the host of our most glamorous parties. But he

lives in Burford, which to most people in Chipping Norton –
myself included – is basically France.

Then there's Steve Hilton. Apparently, he's a Tory adviser,
but I've never met him. Nor have I met another chap who has
been mentioned, Sir Howard Stringer. But that's probably
because he lives in Chinnor, which is as far away as Russia.
Last weekend the *Mail on Sunday* suggested Nat Rothschild is
also involved simply on the basis he once used the M40.

I'll let you into a secret, though. There is a group of Chipping Norton people who do live close to one another and
who do meet up most weekends for wine and cheesy things
on sticks. I am one of these people. And so is the Blur bassist
Alex James, who often brings his children round to swim in
our pool.

We have other friends, too. There's Tony and Rita and
James and Annabel and Dominic and Caroline. Bored yet?
No? Well, that's because I haven't got to Emily and Miles,
who have the pub.

Of course, there are some other people in the group who
have been in the newspapers recently. There's Cameron and
his wife Sam, but we don't see much of them these days,
partly because he is jolly busy running the country and partly
because Sam is one of those non-smokers who suddenly
remembers when she's presented with a smoker like me
that what she'd like to do is smoke all my bloody cigarettes.
And then send me out to get some more.

Then there's Rebekah Brooks and her husband, Charlie.
They actually met over supper in our house one night and
are the most fantastically kind and generous people we know.
I feel desperately sad that Rebekah has had to resign but the
cloud does have a silver lining – I can see more of her. She
has been a friend for a long time. She is now. And she always
will be.

And now let's get to the meat. The question that has burnt brightly in the *Guardian* for the past six months. The infamous Christmas-time party at Rebekah and Charlie's house. Investigative journalists have established that the Camerons were there but they have not been able to establish what was discussed.

I'm going to tell you everything. I was there with my wife – and that's a story already for the *Mirror*. James Murdoch was there too, with his wife. There were two other couples, neither of whom have even the slightest connection to newspapers, the police force or the government. They were simply neighbours.

We began with a cocktail made from crushed socialists and after we'd discussed how the trade union movement could be smashed and how News Corp should be allowed to take control of the BBC, Rupert Murdoch joined us on a live video feed from his private volcano, stroking a white cat.

Later, I remember vividly, a policeman knocked at the door and Rebekah gave him a wad of cash. Cameron tapped the side of his nose knowingly and went back to his main course – a delicious roast fox.

That's what you want me to say happened, isn't it? But what you're going to get now is the truth. I've kept quiet for six months but I feel the time is right to tell all. What Rebekah and Cameron talked about most of all – and I'm a trained journalist so I understand the need to get things right – is sausage rolls.

We were planning a big walk with all our kids over Christmas and thought it might be a good idea to build a fire in my woods and stop off for a picnic. Rebekah was worried about what we'd eat. Cameron thought sausage rolls would be nice. My wife said she'd get some.

Aha, you cry. But what about evil James Murdoch? Was he

not to be found sticking pins into a waxwork model of Vince Cable?

No, actually. James was sitting opposite me and we spent most of the night arguing about the environment. He likes it and I don't. The row only ended when Samantha Cameron suddenly remembered that what she'd like was 400 of my cigarettes.

In other words, it was much like a million other Christmas-time dinners being held in a million other houses all over the world that day. BSkyB was not mentioned. Nor was phone hacking. And it was the same story the next time we all met. That time, we played tennis. You might call this disgustingly middle class. Going for walks and picnics and tennis. And I won't argue with you. But louche? Amoral? Corrupt? No.

Of course, much has gone wrong in recent years and many will spend the next few years wondering what caused the rot to set in. But I can assure you that the root cause of it all will not be found in Chipping Norton.

17 July 2011

Okay, tontine tango birdie, let's baffle 'em with insider talk

British prisoners of war in some of the more barbaric Japanese camps were not allowed to speak to one another. So, to get round the problem, they developed a new language that featured no Bs, Ms, Ps, Vs or Ws. This meant they could at least whisper, without moving their lips, and thus avoid arousing the suspicion of the guards.

People in certain villages in North Wales perform a similar trick even today: when an English person walks into their local pub, they switch to a version of English in which the A, E, I, O and U are replaced by the letter L.

Then, of course, there were the eighteenth-century plantations where slaves, often from different parts of Africa, conversed in English. But not the sort that their English master would have a hope of understanding. The language has lasted, and now I have literally no idea how the courts work in Barbados since the defendant invariably answers all the questions by speaking in a way that is indecipherable to anyone in a suit. 'Dah you own?', for example, means 'Is that yours?' Not guilty is 'Ah'n do dah'. Which is literally 'I didn't do that'.

So, there have been good reasons in the past for using language as a device for not being understood. But today people seem to mangle language just to make themselves sound more important.

This began in about 1840 with the birth of Cockney rhyming slang and is practised extensively in the world of light aircraft. Instead of speaking to the tower in a manner the passengers can understand, the pilot chooses to say things that make the task look much more difficult than is actually the case. 'Whisky Oscar Tango Squawking on niner niner two decimal seven. Requesting basic service ILS Echo to outer beacon.'

We see a similar problem with the practitioners of business who now talk about 'quantum' instead of money and 'P and L' instead of money and 'piece' instead of money.

It's like footballers coming up with a million new words for 'goal'.

Lawyers are also annoying, never using one word when several thousand will do. And then several thousand more, until the reader has completely lost the point and sometimes the will to live.

You think you have just about got to the end of a sentence but then there's a colon and you know that there's at least a fortnight to go before you get to the next verb. I signed a legal document a while ago, not because I agreed with what it said: I was bored.

So, some people talk strangely to hide what they're saying from eavesdroppers. And some because they want to make a simple job look more difficult. So what excuse, I wonder, do golfists have?

Last week there was a golf tournament in Kent that must have been jolly important because it was the only thing on the news apart from the people who knew the person who once met someone at a party who may or may not have illegally listened to Sienna Miller making a hair appointment.

I'm not kidding. Every half hour on every radio station, we had the phone hacking stuff, and then instead of the collapse of the euro, or the famine in East Africa, all we had was a breathless report about the leaderboard at Sandwich. And I'm sorry, but I couldn't understand what they were on about.

A man, whom I'd never heard of, was four under par behind another man I'd never heard of who needed an eagle and a bogey to win. It was as though the reporter were reading a Scrabble board.

No other sport does this. Even if we are not interested in football, we understand who has won when we are told that Manchester United have scored two and Chelsea have scored three. But in a golf report your car radio needs to have the decoding powers of Bletchley Park or you are left completely in the dark.

Golf fever even spread to the traffic reports. Normally, these begin with Scotland and we all think: 'Oh, do us a favour. They have no idea what a jam is.' But last week they all began with news of hold-ups in Kent, caused, apparently, by people going to the golf match.

That's even more baffling than the leaderboard. I can, if I squint, understand why people play the sport – they don't like their wives – but I cannot understand why anyone would want to watch it, because, so far as I can tell, you choose whether you want to watch a man you've never heard of hit the ball or whether you want to watch the ball land.

Isn't that like being forced in a football match to choose whether you want to watch the man take the penalty, or the other man try to save it? Imagine if the bowler and the bats-man in cricket were made to stand three miles apart and you had to choose which one you'd like to see.

Except there is no batsman in golf. A man hits a ball and all you can do if you're at the other end is watch it land. Can you imagine anything in life quite so dreary?

And it was raining. Doesn't that strike you as odd? That you would drive through severe traffic and stand in the rain for hours watching a selection of men in nasty trousers thwack a ball into the clouds. Or, worse, peering into the heavens in the hope that you've selected the right spot to watch it come back down to earth. And you have no idea who's winning because reports of the scores don't make sense.

It's almost like a secret code. Which it is, in a way, since in the early days golf was played almost exclusively by Freemasons. And Freemasons do not make a habit of speaking openly about their activities or their handshakes or their funny words.

Today, of course, most Freemasons are to be found in the police, who don't talk properly either.

24 July 2011

Get on your roof, everyone, and give Biggles an eyeful

In my continuing quest to prove that airport check-in times are fraudulent nonsense, I arrived at Ronaldsway on the Isle of Man the other morning twenty-three minutes before the scheduled departure time.

And made it on to the flight, easily.

I was feeling extremely smug as I cast my eyes over the other passengers. 'Ha,' I thought, 'while I was catching a few more zeds in bed this morning, all you slaves to convention were marooned in the departure lounge, having your hair redone by static electricity from the seats.'

But then the plane took off, and I realized that, unlike everyone else, I hadn't left myself enough time to buy a book or a newspaper.

This meant I had to spend the entire flight looking out of the window. And as we began our descent into London City an hour or so later, I arrived at an interesting conclusion: from the air, England is much too dreary. I realize, of course, that we don't have any Alps and there's no desert – apart from a small one between Birmingham and Coventry – but we do have many towns, and from the air they're all extremely similar and very horrid.

Stoke-on-Trent looks exactly like Stafford. Milton Keynes looks like a retail park. Lichfield appears to serve no purpose at all. And every building you see looks like a prison. Except for all the actual prisons, which look like supermarkets.

There's a very good reason for this. It's because the planning rules were drawn up when only the very tall had an aerial view of anything. Architects therefore concentrated hard on frontal aspects and put all the flotsam and jetsam and the air-conditioning plant on the roof where no one could see it. Now, though, thousands of us can – and do – see it every day.

There's more. Think how much effort is put into a town's ground-level entry points these days. You get a little gate, and some flowerpots, a sign asking you to drive slowly and often a reminder that back in 1996 the Britain in Bloom judges had bestowed upon the council a special commendation. All this effort for a few people in cars.

Whereas people flying overhead are given nothing. It's just a big brown splodge that looks exactly the same as all the other big brown splodges.

So what about a bit of civic advertising. 'You are now flying over Rutland – the best little county by a dam site.' Or 'Mansfield – birthplace of Rebecca Adlington *and* Richard Bacon'. Or 'Chipping Norton – nothing to see here'.

From the air, there seems to be no point at all to Preston. You realize why it was the first town to be given a motorway bypass. There was simply no need to go there. But this was the first British town outside London to be lit by gas. So why not light it up by gas again?

Think of all those eager little American faces, pressed to the windows of their planes, straining in the pre-dawn light to get a better look at Britain's only town to be completely on fire.

Companies, too, could get in on the act. They spend a fortune getting their message across to motorists who have better things to do than look at billboards.

But they spend not a single penny pushing their slogans to the thousands of trapped businessmen who fly over the factories every day.

We know of the story of a man in Wales who became so

fed up with low-level RAF sorties that he put a message on his roof saying 'Piss off Biggles'. Inevitably it backfired because when news broke of his stunt, everyone with a pilot's licence flew over his gaff for a gawp.

But you can see from this story that rooftop advertising has power. Pilots will fly hundreds of miles out of their way, just to be abused. That's how boring Britain is from the air.

As you come in to land at Heathrow, there are thousands of nondescript warehouses on either side of the final approach and I think I'm right in saying that only one owner has had the gumption to festoon his otherwise useless roof space with an advert. That's madness.

At present, escort girls ply for trade by leaving cards in telephone boxes. Why? The only people who use a telephone box these days are people who are desperate for a wee. So why not put a photograph of yourself, a phone number and a brief list of the services you offer on the roof of a warehouse in Hammersmith? One Korean jet and you'd be rushed off your feet, literally, for a month.

It's the same story with Windsor Castle, over which you descend when the wind's blowing from the east. I'm pretty sure that most airline passengers haven't a clue what it is, so why not use a banner to tell them of opening times and ticket prices? Mrs Queen would have enough for a new royal yacht in weeks. And airline passengers would have something to read.

But it's farmers with whom I have the biggest gripe. Who says that crops have to be planted in squares? What's the matter with a good old-fashioned cock and balls?

In Oxfordshire there's an estate on which all the woods were planted in the precise formations of various troops at some battle in the Crimea. The old buffer who did this could not possibly have known that one day people would be able to enjoy the fruits of his imagination. But today, every time I leave Heathrow, I do.

And certainly, if my farm were on a flight path, I'd be doing all sorts of things that would be invisible to arbiters of good taste on the ground but clear as day from 30,000ft in the sky. Some of the things I have in my mind would involve messages, perhaps about Gordon Brown. And if I had some land in Sussex, I'd plant a wood in such a way that Lufthansa's passengers would know that I shared their view of the Greeks.

My plans are good news for everyone. They are good for business, good for tourism, good for civic pride and good for those airline passengers who see the airport as a glorified bus stop. And not a two-hour compulsory shopping trip.

31 July 2011

That's it – one fluffed backhand and I'm broken as a father

As we know, it is much better to lose than to win. First of all, losing requires much less physical exertion. If you want to win a game of tennis or squash, you have to try very hard, which involves a great deal of running and sweat. Whereas if you really couldn't care less, you can spend an enjoyable hour sauntering about, hitting the ball only if it happens to be passing close by.

It's the same story with chess. If you set out to win, you really have to concentrate hard on what you are doing, anticipating all of the moves your opponent could make and deciding how you might respond.

Whereas if you don't mind losing, you can spend the time when it's not your turn drinking martinis and flicking through powerboat magazines. This is much more enjoyable than doing mental maths.

There's another big advantage to being the plucky Brit who comes home second. It's this: if you win, it is almost impossible to get your face right. You have to look pleased but not smug. And you have to walk that tightrope while making magnanimous noises to your opponent. This is tricky.

Whereas if you lose, you can shrug your shoulders and make all sorts of jokes about how useless you are at everything. There is comedy to be had from being a loser, and none at all from being a winner.

That's why I have spent all of my life ensuring that I am no good at anything.

However, there is an exception to all of this. A time when you must risk a heart attack and a seizure to ensure that you wipe your opponent off the board, or the court or the pitch or wherever you might be. This is when your opponent is one of your own children.

I spent some time yesterday with a fifty-three-year-old man who was absolutely charming, until the conversation turned to his fondness for running half marathons, and how he is driven every year on the Great North Run not to just beat, but to humiliate his twenty-seven-year-old son. I understand this very well.

One of the sports at which I don't excel is table tennis. That said, I'm not a complete numpty. Obviously, I won't spend the game standing fifteen yards from the net making stupid spin shots and sweating like an Egyptian burglar. And you can be assured that if you've moved me to the left side of the table and then suddenly sent a shot to the right, I'm not going to risk a coronary running for it. That would be undignified.

However, while playing my son the other day, all of this changed. It was 8-1 to him. A score that was not possible. It's my job as a dad to be better than him and better than all the other dads, too. It's my job to win.

And then it was 10-1. And then 11-1. At this point, I'm ashamed to say, I changed into a pair of training shoes. Then I went outside, took some deep breaths and came back a new man. I may have even been growling a bit.

I sent my serve deep into the bottom corner. It skimmed the very edge of the table, and whooshed under his armpit. 'Yes!!!' I cried, punching the air, my face contorted with determination and rage.

And so it went on until the score was 21-20. To him. He was serving. He took his time. Wondering, perhaps, what the snarling, sweat-soaked monster at the other end of the table had done with his dad. He pulled his hand back, and this was it.

My life hung in the balance. If I messed up, I would have lost to my own son. I focused. The ball came, I sent it back, with some side. He whipped a fast one hard into the left court but I was ready with a chip. Which he reached, sending a short ball back. I smashed a backhand at it. And knew the instant I made the move, it wouldn't work. I was right. The ball sailed into the pile of boxes at the far end of the room and was lost. So was I.

The boy was very kind and said all the right things. He had been lucky. I hadn't been concentrating properly at the beginning. It had been a good game. And so on.

But I knew that what had just passed between us was not a fluffed backhand in a game of table tennis. It was the moment when the line of his ascent to adulthood passed my line of descent into an old people's home.

For fifteen years, I have encouraged my son and taught him things. I have watched him grow and learn, safe in the knowledge that, of course, I will always be faster and cleverer and stronger. And then comes the moment when you are forced to face up to the fact that this just isn't so.

The fluffed backhand was that moment, that pinprick of time when I realized he is now faster and stronger than me, and that one day soon, he will be cleaning up my faeces and holding my hand when I cross the road.

The only good thing, of course, is that despite his new-found strength and agility, he would never have the same level of wisdom. The young bull knows that he can charge into a field of cows and have a couple. The old bull knows that it's better to stroll into the field and have the lot.

So, even when my son is having to wipe my bottom, I will

still be able to offer him advice on the ways of the world – because I will always be thirty-six years older. He will always have thirty-six fewer years to have experienced things. As a result, I will always have the ability to think more strategically than him.

That's why, after I'd smashed my table tennis bat into a million pieces and fed the remains into a wood-chipping machine, I agreed to sit down and play him at chess.

I poured myself a glass of Ribena so that I would go into the match sober. I turned off my telephone. We began.

And he won that, too. I'm now thinking of killing myself.

7 August 2011

French porn and a little software can save our schools

As you are no doubt aware, every single young person in Britain discovered last week that they had passed fifteen GSCE exams with A* grades. This means they are now able to sit their A levels, which they will also pass with flying colours, and pretty soon they will be at university studying, oh, I don't know, 'dance and waste management' or 'Third World development with pop music'. Both of which are real courses, incidentally.

When they have achieved first-class degrees, they will emerge into the workplace fully formed and educated to a higher standard than any other young people in history. Or will they?

Because if you look carefully at the results you will note that many of the successful children passed in subjects such as ceramics, or needlework, or PE. So while the child may be capable of making a flowerpot and doing a forward somersault, he or she may not be able to go to Paris without ending up in Rio de Janeiro.

Some lay the blame for this fairly and squarely at the door of league tables. They argue that to get a tick in the box from the government, each school must ensure that as many kids as possible get as many passes as possible. This means pupils are discouraged from taking an exam in physics, which is hard, and encouraged instead to sit papers on dusting, or using a urinal.

This is undoubtedly true. I know of one girl who insisted on taking various science subjects for her A levels. Her head teacher argued strongly that she should not but she was adamant and scored a C and two Ds. As a result of this – just one pupil – the school fell fifty places in the league tables.

However, league tables are not the only reason for the shift. There's another which comes to light when you note that this year the number of pupils sitting a geography GCSE fell by a whopping 13,800.

When I was at school, geography was a doddle. We learnt about capital cities and American states and then occasionally we were taken on a field trip to the Peak District so we could stand behind millstone grit outcrops, smoking Player's No. 6s. I loved geography and still do.

However, today the geography syllabus has changed beyond all recognition. Instead of learning which countries are next door to Libya, which is interesting and useful, the subject has been hijacked by eco-mentalists.

Yes, there's a bit of interesting stuff on tectonic plates, but mostly it's a non-stop orgy of weird-beard nonsense about man's impact on the ecosystem and why snails are more important than bypasses. Kids are taught to 'appreciate the ways in which people and environments interact and the need to make developments sustainable'. It sounds like a local council pamphlet.

They're also taught about climate change and hazard management, which is another way of saying health and safety. And then, if they are still awake, they are made to sit through hour after interminable hour of the teacher droning on about the green revolution, globalization and how best to manage the world's resources. This isn't education, it's propaganda. And, worse still, it's boring.

We have the same problem with English literature. Instead of getting children to study books such as *Matterhorn* or *Birdsong*, which are exciting and well written, they are still made to read Shakespeare. If I were running the education system, Shakespeare would be banned. His plots are simplistic. His characters are unfathomable. He is only of use to postgraduate dweebs interested in what was going on with the language in the sixteenth century. He should be removed from the curriculum and take Chaucer and bloody Milton with him.

Then there's maths. What in God's name is the point of learning algebra and cosines and long division? Maths is not necessary once you are past the age of four because anything more complicated than adding two and two can be done on a telephone.

To make matters worse, maths is compulsory. Which is almost certainly why so many children choose to spend their days sitting around in an Arndale centre frightening old ladies.

As a country we need a rethink on not only what we teach our children but also how we teach it. Take French. Like geography, it, too, is less popular now than PE and ironing but I know how to reverse that trend. I know how you could make every single child in the land fluent by the time they are fourteen. It's simple. Instead of teaching them that a table is female and how to conjugate verbs, simply play them French – ahem – 'art' films with the subtitles turned off. They'd get the gist pretty quickly.

What's more, when they are in France they will find it much more beneficial if they can say 'My dear, your thighs are exquisite' than if they can only say 'The pen of my aunt'. Just one word of warning. It's probably best not to let children see German 'art' films. Not unless they want to take a GSCE in moustaches.

Let me give you an example of how a change in teaching methods has revolutionized life in my house. Ever since they were old enough to walk, my children have had music lessons.

They've done their scales and learnt to play stupid bits of Bartok and as a result none of them can play an instrument.

But yesterday I was sitting watching television when I heard my youngest daughter sit down at the piano and play 'Clocks' by Coldplay absolutely perfectly. I was so staggered that I went next door to find out how this had been possible.

It turns out she had downloaded the score, which was displayed on an iPad like a Space Invaders game. I had no clue what was going on but, her being twelve, it all made perfect sense. This morning she bashed out the second movement of the 'Moonlight Sonata' so beautifully I thought Beethoven had dropped in for breakfast.

If schools can use technology like this and French pornography and get rid of Shakespeare, the nation will once again be full to the brim with educated people. Rather than people who have a lot of GSCEs.

28 August 2011

Oh, Berbatovs – I've got to learn footballspeak

Back in the 1960s there were many things to occupy the mind of a small boy, many rivalries to be discussed in the playground. There was music, for starters; lots of it and all so very different. There were tunes for mods and rockers and hippies, and there was bubblegum pop for people with pigtails.

Later we would discover Led Zep and the Who and the Stones and I would argue until well into the night about who were best. And this was just the tip of the iceberg. Was *Crime of the Century* better than *Rumours*? Was Mitch Mitchell a better drummer than Nick Mason? Who was better-looking, Christine McVie or Stevie Nicks?

And when we tired of music, there was still a rich seam of debate to be explored. Ferrari versus Lotus. Chelsea versus Leeds. England versus Australia. Communism versus capitalism. America versus Vietnam. The nearest I ever came to an actual schoolboy fistfight was with an idiot who really and truly believed Wrangler made better jeans than Levi's.

Now, though, all this is gone, swept away by the rise and rise of Premier League football. Today, if you listen to children talking, it's not about whether McDonald's does a better fry than Burger King or whether the Taliban have more of a point than Obama. No. There's an occasional discussion – usually among girls – about which *X Factor* contestant is most likely to end up back behind the counter at Asda that week, but mostly it's football.

In our house it's constant. My fifteen-year-old boy is a

fanatical Chelsea supporter and I like to play a game with him: starting the conversation as far away as possible from football and then seeing how long it takes him to get it back to Stamford Bridge. His record is pre-Byzantine architecture to John Terry in three moves.

His fanaticism has even had an effect on me. Until quite recently I saw football as twenty-two overpaid young men with silly hair kicking an inflated sheep's pancreas around a field. Yes, I was able to recite the Chelsea and Leeds teams that played in the 1970 FA Cup final but I only chose to do so, in my head, when I felt I needed to last a little longer in the bedroom department. I would even pray for England to get knocked out of tournaments so that television programming could return to normal and I could get back to discussing the Rubettes and the joy of a pleated Ben Sherman shirt.

Not any more. Last year I flew all the way to South Africa – at my own expense – to watch Holland and Spain play in the World Cup final. Then, last weekend, I voluntarily sat down and watched Tottenham play Manchester City, two teams in which I have absolutely no interest. Because unless I know what's going on these days, I'm useless to my son when I'm at home and in a conversational cul-de-sac when I'm out.

I met a chap last week who drives a Toyota Prius and thinks it's unkind to shoot a pheasant in the face. I was very much looking forward to talking to him about these and other things. But no. We started with football over the prawn cocktail and were still at it as we finished the Black Forest gateau.

It's not just a religion here, either. Premier League football is now screened in more than 200 countries around the world. And we're not talking 'screened' in the same way that Piers Morgan's chat show is 'screened'. I mean watched. And not just casually, but fanatically.

Because the big teams field players from all over the world, pretty well every country has a local hero for whom they can cheer.

Nigerians can support Chelsea because they have John Obi Mikel. Bulgarians can support Manchester United because they have Dimitar Berbatov. Scandinavians have a fondness for Liverpool because the Reds once employed a Nor called John Arne Riise.

This means that wherever we go in the world my son is always first to make friends with the locals. I caught him in earnest conversation with a known Caribbean drug dealer the other day and was very angry, until I realized that they were actually discussing Arsenal's chances this season.

And while it's undoubtedly sad that football now sits in humankind's conversation pit like a gigantic elephant, it's good news that Britain gets to sit in the spotlight every weekend.

There is, however, a problem. According to all the experts, the league will be dominated this year by just two teams: Manchester City and Manchester United. That's not good, because what makes the Premier League so much better than any other in the world is the sheer number of teams that start every season with half a chance. If it's a two-horse race, between the teams from just one city, new boys like me are going to struggle to stay interested.

Which brings me on to an idea suggested by John Timpson, the shoe-repairs magnate, whom I met on holiday last month. He reckons that the Football Association should work out a formula based on a club's finances to determine how big the goalmouths should be.

This is inspired. It would mean that when a rich side such as Manchester City plays a less well-off side such as Norwich, the East Anglians would be aiming at a goal that's about the same size as their home county, while the Mancs would be trying to get the ball through what was basically a letter box.

Obviously it needn't be that pronounced. A few inches either way should be enough to level the playing field. Rich owners could then continue to field great teams playing great football. But the result? Deliciously, it could go either way.

Then – and this is my little twist – if it's 0-0 at half-time, the second half should be played with two balls on the pitch at the same time.

Oh, and finally, this is from my son: anyone appearing for a team with Manchester in the title must play while wearing a bag on his head.

4 September 2011

My daughter and I stepped over the body and into a brothel

There is a terrible famine in East Africa, which is great news if you're a celebrity.

Because it means you can head off to Ethiopia for some nice PR and a spot of late-summer sunshine.

It's a great gig.

All you have to do is walk about on a rubbish tip, looking despondent, and then cuddle a baby with flies in its eyes while pulling your best kid-in-a-wheelchair charity face.

Bang in a couple of shots of you pretending to listen to a starving mum, plaster the finished film with a veneer of 'Everybody Hurts' by REM and it's back to the hotel for a few beers and a sixth-form debate with the charity bigwigs on the injustices of the World Bank, Swiss drug companies, General Motors, climate change, McDonald's and the bloody Tories.

Meanwhile, back at home, everyone is bored to tears. Legend has it that Bonio once told an audience who'd come to hear him sing 'Wiv or Wivout You' that every time he clapped his hands a child in Africa died, prompting one wag in the crowd to shout out: 'Well, stop clapping your hands then.'

Deep down we all feel very sorry for the starving masses but the compassion is buried under the blanket of certainty that Africa is basically screwed. Russell Brand can walk about on a rubbish tip till the cows come home but it'll make no difference to the fact that the leaders are corrupt, violence is a way of life, the Sahara is getting bigger and there's not a damn thing anyone can do about any of it. It's just a question of what wipes them out first: starvation or AIDS.

I've always felt this way. Bob Geldof may have it in his head that I went to Live Aid so that others, less fortunate than me, might have a happier life. Well, I didn't. I went because I wanted to see the Who. And despite constant denials, I've always harboured a deep-down belief that the money I paid for the ticket was used to provide the Ethiopian president's personal bodyguard with a new Kalashnikov.

Anyway, moving on, I have a strict policy with my children about their holidays. They can do their snogging and drinking in the Easter break but in the summer they have to go somewhere a bit more educational. Which is why, last weekend, my eldest daughter and I set off for a mini-break in Uganda.

A few facts. Half the population of this landlocked East African country is fourteen or younger and the gross domestic product is £11 billion or, to put it another way, about a tenth of what Britain spends on the National Health Service alone. It's very poor, but in Entebbe, which is used by the United Nations as a hub, the whole place looks like Surrey. Except for the shops, most of which are named after the baby Jesus. You have the Blessed Lord butchery and the Praise Be to the Almighty banana emporium. You also have a lot of roadside stalls selling double beds. No idea why.

The capital, though, Kampala? That's a different story. I've seen poverty in my travels. I once saw a woman in Bolivia having a tug-of-war with a dog over an empty crisp packet and in Cambodia you get the impression that pretty well everyone has had their legs blown off by landmines. But nothing prepares you for the jaw-dropping horror of a Ugandan slum.

We stepped out of the car, over the body of a man, and

moments later we were surrounded by solid proof that Dante completely miscalculated the number of circles in hell. We'll start with sanitation.

There isn't any. Well, there are a couple of public bogs, but since they cost 200 shillings to use, everyone simply uses what passes for the street. At one point we were taken to a 10ft x 10ft brothel, which in the rainy season floods to a depth of 2ft with raw sewage. This means customers have the opportunity to catch cholera and AIDS in one hit.

You may wonder why anyone goes there. Well, it's simple. In a two-hour walk I didn't see a single girl under the age of eighteen. 'They don't survive,' said our guide. Which, when translated, means they are either raped and then murdered to shut them up or they are beheaded by witch doctors in the daily child sacrifice ceremonies.

Not that most of the boys seem to care very much since almost all of them are completely off their heads on solvents.

They lie there – some of them just three years old – entirely unaware of the fact they're in a puddle of someone else's piss.

You know the cupboard under your stairs? In a Kampala slum this would be considered a luxury house and at night it would sleep seven people. I could not see how this would be possible unless they all stood up. Which, when the rains come, is necessary anyway.

On the upside, we did find a lovely place for lunch. A few miles away from the slum, in the shadow of an amazing new hotel complex owned by the president's wife, was a Belgian restaurant where we had a Nile beer and an excellent beef stew. It cost more than most people in Uganda will earn in a lifetime.

Over coffee, which is delicious in this part of the world, we talked about the Lord's Resistance Army, which runs about in the north of Uganda torturing, mutilating, murdering and raping pretty much anything that hasn't already died of starvation.

Over the obligatory corporate greed and climate change debate on what's to be done, we concluded that Live Aid didn't work. Live 8 didn't work. Nothing's worked. And, yes, while it's good that David Cameron has pledged to keep Britain's foreign aid at similar levels, we shouldn't forget that last year the Ministry of Defence spent £1.7 million on body armour and helmets for the Ugandan army which, honestly, isn't really what most people think of as 'aid'.

All I know is that when you've been there, you feel compelled to do something. Appear in a charity video, walking about on a rubbish tip, wearing a compassionate face? Yup. Count me in.

11 September 2011

Own up, we all had a vile streak long before going online

Every week we are presented with supposedly conclusive proof that Britain is broken. The summer was marked by riots; you get five minutes in jail for murdering a baby; our education system is worse than Slovenia's; and we're told that it's perfectly natural and traditional for travelling people to keep a handful of slaves in the shed. Meanwhile, register offices are full of people who've never met; your village bobby can neither read nor write; your MP is an imbecile; burglaries aren't investigated; the banks are back in cloud cuckoo land; and the rivers are all full of excrement.

Swim down the Thames these days and you really will be 'going through the motions'.

Those who seek to make gloom and doom from all of this say that Britain was much better when everything was in black and white and we had the reassuring spectacle of *Dixon of Dock Green* on the television every week. But this is rubbish. Because back then everyone died of pneumoconiosis when they were twelve, immigrants were routinely poked with sticks, tea was considered exotic and Ronnie and Reggie Kray were running amok in the capital, nailing people's heads to the floor.

If you developed cancer in 1956, you'd had it and would welcome death's cold embrace with open arms because it was a ticket out of the grime and the misery and the unfunny television shows and the soot and the socialism.

The fact, then, is this: life's better now than it has been at any point in human history. It's better than it was ten years ago. It's better than it was yesterday morning. Except for one thing.

You may have read last week about a young man called Sean Duffy, who took it upon himself to post revoltingly unkind internet messages about teenagers who had died. He superimposed the face of one, who had committed suicide by throwing herself in front of a train, on to a video of *Thomas the Tank Engine*. And he put up pictures of the site where another had lost her life in a road smash with the caption: 'Used car for sale, one useless owner.'

It's impossible to conceive how much anguish this caused the families, and that's why you were no doubt delighted to hear that Duffy was given the maximum jail sentence of eighteen weeks.

But hang on a minute: is he so very different from everyone else? Last week one newspaper ran on its website some photos of an actress who had been knocked down by a car. People in their droves left unbelievably unkind comments about her face and her children. There was even worse abuse for Jade Jagger, who had been photographed topless on a beach. She was described as 'ugly', 'fat' and a 'spoilt rude cow'. Elsewhere, Elton John was 'greedy', the Duchess of Cornwall was 'lazy' and Simon Cowell's legs were 'too short'.

If you plunge even more deeply into the darkest corners of cyberspace, you will find websites that show people with severed arms searching for the heads of their loved ones on the hard shoulder. People being eaten by tigers. People after they've jumped from the top of a skyscraper. And each is accompanied by amusing observations from the folks at home. If you die now, you'd better make sure no one has a camera, because if they do, the event is almost certain to end up on the web.

The internet is now just a receptacle for vitriol. It's malice in wonderland. And that's before we get to Facebook – which, let's not forget, was set up as a place where men could go online to make judgements about a girl's appearance – or Twitter.

You may say this is a new phenomenon – another example of the sick society we've created – and that it's caused by the anonymity of the internet. But is it? Long before you had a domain and an email address, you would sit in the safety of your car, muttering abuse at other drivers. Which amounts to exactly the same as muttering cyberspace abuse at Cheryl Cole's hair from the safety of your home or office.

And even before people had windscreens to hide behind they would go home after a hard day down the pit and mumble about the shortcomings of their neighbours, their colleagues, their bosses, the government. This is the way we are. It's just that now the internet lets us grumble in public.

Time and again a mother has presented me with her new-born and I've wanted to say: 'Holy cow. It looks like a smashed ape.' But I've been forced by my frontal lobes to *um* and *ah* until I can find a compliment of some kind. It's usually about the pram.

Once, I was taken backstage after an appalling play to meet the actress who had been simply dreadful in the lead. But, instead of saying she was dire, I cracked my face into a beam and said she'd been 'amazing'. Which was also true. She had.

Then there was the time I interviewed Chuck Yeager, the sound-barrier-breaking former test pilot. I wanted to say afterwards that he had been, without a doubt, the most unpleasant man in the entire world and that he was living, breathing proof that you should never meet your heroes. But instead I thanked him for his time and drove away.

In her latter years my grandmother lost the brake on her brain and would spend her days in the local dress shop, howling with derisive laughter at everyone who came out of the changing rooms. Secretly, I've always wanted to do the same. I bet you have, too.

Well, now the internet lets you. No longer do you have to sit in a fog of impotence during a television show that you dislike. You can get on your phone or computer and let the world know. Last week, for instance, Lily Allen saw a picture of me in the paper and tweeted one word: 'vomit'.

The internet hasn't caused any of this. It isn't, as some would have you believe, another example of Broken Britain and a fractured society. No, the internet is just a tool, which has demonstrated that behind our smiles and our cleverness, human beings, actually, are fairly terrible.

18 September 2011

Down, boy! Fido's fallen in love with the vacuum cleaner

There are many reasons why people choose to own a pet. To stop a daughter's endless nagging; for companionship; as an excuse to take the occasional walk; or because you won it at a fair and it seemed cruel to flush it down the waste disposal unit. Cruel, and difficult, especially if it was a horse.

However, according to a recent survey, 39 per cent of pet owners say they invested in their furry friend to replace a husband or wife. And I'm sorry, but I find this a bit alarming, because how can a pet possibly do that? It can't cook, or iron, or clean the air filter on a 1973 Lotus Elan.

And if you try to use it for a spot of jiggy jiggy, you can be fairly sure the police will want a word.

The trouble is, of course, that we all love animals a lot more than we love people. And the animal we love most of all is the dog. Dogs make us soft in the head.

In the disaster movie 2012, thousands of Chinese people are killed by a tsunami. But that's okay because we are treated to a close-up of the heroine's King Charles spaniel boarding a rescue ship in the nick of time. Then you have *Armageddon*, in which giant meteorites wipe out half of New York. But this is no problem because when the destruction is over, we see that the dog that we thought had been killed is in fact perfectly all right. Phew. It was only people that got flattened and blown up.

Such is our love for the dog that there are now 1.2 million Pakistanis living in Britain, 154,000 Nigerians, about a million Poles and 7.3 million dogs. Many of them live in my house.

On the face of it, it's an excellent idea to keep a pooch. It will bark at burglars and sit by the fire in the evenings, looking all sweet and cuddly. And all it demands in return for its sweetness and its Group 4 policy on security is a handful of biscuits and a bowlful of tinned meat from a company that did somehow work out how to push a horse through a waste disposal unit.

Unfortunately, it doesn't work out like this in reality. Let's take my West Highland terrier as a prime example of the problem. She is very cute and has fully jointed ears that swivel about when she is excited. On the downside, she is very violent. In the past two months alone she has eaten the lady who delivers the papers, the postman and the man who came round to mend my computer. She's like Begbie from *Trainspotting*.

Then there's a labradoodle, which is about the same size as an elephant. This means that no matter how high the shelf on which we put leftover chops and joints of lamb, he can get at them no problem at all. He also manages to look fantastically indignant when you tell him off.

There's also an elderly Labrador, who is now blind, deaf, arthritic and bald. Technically, she isn't really a dog any more. And then there's a young Labrador, who recently had her first period. This drove the labradoodle stark staring mad. He became a sex-crazed elephant-wolf who spent his entire time trying to put his ridiculous dog lipstick into the back of the stricken Lab, until eventually we had to send her away to the kennels.

This made things worse because he was now cut off from the target of his lust. So he began to mount everything else. The dishwasher, the keyhole in the front door, me, my daughter's friends and the exhaust pipe of my bloody car. At one point he attempted to rape the newspaper columnist Jane

Moore's dog and didn't seem to realize that a) it was male and b) he'd accidentally climbed on to the damn thing's face.

We locked him in a fenced-off part of the garden and he tried to eat a metal gate to get out. And then, with blood pouring from the wounds he'd inflicted on himself, he scampered off to the hen house. Nobody in human history has ever thought, 'Hmmm. I fancy a go on that chicken.' But he did.

Meanwhile, the housekeeper's Lab had been similarly affected and had tried to mate with the cat, my wellington boots and the lawnmower. Six months from now I won't be at all surprised if one of my donkeys gives birth to a dog. It's been like living in an inter-species free-love commune. Only with added howling.

You don't think of any of this when you are buying a puppy. You think the worst thing that could happen is that it will unravel the occasional loo roll. Nobody at Battersea Dogs Home ever tells a prospective customer that one day the scampering little mite in which they're interested will try to have sex with the vacuum cleaner.

My wife suggested that we really ought to relieve the pressure by, ahem, giving the maniacal labradoodle a helping hand, but I'm sorry, no: that's up there with morris dancing and incest. And so we took him to the kennels and brought the bitch home.

When she had finished filling the house with what to a doggy nose is Impulse body spray we brought him back and were looking forward to some peace. But no. Because while he was away, he had caught something called kennel cough. It doesn't sound so bad, does it? You think you could live with a coughing dog. Well, you can't, because a more accurate name for the disease would be 'explosive vomiting'.

So now he helps himself to a leg of lamb that we'd stored on top of a pylon, and just a few minutes later it shoots back out of his mouth all over whatever it was he broke last week by trying to have sex with. This upsets the Westie, who decides to bite another visitor, and when you tell him off he has the cheek to look affronted.

This is the reality of dog ownership. Fluids. Mess. Stolen food. Expense. Savaged paper boys. No post. Vets' bills. Broken vacuum cleaners. Ruined washing machines. Chewed shoes. Unravelled bog rolls. Endless barking, and then terrible, aching sadness when they die.

I can understand, therefore, why they make such an ideal substitute for a husband or a wife. There's no real difference.

25 September 2011

Street lights and binmen? Luxuries we just can't afford

So let's see if I've got this straight. If Italy goes belly up, any bank that has lent Mr Berlusconi money will go belly up, too. So will the people whose savings were held there. And all the shops where they used to buy provisions. And the airlines they used to fly with. And the banks from which the airlines had borrowed money. And their customers. And their local shops. If Italy goes, we all go. Plainly, that would be bad.

The experts are sitting around in huddles with their political masters, and the general consensus seems to be that no one has the first clue how to stop this happening. Well, unless I'm being thick, I do.

At present, various bits of British government expenditure are being ring-fenced because, it's claimed, no civilized country can do without them. The National Health Service is an obvious example, but the fact is, we may have been able to afford healthcare for everyone when the most expensive drug on offer was an aspirin and teeth were removed with a hammer; now that we have complex operations and lasers and colonoscopies and people with exotic diseases such as AIDS, we cannot afford it any more.

Nor can we afford an aircraft carrier. Or bypasses. In August alone this country had to borrow £16 billion to meet the gap between what it spent and what it earned. Obviously that's unsustainable.

The problem goes way beyond the big stuff. Because of global warming, or intensive farming, or possibly the satellite that crashed into Canada recently, Britain's waterways are being overrun with blue-green algae that make them extremely pretty. Unfortunately, if you choose to swim in an affected waterway, your skin will itch and you could end up with a poorly tummy.

You can see what's going to happen next. A small boy with freckles and a cute nose is going to end up on a BBC regional news programme all covered in diarrhoea, and his sobbing mum is going to say that someone should have done something about it. To prevent this public relations disaster from unfurling, water companies are being forced to spend millions of pounds clearing it up. That's millions we don't have being spent on some algae. Just so some kid doesn't end up with an itchy botty.

It's absolutely insane. Over the years, my kids have trodden on venomous stonefish and been attacked by jellyfish and battered to pieces by storm-tossed coral. And I don't complain to the authorities in Barbados. It's one of those things. But now, here, it's somehow become a government's job to prevent it from happening. And to provide lavatories for dogs.

In fact we've become used in recent years to the government providing us with everything. We expect it to protect us from algae and take away our rubbish and educate our kids and look after us when we are poorly and have a bobby on the street corner and fight Johnny Taliban and put up park benches and keep the libraries open and stop planes blowing up and build roads and send round an appliance when we've caught fire and make sure the food we eat is delicious and nutritious and lock up vagabonds and house the poor.

Fine, but have you noticed something? All the countries that share this view are now in a complete pickle while countries such as India and China, where shoes are considered a luxury, are doing rather well.

Last weekend the Labour party said that it would solve all our problems by cutting university tuition fees to £6,000. But that's like Dawn French cutting her fingernails to save weight. It's a pointless, meaningless, futile gesture and demonstrates clearly that Ed Miliband must be an imbecile.

We read all the time about people who borrow vast sums to fund their sports cars and speedboats, and we tut and think that they must be very tragic people with many complex problems. The government is behaving in exactly the same way, fearful that if it actually makes the necessary cuts, the country will be cast into poverty and the chance of a second term will be lost. Well, let me make a suggestion. Screw the second term and ask a question instead: what exactly is poverty?

An Eton schoolboy was once asked to write on the subject, and he began thus: 'There was once a very poor family. The father was poor. The mother was poor. The children were poor. Even the butler was poor . . .'

In the olden days you could tell at a glance if someone was existing below the poverty line because they were eight years old and sitting in a gutter with a dirty face, eating a turnip. Now it's more difficult. People claim to be poverty-stricken even when they have mobile phones and a television set and an internet connection. And when you've seen a woman on a Bolivian rubbish tip having a tug-of-war with a dog over an empty crisp packet, it's hard to stop yourself punching people such as this in the middle of their face.

The European Union defines poverty as any household that exists on an income that is less than 60 per cent of the national average. In Monte Carlo that sort of guideline would put Elton John on income support.

Here the average household income is about £35,000 a year and it's said that in the region of one in five exists on less than 60 per cent of this figure. But it's confusing because many pensioners fall way below the threshold in terms of income but own the house in which they are starving to death.

I read one report recently that says poverty should be measured on how poor you 'feel'. Well, I was at a charity fund-raiser the other night and, trust me, among all the Russian oligarchs I felt very poverty-stricken indeed.

The solution is that we all need to be recalibrated. Not just us, but the whole stupid Western world. We all think that street lights and having the bins emptied are essential. We must start to understand that, actually, they're luxuries. And we can't afford them any more.

2 October 2011

Ker-ching! I've got a plan to turn India's pollution into pounds

Over breakfast at a 700-year-old Indian fort that had been lovingly converted into a wonkily wired, no-smoking youth hostel, I met an Englishman who was planning to drive all the way across the subcontinent in an electric Reva G-Wiz. This seemed an especially pointless thing to do.

It turned out that he worked for the British government and was setting up a team to advise the emerging economic superpower on how best to cut its carbon emissions. As you can imagine, I had many questions for him on the matter.

Starting with: right, so you walk into a meeting with Mr Patel and you say . . . what exactly? 'Hello. I come from a country where everyone has musical loo-roll dispensers and patio heaters and enormous televisions, and we recognize you'd like some of that action too. But we feel it would be better for the polar bear and the Amazonian tree frog if you stayed in the Dark Ages.'

I imagine that Mr Patel might not be very sympathetic to this argument. Especially if his next meeting was with a representative from the German government who was going to say exactly the same thing. And doubly especially if he had hosted similar meetings the previous day with the Americans, the Canadians, the French, the Italians and so on.

The idea that Western governments should lecture India on how to conduct itself is absurd. It's like Simon Cowell popping into the terraced home of a lottery winner and telling them it would be better for the planet and their soul if they gave the jackpot to charity.

There's more, too. As we know, the government in Britain is cutting many services as it desperately tries to reduce the nation's debt. The streets are packed with homeless ex-librarians whose places of work have been boarded up in the never-ending quest to save cash. We have the prime minister on the Tube and the mayor of London on a bicycle, the lights are out at Buckingham Palace and BBC2 is showing pretty much what it showed in 1972. We understand that there is a need for all this. It makes sense. And we like to think that, day and night, every single government minister is sitting in a candlelit office, in mittens, desperately thinking up new ways of getting the debt down.

So what in the name of all that's holy are we doing funding a team of people whose job it is to tell the Indians to stick with their oxen? No, really, I mean it. How can we be turning off our street lights and planning to kick-start the Olympics with a pigeon and a box of sparklers when we are running a climate change department in Delhi?

What is Chris Huhne thinking of? I realize that the energy secretary is jolly busy dealing with his speeding ticket and the recent World School Milk Day but I urge him to have a long, hard look at the team in India and think: 'How can I be responsible for putting a million people out of work in Middlesbrough while funding this claptrap on the other side of the world?'

Of course, there are those who think that global warming is the greatest threat to humanity and that if any spending is going to be ring-fenced over the next few years, it must be money used in the war on carbon dioxide. They would abolish the army, the National Health Service, the north and those who live in it if they thought it would keep the polar ice intact. They would even seek to make it a crime to disagree with them. But that hasn't happened yet, so . . .

For sure, the air quality in India is extremely poor. When you come in to land at Delhi airport, it's like descending into a big airborne cloud of HP Sauce. At ground level, life's better – the air is like a consommé – but after a day it still feels as though you've been sucking furiously on a lozenge made from crude oil.

Sadly, though, air you can eat has nothing whatsoever to do with carbon dioxide. If you want to make it go away, you don't send climate change experts. You send mechanics to service the buses properly.

I also recognize that India is committed to reducing its emissions – well, that's what it says in meetings – and that there may be a couple of businesses here that could make a bob or two from popping over there and helping out. But India is a country on the move. And if we in Britain want to make a few quid out of its growth, isn't it better to sell it our jet fighters and our diggers and our bladeless Dyson fans? We should be milking its growth, not trying to stifle it with pious words and Uriah Heep hand-wringing.

It's rare that I actually get cross about something. But I am cross about this. The high commission in India has an important function. It is there to help British nationals who have lost their passports or who have become so incapacitated by diarrhoea that they've just excreted their own spleen.

It is there, too, to promote British business and, most of all, it is there to foster good relations between India and Britain. How are any of these things helped by a team of mean-spirited eco-ists who want to stand on the hose that's fuelling India's growth?

I don't mind that my taxes are used for schools I don't use, street lighting that doesn't shine on my house, hospitals I don't need and a police force that most of the time is a bloody nuisance. I understand that this is how the world works. I pay for a system in which I play no part.

But I really can't get to sleep at night knowing that some of the tax I pay is being used to fund a climate changist to drive across India in a G-Wiz. The only good thing is that it will take him several years, during which time India can choose life, choose a career, choose washing machines, cars, compact-disc players, electrical tin openers, good health, low cholesterol, dental insurance and a nice set of matching luggage.

23 October 2011

Look out, dear, a carbuncle is heading your way

As I'm sure you know, it is very difficult to get planning permission these days. Unless, of course, you are a Freemason. Even if you want to add a small side extension to your kitchen, the council's inspector will raise all sorts of issues about the neighbour's right to light, the need to protect the original style of the house and what provisions you intend to make for off-street parking.

And even if you cover all these bases, he will usually find a bat in the attic, and that'll be pretty much that.

So imagine how hard life must be if you are a developer and you want to build a 1,000ft skyscraper in the middle of a big city such as London. You'd need to be the Duke of Kent, or at the very least a grand wizard, to stand even half a chance.

And even if you manage to convince the local council your design is sound, that the foundations won't impede progress on the District line and that no bat will need to be rehoused, you will still have to get past the man I met at a dinner last week. The man whose job is to protect 'the look' of London. This must be the hardest job . . . in the world.

Because it's all very well saying now that London is perfect, but what if someone had done that in 1066? 'I'm sorry, William, but you cannot build a tower on the Thames because it would spoil everyone's view of the inner-city farm on Watling Street.'

It's like those morons who have decided that Britain's countryside was absolutely perfect in about 1910 and that every effort must be made to keep the dry-stone walls and the hedges and the village idiots.

Or, worse, the climate. The temperature has shifted dramatically over the millennia, so which crackpot has decided that it's correct now? Because it absolutely isn't if you live in Sudan.

Then there's the case of Scotland. It began life as part of America, although at the time this was down near the South Pole. Gradually it broke away from Iowa and began its move northwards, until around 400 million years ago, when it sank just off the equator.

What if someone had decided then that the world should be preserved just as it was? We'd have no tarmac. No phones. No penicillin. No Highland bagpipes. No bolshie trade unionists. No Labour party. So, on balance, it wouldn't have been all bad.

Of course, at the other end of the scale, we have the problems of rampant development trampling all over the bedrock of history. Cape Town springs to mind here. From the sea, this used to be one of the world's most attractive cities, but now your eye is drawn to the World Cup stadium that sits in the view like a giant laundry basket.

Then there's Birmingham. Such is the prominence of the Selfridges building that you no longer notice the tumbledown, smoke-stained old factories or the canals full of shopping trolleys.

The history has been obliterated by something that appears to have come from the opening credits of *Doomwatch*.

The man I met at the party wholeheartedly agrees that balance is everything. He knows that new buildings are necessary but has to temper that with various established views and sightlines that should be preserved for the good of our souls.

For example, when you climb up Parliament Hill in the

north of London and turn round, you don't want to be presented with a city that looks like Manhattan. You want the London Eye but you also want to be able to see the things that your forefathers saw. Apparently, it is writ that visitors to Richmond Park in the south-west must be able to look down an avenue of trees and see St Paul's Cathedral in the City. And it doesn't matter how much wizardry developers deploy or how silly their handshakes, that's that.

Here's a good one. As you may know, the Americans decided quite recently that it simply wasn't possible to butcher Grosvenor Square any more and that it was time to move out of their current fortress to a new super-embassy on a five-acre site in Nine Elms, south of the Thames. Everyone was very supportive of this. It would provide many jobs and keep alive the special relationship in which they decide what they'd like to do and we run about wagging our tails, hoping that if we look sweet, they will give us a biscuit. Frankly, if they'd wanted to build their new embassy in the Queen's knicker drawer, we'd all have said, 'Oh yes, Mr Obama. And can we have some more Winalot?'

Happily, however, we have a man in charge of 'the look', who pointed out that if you stood on Vauxhall Bridge, the new embassy would sit slap bang in the sort of view immortalized by Turner. He saw no problems with the building they were proposing but realized that it would undoubtedly have a flag on the roof. So right in the middle of this much-photographed all-English scene would be the Stars and Stripes.

I'm sure the Americans find this objection very petty, and that Mr Cameron has been made to sit on the naughty step, but would they let us fly our flag in between the Capitol building and the Washington Monument? My guess is ... probably not.

That said, I do wish London were a bit more high-rise. Out in the east there are a few tall buildings shielding us like giant glass leylandii from the views of Essex. But there are nowhere near enough. And there won't be any more because of London City airport and the problems of coming in to land between Barclays' boardroom and the executive fourty-fifth-floor bogs at HSBC.

We need to look elsewhere and find a site where designers and architects can run amok with their gigantic cathedrals to capitalism. A site where there are no snails and where there are no ancient views to worry about. A site where we don't worry about what's been lost, only about what we have gained. And I think I have just the spot: right on top of my ex-wife.

30 October 2011

Oh, the vita is dolce. But the music? Shaddap you face

Perfection varies. One man's dream is another man's gangrenous knee. For some, perfection is a Riva Aquarama and Kristin Scott Thomas and getting ready to go to a party on a warm night with friends. For others, it's a damp hillside and a tent. There is, however, one constant. Everybody is in agreement that while the actors and the scenes and the plot may vary, the location is always the same. The location has to be Italy.

Nearly all my favourite places in the world are in Italy. Lake Como. Capri. Siena. And last week I found another.

It's a little restaurant called Volo in the southern city of Lecce, where you can sit outside in the evening, even in early November, and startle yourself with the swordfish carpaccio and the cheese and the local wine. The owner's almond cakes were the nicest thing I'd ever put in my mouth.

The couples that walked by were dazzlingly beautiful. It was impossibly perfect.

It's in a back street, far from the main squares, but even here the lighting is as carefully considered as if it had been designed for Pink Floyd. Where the narrow street went round a corner, someone had lit a candle. Why? Just to bring a bit of warmth and interest to a small place that would otherwise be lost to the night. That's the Italian way.

I think it's true to say that everyone I've ever met has at some point harboured a secret little dream that one day they will have a house in Umbria, where they will sit under the wisteria eating olives they have bought in the local market that morning. It's one of the things that makes us British: wanting to be Italian. They're everything we're not. And they're everything we want to be. Stylish, unconcerned with petty rules, expressive and well-endowed.

Once, I said that to be born Italian and male was to win first prize in the lottery of life. Nobody argued. Nobody wrote to say: 'No. I wish I were Swedish and gay.'

However, while Italy has many things that we can admire and envy and dream of, there is one big thing wrong with it. It has the worst soundtrack in the world. And I'm not talking about the barking dogs that wake you up every morning. Or the idiot with the strimmer in the next valley, or even the swarms of two-stroke motor scooters. No. I'm talking about the radio stations.

Just as it is everywhere else in the world these days, the dial is rammed full of choice. But actually there is no choice at all because, as with the menu in a TGI Friday's, you don't want any of it.

Music snobs have sneered for years about the awfulness of Europop – and with good reason. It's shocking. Things I'd rather listen to than a Belgian Eurovision wannabe include the sound of my own firing squad. Pop radio is just as bad in France and Spain and Germany – home of the Scorpions – but it reaches the fourteenth circle of hell when you arrive in Rome. I heard one tune on the car radio that was so bad, I felt compelled to find the man who'd written it and cut his head off. So imagine my surprise when the next thirty-six songs were even worse.

How can a country that has given the world so much art and literature and electricity possibly think it is acceptable to drive along listening to home-grown synthpop?

How can a country capable of making an engine sing like the best tenor of all time say that Gabriella Ferri sounds like

Janis Joplin? The only way you could have made Ms Joplin sound remotely similar would have been to plug her into the mains.

You think Italian television is bad, and you're right: it is very bad. But it is a haven of highbrow peace and summer'-s-afternoon tranquillity compared with the non-stop barrage of electronic trash that the radio pumps out. All of the shows are hosted by two people – usually a man and a woman – who argue furiously for a few minutes and then play a noise that sounds like a flock of tomcats being killed with a buzz saw.

And then, just when you think it can't get any worse, some-one starts to sing. And the problem with that is: they are singing in Italian. And while Italian is good when you are making love or ordering lunch or even shouting at another motorist, it really doesn't work in a pop song.

'Yes, sir, I can boogie' becomes 'Si, signor, posso boogie'. Which doesn't sound quite right, somehow. And neither does 'Bambina, puoi guidare la mia macchina', which is Italian for 'Baby, you can drive my car'. Singing anything other than opera in Italian is like mixing cement in a tutu or swimming in a ballgown. Messy and wrong.

Plainly, Silvio Berlusconi knows this, which is why he has chosen to release a CD of love songs. I'm not making that up. He really has. Mr Bunga-Bunga used to be the singer on a cruise ship and . . . oh God, I've just thought of something. What if it was the one that employed John Prescott as a stew-ard? It's hard to think of anything worse than being on a cruise ship, but being stuck out there with a million old people, and two million desperate divorcees, being served by Mr Bolshie and crooned at by Silvio? Honestly, I'd rather fire a nail gun into my testicles.

Anyway, Berlusconi fancies himself as a singer and lyricist, and he has a mate who used to be a traffic warden who fancies himself as a guitarist, and the two of them have battled their way through Italy's increasingly difficult financial problems by staying up late into the night writing a selection of smoochy love songs.

I can give you a taste of the lyrics: 'Listen to these songs. They are for you. Listen to them when you have a thirst for caresses; sing them when you are hungry for tenderness . . .' And now, if you don't mind, I'm going to be sick.

Sadly, the album's release date has been put back because of the eurozone problems, but we are assured it will be out in time for Christmas. It will be the ideal gift for someone you don't like very much.

6 November 2011

Down periscope! I've found an airtight way to quit smoking

Over the years, I've done pretty well all the 100 things you're supposed to do before you die.

I've vomited in a fast jet, met Nelson Mandela.

Broken a bone, been arrested and driven a pick-up truck across the English Channel.

However, there is one piece of the jigsaw missing: I've never been on a nuclear-powered hunter-killer attack submarine.

Most people say that subs are their idea of hell.

Living in a narrow tube, hundreds of feet below the churning sea, pooing in plain view, sharing a bunk that's a bit too small with another man and knowing that your wife is at home porking the postman and that you won't have anything remotely interesting to do until your family and everyone you know has been turned into a whiff of irradiated dust.

Pah! If the balloon were to go up tomorrow, I'd break out my white polo neck and join the submarine service in a heartbeat. I know the Royal Navy once dismissed subs as 'underhand and ungentlemanly' but that's precisely why I like them. You sneak up on an enemy, in big, atomic, softly-softly slippers, flick his ear and then run off and hide. He simply won't know you are there until he has exploded.

And have you ever seen a bad submarine film? *Crimson Tide. Morning Departure. Das Boot.* It is impossible to make an underwater movie dreary. Unless you are the Beatles, of course.

As a result of all this, I was very excited when I was invited recently to spend some time aboard the brand-new HMS *Astute*. I knew that early in its life it had crashed into Scotland and then been hit by the tug that came to rescue it. Really it should have been called HMS *Vulnerable*. But I didn't care. I wanted to spend time on a vessel that is as long as a football pitch but which can barrel along, in reverential silence, at more than thirty knots.

Sadly, the trip was cancelled because of what the navy called a 'technical problem'. This turned out, I think, to be a crew member who had run into the control room and opened fire with an SA80 assault rifle. Maybe a better name would have been HMS *Unlucky*.

No matter. I did not hesitate when another opportunity presented itself. This time, I would join *Astute* as it sailed past Key West in Florida to conduct a test-firing of its missiles. Can you honestly imagine anything you'd like to do more than that? Well, Anne Diamond probably could. And those people on *Loose Women*. But I couldn't and so I packed my little bag and last weekend headed over to Miami.

Unfortunately, by the time I arrived, HMS *Unreliable* had had another 'technical problem'. It had flooded, apparently, and was limping north for repairs. So I spent the night in an airport hotel, watched *The Hunt for Red October* and, with a little tear in my eye, came home again.

It wasn't just the disappointment that made me sad, or the wasted trip to Florida.

No, I was looking forward to spending three days in an environment where smoking is banned and you can't just pop outside when you're desperate.

That trip around the Gulf of Mexico was going to be my cold turkey.

Yes, I admit that the multi-billion-pound HMS *Unlucky* is not the best place for a sixty-a-day man to kick the habit of a lifetime. Not with that nuclear reactor humming away in its bowels and all those cruise missiles in its nose. Perhaps this is why other people choose less extreme methods to give up.

Hypnotism, for example. Well, I tried that and it didn't work because when the man with the half-hunter and the husky voice said, 'Right, you're under now,' I put my hand up and said: 'Er, actually I'm not.' This turned into a heated debate that ended when I tried to leave and he said he needed to bring me round first. I let him go through the motions, then I slipped away.

An alternative is nicotine patches. They work for many people – a point proved by the massive private jet owned by the man who invented them – but they make me itch. And gum is equally ineffective, because it makes you look slovenly and possibly American.

Willpower is obviously the best solution but I have the backbone of a worm and the resolve of a field mouse. The idea of striding purposefully past a newsagent with nothing but my head to stop me going inside and buying a glistening pack of Marlboro is as idiotic as setting a lamb chop in front of a Labrador and asking it not to eat.

However, the fact is that I can do without fags. At the moment, I'm spending about twenty hours a week in aeroplanes and at no point have I ever felt the need to attack the stewardess or murder the fat man in the seat next to me. When I can't smoke, I can cope.

Which is why I was so looking forward to breaking the habit on that sub. However, I do think there is another alternative.

Almost every week, *Country Life* is full of islands off the coast of Scotland that are for sale and it strikes me that these would make ideal getaway hostels for weak-willed, unhypnotizable people like me who want to give up smoking but can't.

There would be no handy branch of WH Smith. No nicotine at all between the shoreline and Glasgow. And the only visitors would come from out-of-control submarines that have crashed into the beach. And they wouldn't have any tabs either.

We could therefore head north and have our withdrawal tantrums away from our families and loved ones. Furniture could be provided for us to smash. And Wi-Fi so that we could do a bit of work.

I even believe the government should fund this idea. We are forever being told that smoking costs the country £5 billion a year: well, for half that ministers could turn Scotland from what it is now – a handy storage base for submarines – into a health farm.

13 November 2011

No more benefits: I'm putting the idle on the bread and sherry line

Put your hand on your heart and answer this question honestly. Do you have the faintest idea what's going on in the eurozone? We are told there's a terrible crisis that has mutated and gone airborne, but it's like the worst kind of bad dream, the sort where you can't actually see what's in the shadows. You're running and you're terrified and now you're on an escalator and, aaaargh, it's going the other way!

Angela Merkel, the German chancellor, likened it last week to the Second World War but I think she's wrong. People knew at the time what caused that and they knew what had to be done to solve it.

The current problems facing Europe are more like the First World War.

There are many historians who have spent their lives trying to work out why millions of young men were forced to die in a bloody, muddy French trench, and the upshot is: no one has a clue. The Serbs wanted a port in Turkey. This enraged the Austrians. And they were enraged even more when a Serbian gang shot one of their royal family. They were so cross in fact that Germany decided to attack Russia.

Then, like your big mate in the playground, it declared war on France and, for no reason at all, thought Belgium ought to be roughed up as well. What the Belgians had to do with a dispute between Serbia and Austria, God only knows, but this was the trigger that brought Britain into the war. And for reasons that are as transparent as concrete, that brought Japan in as well.

Of course, they said it would all be over by Christmas. In the same way as they said the financial crisis was solved when the US insurance giant AIG was rescued. But it wasn't. Millions and millions of people were being killed and this caused the Americans to think: 'You know what? We should send some of our young men over to Europe so they can be killed as well.'

People must have sat about back then thinking, 'What the bloody hell is going on?' in much the way that people are sitting around now trying to get a handle on the eurozone crisis. It is unfathomable, a big potpourri of vested interests, national stereotypes, market reactions, furious students, gormless politicians, petrol bombs, trillion-euro debt and unbelievably complex economics. Trying to sort it out is like trying to untangle the headphone lead to your iPod while blindfold, wearing mittens and being attacked by a bear.

What they seem to be doing is throwing out the concept of democracy by replacing elected leaders with backroom technocrats. And hoping that this will appease the computer that controls the markets.

At times such as this the world should turn to the motor industry for help. In the First World War Henry Ford spent time and money trying to organize a peace conference, and few would disagree that the recent problems in Iraq could have been solved more cheaply and with much less death if every single person in the country had been given a Cadillac. This time round, though, it falls upon me to come up with a solution.

We watched last week a new Greek prime minister being sworn into office and, wow, what an office it was. There were elaborate rugs on the floor, ceilings high enough to stage an air display and furniture so expensive that Andrew Lloyd Webber could only dream about it.

This is a country that's preparing austerity measures that will make 1930s Germany look like Donald Trump's bathroom.

And yet it still owns works of art and buildings that are worth millions. Well, all of it has to go. All of it, d'you hear? Including the Parthenon. Sell it to Coca-Cola, McDonald's, anyone. Just sell it.

Europeans are going to have to get used to the idea that, actually, people in India and Brazil and China have got it right, while we are living a life we cannot afford.

This brings me on to the thrust of my brilliant plan. Benefits. At present you go to the doctor and tell him you have a bad back. He confirms this without looking up and as a result the government gives you a box of money every week that you use to sail across the Atlantic or start up a rock band.

Then you have the Jobseeker's Allowance. If you can show that you spend twelve seconds a week looking for work, you are paid to sit about all day, eating chips, drinking Ace and watching DVDs on the obligatory plasma television to which everyone feels entitled. One woman complained recently that the Jobseeker's Allowance was not big enough to pay for her son's funeral and he was lying on the mortuary slab as a result. Yes. Well, there you go, dear.

Obviously, all of this has to stop, and here's what I suggest. Instead of paying people benefits in cash, why not remove them from the decision-making process and instead give them what they need to live? They go round to the benefits office once a week and are given some bread, some meat, some toothpaste, a schooner of sherry and, at Christmas, one or two wooden toys for their children.

This system would reduce the amount of public drunkenness, because those on benefits would have no cash to spend on beer. It would reduce obesity, because they would be given only healthy food. And it would reduce debt, because they would no longer be able to buy hideous settees using money they have no chance of paying back.

More importantly, it would teach us what the rest of the world already knows: that if you want to watch *The X Factor* from the comfort of a button-backed, reclining La-Z-Boy, you are going to have to work.

That would reduce unemployment, stimulate growth and show our friends in southern Europe that the solution to their woes is not replacing the government, or throwing petrol bombs at policemen, or getting the Germans to attack Russia. No. It shows them that if they want to be part of Europe, they need to get off their arses and get a job. Yours sincerely, Norman Tebbit.

20 November 2011

I walked tall into Savile Row – and left a broken man

For years, short people have blamed hereditary variations for their tragic disorder, but scientists announced last week that, actually, shortness is caused by missing genes and wonky DNA.

And since we know that, genetically speaking, human beings are extremely close to plants and animals, we can deduce that people such as Tom Hollander, star of the hit show *Rev*, Richard Hammond and Ronnie Corbett aren't actually people.

They may have arms and lungs but in fact they are shrubs.

I should imagine that if they are capable of thought they will be very troubled by this. Short people have enough on their plates without being told that they are subhuman. They can't see the action at football matches, they have a bad temper and they cannot play basketball very well. But, speaking as someone who has more genes than usual, and extremely strong DNA, can I just explain that being tall is even worse?

Tall people may be more civilized and cleverer than average but on a clothes-shopping expedition we get some idea of what life must have been like for a black person in South Africa during the time of apartheid. Especially if we are a bit fat as well.

We pick out a garment that we like and then we go through the piles to see if there is one in our size. And even if by some miracle there is an XL, it's still suitable only for a mouse. And now some makers are labelling their clothes XXXL, which I'm afraid is offensive.

How dare some anorexic Italian with his missing genes and his defective DNA call a fine human specimen such as me extra-extra-extra-large? I'm not.

Yes, I have long arms, but they are not so long that people point at me in the street and make baboon noises. However, despite this, shirtmakers, with the notable exception of Thomas Pink, have it in their heads that every single adult male in the world has arms like a T. Rex's.

It's the same story with shoes. If you are a girl and you have size 9 feet, which is not exactly going to get you a job in the circus, you will face a choice. Either you become a hippie and go about your business in bare feet, or you go to a shop that caters for transvestites.

I appreciate, of course, that people who make clothes need to earn money and they will achieve a higher turnover if they cater only for Mr and Mrs Average. But clothing is an international business, and in Holland – home to the tallest people on earth – I'd be the man in the middle. Whereas, in fact, I'm the man on his way to get a suit made to measure.

As you probably know, I am not a fan of the suit. It is fine for newsreaders, but I do not see why the world thinks you are being respectful just because your trousers match your jacket. It's idiotic. But the world does think this way and from time to time my jeans won't cut the mustard.

I have had a suit for some time but just recently I've noticed it has started to shrink. The trousers will no longer do up properly, and the jacket feels very tight. It must have been a fault in the manufacturing process. But, anyway, I decided a new one was in order.

Like all sensible beings, I wish to get my clothes shopping done as quickly as possible, but this is not allowed when you are having something tailored. First of all, the man in the shop will want to measure every single part of your body and

I'm afraid his tape measure is made by the people who make bathroom scales. I don't care what it says: I do not have a 38in waist. Just as I do not weigh 16 stone.

After you have been humiliated, and fondled, you will sit down with a book full of nothing but material. All of it is exactly the same. The tailor can do his best to tell you that some of the fabric is heavier, or warmer, but frankly you can pick one blindfold and it won't make a jot of difference. It'll be grey and fine.

At this point you will be asked to choose a lining and, while you know it doesn't matter, you will feel tempted to go for something a bit mad. You want to present an outward appearance of sober restraint, but you want to know that behind the façade of sobriety beats the heart of a Californian surfer. Lime green was my selection.

Then I was asked how many buttons I'd like on the front and how many I'd like on the cuffs – none isn't an option, for no reason at all – what sort of pockets I'd like, and where they should go, and how far down the heel of my shoe the strides should reach. It was like doing a test in a subject about which I knew absolutely nothing.

However, with that done, there was a sense I could get out of the shop and back to the bothersome business of making a living. But no. You then have to make an appointment to come back for a fitting, and your head is screaming, 'Why?'

You can see short people coming into the shop, selecting a suit that fits just fine and getting out again in five minutes flat. You've been there a year, and now a further day is needed for a fitting. Just because you're tall. It's racism. That's what it is.

Eventually I received a call to say that my new suit was ready. And so, having primed my credit card for what would be a eurozone assault on its core, I made yet another trip to London to collect a garment I didn't really like or agree with.

Then, on Monday last week, I was due at a charity event and felt that my new suit could be given its first outing in public. It fitted very well, it was very grey and it made me look very like an accountant. However, I looked very smart right up to the point where someone threw an ice cream at me.

It hit my jacket square on, and yesterday the dry-cleaner said it was ruined.

27 November 2011

Harry's chopper makes mincemeat of Will's whirlybird

This is a tale of two princes. On the one hand we have Harry, a tanned and muscular Adonis who has just returned from two months in the Wild West of America, where he spent a couple of weeks charging about on a Harley-Davidson motorcycle while learning to fly the fearsome Apache helicopter gunship: an airborne dealer of death with the face of a bulldog and the strike of a stingray.

The gunner, who sits in the front, aims by simply looking at a target and then he chooses how the baddie will go to meet his maker. In the explosion from a tank-busting Hellfire missile, or having been hit between the eyes with a bullet from a 30mm chain gun.

Meanwhile, in the back, we find Prince Harry, who will have learnt how to operate each of his eyes independently. One is used to look at the dashboard while the other is focused on a helmet-mounted monocle that keeps him abreast of combat developments. It's a tricky job, flying at about 150 knots, 50ft from the ground, at night, with each of your eyes doing something different. It's also very glamorous and exciting. Which makes Harry a bit like Robert Shaw in *Battle of Britain*. A skilled and brave killing machine in a white polo neck.

Then we have his brother, William, who is also flying helicopters for a living. But in a very different way. He is sitting on a lump of rock in the Irish Sea, watching his hair fall out and waiting for the fog to lift so he can take to the skies in a lumbering Sea King – a top-loading washing machine that is about as advanced as a Morris Minor's trafficator.

While Harry is learning in the desert sun how to take out underground bunkers, William is clumping about in the heavy, swirling skies of Wales, rescuing idiotic ramblers who have forgotten their shoes and Filipino container ship captains who have driven into the side of Pembrokeshire.

Last year crews at William's remote base rescued 244 people, and I'm sure every single one of them gives thanks on a daily basis that the pilots had the necessary skills to pluck them from the icy-cold jaws of death. But what about the rest of us?

Every year I am invited to be a judge for the *Sun* newspaper's military awards and every year I'm racked with guilt. Because I'm always given four options in each category. Three are always men and women from Afghanistan who have defused a bomb with their teeth or taken out a battalion of Taliban with nothing but a spoon. Then there's the fourth, and it's almost always a search-and-rescue chappie who has saved a kid who had been blown out to sea on his lilo.

And I'm sorry but, with the best will in the world, it's hard to give my vote to the chopper man. It just isn't glamorous enough, somehow.

Yes, I know they must get airborne in fifteen minutes and they are rarely called upon on balmy June days, but no matter how difficult it is to hover above a stricken sailing boat, near an invisible cliff, in a force eight gale, it's not quite as gallant as charging down an enemy machine-gun nest armed with nothing but a square jawline and a sense of moral outrage.

Or, if we are sticking with helicopters, it's not quite as *Boy's Own*, *Commando*-comic heroic as the men who land their monstrous Chinook choppers in a sandstorm, under enemy fire, to rescue one of their mates who has been shot.

Helicopters are glamorous and the people who fly them do so because they love it.

This is true of the men who ferry oil workers out to rigs in the North Sea and the guys who fly photocopier salesmen into Silverstone. It's true, too, of both Prince William and Prince Harry. But when you are landing a Chinook in the middle of a gunfight and you know that you have just become the biggest, juiciest target of them all – well, you need balls like the moons of Jupiter and a heart of gold to do that.

And, frankly, we need more Chinooks and Merlins for the wars we are fighting now and the wars we will undoubtedly fight in future. That's why I'm not really surprised to hear that the navy and RAF's rescue services will soon come to an end. Politicians say we can't afford them. Military bigwigs say neither service was set up to rescue Janet Street-Porter if she trips up and gets a hurty ankle.

I'm afraid I have an objection, too. I don't mind paying for schools and hospitals because a civilized country must help those who cannot afford to help themselves. But why should I fund the rescue of a rambler? He or she chose to go out there in the mountains. He or she knew the risks. And I'm sorry, but if they fall over and get gangrene, they can't furtle around in my wallet for assistance.

And, anyway, we have ambulances for rescuing people who are in trouble on land, and lifeboats for those whose boat has run out of petrol. Maintaining a fleet of ageing Sea Kings, then, seems a luxury we don't need and can't afford.

However, there's a problem. Because the service is not being scrapped. It's being privatized. And how, if you don't mind my asking, is that supposed to work?

Are the pilots going to winch up a fallen climber's credit card before they send down the stretcher? Are drowning Fili-pinos going to be expected to remember their PIN codes before the man in the immersion suit is allowed to help them on board? Or is this just a bit of creative accounting? Paying a private company to do what the government used to do for itself?

Isn't it better to use sponsorship? I should imagine that large companies would love to have their brand plastered all over a search-and-rescue chopper. They could film the heroics and use them in adverts. And have all the rescue crews dressed up in their corporate livery. Let me leave you with a mental image. Prince William in a Ronald McDonald outfit. Or PC World purple. Tell me that isn't a deal worth millions.

4 December 2011

A *Daily Mail* scoop: I'm a nurse-killing Hitler in blue jeans

Have you ever had one of those nightmares where you can neither see nor feel the monster that's attacking you? But you know it's there all right, and unless you can get away, it's going to gobble you up, burn your house down and sell your children for medical experiments.

Well, let me tell you, such a creature exists in real life. It's called the *Daily Mail*.

Like a Terminator, it doesn't know right from wrong. You can't reason with it.

It has no sense of remorse or humility. It's fuelled by hatred. It hates people who are successful. It hates people who are not. It hates people who are fat just as much as it hates people who are thin. It hates everybody. But for some reason it seems especially to hate me.

So, with hindsight, I should have been a bit more wary when the presenters of *The One Show* asked me a few weeks ago what I thought of the public sector workers who had gone on strike. Knowing that a show such as this, with its skateboarding ducks and neat haircuts, isn't really a platform for serious debate, I gave a wishy-washy *Guardian* answer, saying the walkout had made me all gooey and homesick for the Seventies.

And then I said that because I was on the BBC, I ought to be balanced, so I launched into a right-wing tirade, saying they should all be executed in front of their families. We then moved on to a funny-shaped carrot, and that was that.

But, as you may have noticed, it wasn't. Because someone

took the rabid second part of my answer and put it on YouTube. Someone tweeted it. Someone Facebooked it. And then someone asked one of the trade unions behind the strike what it thought about the madman who had suggested on a fluffy-wuffy early-evening show that teachers and nurses should be shot as their children looked on.

Understandably, it thought I should be sacked. Then it had a rethink and suggested it might call in the police. Yes, it wanted me in jail. And so, out of nowhere, a story was born.

The following morning even the prime minister was asked for his views. Happily, he had gone to the trouble of finding out what I'd actually said and suggested I was just being 'silly'. Downing Street even made a joke, saying: 'Execution is not government policy and we have no plans to make it government policy.'

Sadly, his opposite number from the Labour party – a man called Ed Miliband – hadn't bothered to research the issue so, when he was asked for an opinion, he resorted to the reptilian response of every political nearly-man and said my remarks were 'disgraceful and disgusting'. The story was really burning now.

By this stage almost 5,000 people had complained, so the BBC and I decided we really ought to say sorry.

Sadly, this was like pouring petrol on the flames. Ha-ha. So he really did believe that Florence Nightingale should be tied to a post and machine-gunned in front of her mum. The hysteria became worse.

My house was surrounded by photographers. I was doorstepped by an ITN film crew in Beijing. I was papped constantly in Australia. And in Singapore airport on the way home I was patted on the back by the sort of idiotic right-wing lunatic I'd been mimicking on *The One Show*. I'd become a poster boy for the British National Party. I was Adolf Hitler in Levi's.

And it was all ridiculous. During Wimbledon one year I seem to recall that Terry Wogan said he'd like to take a machine gun to all the people on Henman Hill. No one took him seriously, but me, the two-bit presenter of a poky motoring show on BBC2? Somehow an opinion that wasn't even mine had become the nation's No. 1 topic of conversation.

Apparently I had top billing on that week's *Question Time*. I was front-page news for days. Even Bill Oddie was dragged away from his beavers and asked for an opinion. The worst, though, came from the *Mail*. It said that I was a mental, that my mother had been extremely right wing and that my parents had had little empathy with those less fortunate than themselves. Quite what my poor old mum had done to deserve this after years of unpaid public service, I'm not entirely sure.

But that's the trouble with the *Mail*. There are many creatures on this earth that behave in an unusual way. We can't explain how pigeons find their houses from thousands of miles away or how salmon can find the very spot where they were born. But nothing in the kingdom of nature is quite so unfathomable as a *Mail* reporter.

They look human. They have opposable thumbs and are capable of catching buses. But they don't have the capacity for reason. You can tell them what happened. You can prove it. But it will make no difference.

Here's an example. Last week Mark Thompson, the BBC's director general, was asked by an MP if I was a luxury the corporation could not afford. In the *Daily Mail* this became a statement: 'Jeremy Clarkson is a luxury the BBC cannot afford.' Somehow it had turned a question into a fact. I really do believe that in the whole furore over press standards the wrong newspaper has been closed down.

Anyway, I suppose that while I'm here and there's a little bit of space left, I ought really to set the record straight. So here goes. I absolutely do not think that the public service workers who went on strike should be shot or punished in any way.

But, that said, in these times of great economic uncertainty, when everyone is faced with a need to tighten their belt, it's probably reasonable to take the trade union leaders who organized the strike deep into the Blue John Cavern in Derbyshire and leave them there for a little while.

Clarkson calls for trade union leaders to be buried alive. Read it this week, exclusively, in the *Daily Mail*.

18 December 2011

My RAF training was dull – until I got to bomb Piers Morgan

The Ministry of Defence is said to be worried because the computerized simulations it uses to train squaddies in the art of warfare are not as realistic as the commercially available games that most of their teenage recruits play at home.

Really?

I only ask because I am something of an expert in the *Call of Duty* PlayStation games that allow the player to rush about in various locations around the world shooting down helicopter gunships and planting mines on Russian submarines. I am very good at it.

Sometimes, when I play against my fifteen-year-old son, I can last for three or four seconds before he comes round a corner and stabs me in the heart.

However, this is the problem. After he has stabbed me in the heart, we are treated to a slow-motion replay and then we simply press restart and begin again. That's not how things pan out on a real battlefield, I should imagine.

What's more, when we are playing against computerized enemies, we can be shot with heavy weapons probably seventy times before we are made to go back to the beginning. Hmm. I once shot a railway sleeper with a single round from an AK-47 and it split clean in half. So it stands to reason that if you are hit with seventy rounds from such a weapon, the medical description for your condition would be 'dead'.

Yes, the graphics in the *Call of Duty* games are beyond reproach, but for training to be a soldier, they are about as useful as Lego. I mean it. In my own sitting room, I am an accomplished diver but when I go underwater in a real scuba suit, my ears hurt, my mask fills up with water and I get in a bit of a panic.

It's much the same story when searching house to house for terrorists. In the game, you run into the room, get shot seventy times, and still have the wherewithal to kill the bad guy. In real life – and I've actually done this with proper soldiers – they clipped so many things to my belt that by the time I arrived at the house I was extremely out of breath and my trousers were round my ankles. Then an enormous ser-geant threw me out of a window.

Training to be a fighter pilot is rather less tiring. Yes, the equipment used by the RAF on raw recruits is in no way comparable to commercially available computer games. There are no graphics at all. No realistic noises.

In fact you begin your training with a piece of equipment first designed in the Fifties to train London bus drivers. It's made from wood and brass and you have to weave a pointer round a route, taking into account a delay between any input you make and what happens as a result. It's very tricky.

If you can master this, you are allowed on to the next stage. This is very modern. It even uses electricity. In short, you have four dots moving across a screen. When the green one passes behind a green bar, you hit the green button. When the yellow one passes behind the yellow bar, you hit the yel-low button, and so on. It's a bit like Space Invaders for the terminally ham-fisted and it's very easy.

However, while you are doing this, a combination of ten letters and numbers flash up in front of you. A few seconds after it disappears, while you are still obliterating dots, four more ten-letter combinations appear and you have to say which matches the one that had flashed up earlier.

That makes the game a bit awkward. But what makes it

absolutely bloody infuriating is that at this stage, the dots are getting a bit faster, the combinations are flashing up constantly and you are being asked multiple-choice general knowledge questions that you have just three seconds to answer. It is nowhere near as much fun as *Call of Duty* and it's nigh on impossible for someone like me to get right. Apparently, only about half of those who take this multitasking test emerge with a pass. Doctors call these people 'women'.

Next up is the centrifuge. You are strapped into a large metal egg that is mounted on the end of an arm in a circular room, and then you are whizzed round and round at extremely high speed until sick starts to come out of your mouth.

Weirdly, I was quite good at this. An extremely fit nineteen-year-old cadet who went before me passed out at 3g whereas I took 4g in my stride, no problem at all. This is because I am what medical experts call a 'smoker'. And that means my arterial route map is so clogged up with fat and nicotine my blood is less likely to pool in either my head or my feet. I am therefore less likely to go unconscious.

Annoyingly, the women who pass the multitasking test usually fall down badly when exposed to g. Because according to one man with whom I chatted, the womb is not fastened in place very well and can, when exposed to sustained g, come detached.

So far, then, your training has been nowhere near as much fun as an afternoon in front of the television shooting Russians. Plus, your womb's come off. But then you get to the Eurofighter simulator. And let me tell you this: there is no game on earth, no fairground ride, nothing, that is half as much fun.

In the middle of a giant dome, you sit in an actual

Eurofighter cockpit and in front is a screen that fills all of your peripheral vision. It is showing Britain in minute detail and your job is to fly under bridges in the Lake District, bomb the houses of people you don't like and shoot down other Eurofighters, which can be given Luftwaffe symbols, if that's what you want.

I spent hours bombing Piers Morgan's house and it was so much fun that I had an idea. Instead of spending a fortune making better graphics for wised-up gamers, the MoD should think about doing things the other way round: making a fortune by licensing its Eurofighter simulator to people who have wombs and a tendency for nausea if they ever had a go in the real thing.

Happy new year to everyone.

1 January 2012

A Commons or garden blunder by the duke of digging

Alan Titchmarsh said last week that he had little time for politics because it was always changing. One minute you have the third way and then it's the big society and it's hard to keep up and stay focused. Gardening, he says, is much more important because it always stays the same.

Now when it comes to deadheading and hoeing, I am not really in a position to argue with the son of Yorkshire. But I will have a go anyway. Because, in truth, gardens have changed hugely even in my lifetime and the main reason for this is – drum roll – Alan Titchmarsh.

Every week for many years he told us that our gardens should incorporate stainless steel and other materials that would have been wholly unfamiliar to Peter Rabbit. Then a woman with no bra would make a water feature and someone with sturdy shoes would put up a pergola. None of these things would have been found in any British garden until 19 September, 1997 – the day *Ground Force* was first broadcast.

I can even give you some numbers. B&Q reported that in 1997 it sold about £5,000-worth of timber decking. After *Ground Force*'s love affair with the stuff, the figure had leapt to £16 million. That's a lot of dug-up lawns. And, after a shower, it's also a lot of sprained ankles. It's a lot of change.

But Mr Titchmarsh goes on undaunted, claiming that, in general, views in the countryside haven't changed all that much in the past 200 years. That may be true if you are the

Duke of Marlborough or Prince Charles, but the rest of us? Once again, Alan, I'm afraid I disagree.

Two hundred years ago Britain was a green and pleasant land because cows lived on a diet of grass. However, a cow that has spent its whole life eating turf doesn't look or taste so good when it's reduced to its component parts and displayed in jigsaw form at the supermarket.

We like fat. Which means feeding our cows on foodstuff made from oilseed rape. And that's why Britain is now, mostly, a yellow and pleasant land full of people sneezing and asthmatics searching their pockets for Ventolin.

Our love of fat has had another effect. When I was growing up, the woods were full of children building dens out of twigs and roasting scrumped apples in bonfires made from stolen wheelchairs. That's what I did, anyway. Now the children are all at home eating fat and sitting in front of computer screens.

All you ever hear in a wood these days is the wind caressing the nearby eco-windmill and the occasional blast from a drunken businessman's twelve-bore.

Not that there are many woods because most trees have died of one disease or another over the centuries, or they've been chopped down and turned into decking to feed the trend started by Alan.

There's more. Two hundred years ago the country was crisscrossed with millions of miles of hawthorn, blackthorn and possibly hazel hedgerow, some of which would have dated back 8,000 years. Then along came the tractor and with it the need for bigger fields. Today the countryside where I live looks like the Nullarbor. Only there's more wildlife in that Australian plain.

Despite the best efforts of Kate Humble to convince us

that Britain's yellow bits are teeming with interesting birds and other animals, the fact of the matter is they aren't.

There's plenty of evidence that woodland creatures live on my farm, but thanks to the way we live today they won't be around for much longer.

The badgers will have to be shot because they are killing all the cows, the squirrels because they ruin the trees, the deer because they eat the saplings, the crayfish because they are like aquatic neutron bombs and the pheasants because they are delicious.

So what of the buildings? Yes, the planners do their best to make sure they are broadly similar to how they were 200 years ago, but it's a lost cause. Because a barn conversion, no matter how sympathetically it is done, never looks like an actual barn.

The biggest change to the countryside is the people who live in it. Two hundred years ago the fields were full of people in smocks with nasty teeth, moulding mud into small mounds. Today the only people you see in fields are ramblers. The teeth are the same but the motives are different: they aren't there to make a living; they are there to make sure someone else can't.

They do this either by tearing up crops with which they have a political issue, or by staking a claim to the land, or by walking up and down on footpaths that haven't been used or needed since the invention of the bus.

Then there are the villages. Back in the time when George III was running around Windsor Castle imagining that he might be a hovercraft or a parsnip, most small settlements in Britain were full mainly of terrible debilitating diseases. Now they are full of investment bankers and lovely children called Sophia. Today the average hen is treated more kindly than most people were in the nineteenth century, and you're more likely to have an SUV than an STD.

Mead has become Mouton Rothschild. Bread has got bits in it. Pigs are pets. People think they are clinging on to the olden days by having an Aga, but in fact this wasn't invented until 1922. There is absolutely not one thing that the people who live in the shires today have in common with the people who lived there 200 years ago. Nothing.

The truth is that Alan Titchmarsh got things the wrong way round. The views from our kitchen windows have changed beyond all recognition in the past couple of centuries. Whereas in politics they still have a black rod, a mace and a room full of men making silly noises. BBC Parliament is where you go for traditional values. The countryside? It's just a patchwork of fads.

8 January 2012

No, Fido, the law says you can eat Raffles – not Postman Pat

If you get a job as a lion tamer or a shark juggler or an Australian, it is reasonable to assume that at some point in your career you will be eaten.

But it turns out that the people most likely to be gobbled up by a savage animal are British postmen.

According to a man called Dave Joyce, who is the health and safety officer for the Communication Workers Union – jobs just don't get better than that – millions of postmen are savaged by dogs every year. One had his arm torn off, and six have lost fingers in the past eight months alone.

How long will it be before there is a fatality? Well, according to American research, probably not that long. Over there 2 per cent of the population is bitten every year and the number of deaths averages out at about twenty-six a year.

In Britain we have the Dangerous Dogs Act, which forces the owners of various types of dog to keep them in a straitjacket whenever they are out and about in public. But now David Cameron is saying this legislation should be changed because it's racist. And he's right.

How dare someone suggest that a dog is going to nick your wallet just because it's a pitbull? Or that it's likely to walk into an airport check-in zone and explode just because it's a Japanese Tosa?

The fact is that the most dangerous and violent dog I've ever encountered is my West Highland terrier. Aesthetically, she is the canine equivalent of a nine-year-old girl in a nativity play. She looks unbelievably cute, and when she pricks up her ears, you are filled with an overwhelming desire to pick her up and give her a damn good tickle.

But I don't recommend this because, despite appearances, she is a weapon dog. So far she has attacked the milkman, the postman, the gasman, the poor old dear who delivers the papers and the man who came to fix my computer.

When she encountered a pack of hounds the other day she dived straight in and all of them were driven away. She will not leave a wood until every creature in it is dead, and there is no point cowering in a burrow far underground because she will dig you out and rip you up.

It could be that she suffers from SDS (small dog syndrome), but, whatever the reason, she makes Begbie from *Trainspotting* look like Miss Jean Brodie, and it's only right and proper that she should be given one of the government's proposed 'dogbos' – canine ASBOS. Although I suspect she would simply trot over to Mr Cameron's house – he lives quite nearby – and shove her ankle bracelet up his bottom.

I realize, of course, that I should try to stop her doing these things, but whenever I remonstrate with her, she looks at me as though she is imagining what I'd look like without a head.

She's terrifying. And anyway, the Dangerous Dogs Act says that a dog is entitled to behave in any way it sees fit at home or in the garden.

And this brings me on to phase two of the government's proposals. Because it has just announced that soon owners who fail to control their dogs, even on their own property, will be committing an offence. In extreme cases the local authority could order that the dog be executed in front of its family.

Doubtless, Postman Pat will welcome this news with open arms – if he has any left. But I'm a bit worried because ministers are expected to ensure that dogs will still be free to attack burglars and protect their owners from violent assault.

So your dog will be expected to know the difference between a man who is bringing your electricity bill and a man who has come to help himself to your wallet. Which amounts to the same thing, really.

How on earth is that possible? We all know that dogs can be trained to sit, lie down, offer up a paw and round up sheep. But how do you train a dog to work out what someone does for a living?

And, what's more, how long would it take the nation's burglars to realize that if they dressed up as postmen, in high-visibility jackets and shorts, their victim's dog would give them nothing more than a good licking as they crept about in the darkness, helping themselves to various knick-knacks and items of jewellery?

I've no doubt Mr Joyce, the health and safety man, would suggest dogs that are prone to violent behaviour should be locked up when visitors arrive at the house. Sounds reasonable, but these days, thanks to internet shopping – and the inability of the utility companies to specify when their men will come round to read the meter – it would mean keeping the dog locked up between nine and one, when the man from Tesco is due, and from one till June, which is when British Gas is sending someone round. In other words, your dog would be locked up constantly.

And how long are you able to do that before someone from the Royal Society for the Prevention of Cruelty to Animals comes round with a warrant, a serious face and a stun gun?

It is probably easier to accept that dogs are animals, and that animals sometimes behave in strange ways. A killer whale will loyally take fish gently from the hand of its trainer for fifteen years and then one day, for no obvious reason, it will bite off her arm instead.

A tiger will be used as a prop in a Las Vegas variety show for decades until one day it decides that it wants to liven things up by killing its owner.

And a dog, even the most mild-mannered Labrador, will occasionally turn into a great white shark with the teeth of a hippo and the morals of a Hellfire missile.

This, of course, provides no comfort for Postman Pat, but I think that on this front we can all do our bit to help. Whenever possible, we should use emails and internet banking so we remove the need to have postmen in the first place.

15 January 2012

Skis on, break a leg . . . and take Sarko to the cleaners

So where are you going skiing this year? Val d'Isère? Val de Shnoss? Schnoss de Val? Schnoss Nosh Losh de Schoss? Actually, scrub that. I'm not interested.

In fact, I have no idea why we always ask people where they're going because the one irrefutable fact about skiing resorts is: they are all identical.

There are high ones. There are low ones. There are big ones. There are little ones. And they're all full of wooden boxes and they all look just the same.

They're all full of slightly drunk English people called Harry getting cross with the hunky Italian, who has just given Sophia a dose of chlamydia, and Hans, who has barged into the bloody lift queue again, and the waiter, for charging £260 for what is nothing more than a dollop of melted cheese on bread.

And with Mrs Harry, for wanting to ski all day with the chiselled François, who has never said anything remotely funny in his life and probably has a tiny penis but makes up for these shortfalls by having eyes the colour of aquamarine and cheekbones that could be used to saw through a horse's saddle.

Over the years, I've been to quite a few skiing resorts around the world, and I've always reckoned that the best is a small one in Germany called Wank. Although there are no lifts, there are many long runs. Plus it's not very far away, it's not Swiss – so coffee doesn't cost 800 quid – and there's another good thing about it too. But I can't for the life of me remember what it is right now.

This year, however, I reckon you'll be better off going to France. It doesn't matter which resort you select because you're not there to look at Roman remains, or frescos. You're there to get up, sit on a ski lift, wish you still smoked, get cross with the Germans, get cross with your wife for going off with Monsieur Pommette-Stupide again, have lunch, get drunk, fall over, go to the doctor's, see a man with a ski pole in his eye, have some cheese on bread, pay the licensed burglar who served it £400, go to bed and try hard not to think about what the chalet girls are doing in their room. And since that's what you'll be doing every day, just choose a snowy French town near Geneva airport. La Clusaz isn't bad.

There are two reasons I'm recommending France. First, I think it will be very enjoyable to laugh openly at its downgraded credit rating, and second, thanks to a selection of ambulance-chasing Alpine lawyers, soon you won't be able to go there any more.

We tend to think that idiotic compensation awards could not possibly happen in France, where people seem to spend most of their time examining the latest American trend and then doing the exact opposite. But there have been two recent court cases involving accidents on the pistes, and in one a woman who was left tetraplegic was awarded £830,000.

The court decided that the Pyrenean resort had failed to warn skiers there was ice ahead and that it had narrowed the piste by installing a half-pipe – a U-shaped structure used to perform stunts – for snowboarders. And I'm sorry, but is this not the most stupid thing you've ever heard of?

Warning someone on a skiing holiday that there may be ice ahead is like warning morning sunbathers in St Tropez that come lunchtime it may get a bit toasty. Of course there's ice. And it's all part of the fun, suddenly hearing that terrible clatter, feeling the sudden lurch and trying not to soil your ski pants.

Then there's the business of providing separate attractions for snowboarders. If it were left up to me, I'd ban them from the slopes completely and confiscate their stupid clothes, but anything that keeps them away from normal people, who are being propelled by gravity rather than a cocktail of crystal meth and exotic weeds, has to be a good thing.

There's more, though, because when you go skiing, you sort of know that an injury is not just possible or even likely, but inevitable. Terrible, blood-curdling injuries and severe pain? It's the price you pay for hurtling down a slope at a million miles an hour. So how can you possibly decide, as you hobble home looking like a Day-Glo version of Tutankhamun, that somehow the injuries you have sustained are the fault of the resort?

Sure, if your boss makes you go up an asbestos chimney without ropes and you fall and your head comes off, then yes, there needs to be redress. But skiing? I just don't get it at all.

And, of course, now that the French courts have decided to take a leaf from the book of Hank J. Silverman, attorney at law, of Aspen, Colorado, the cost of ski passes will rise to cover the increased insurance premiums. Worse, there's talk of making helmets compulsory.

Aaaaaaaaaaaaaaaargh. Nothing fills me with such despair as the sight these days of the piste jammed full of people dressed up as if they're Valentino Rossi. And the idea that someone is going to force me to swap my Doncaster Rovers beanie for what is little more than a plastic colander fills me with rage. Next thing you know, they'll try to stop me skiing in jeans.

I realize, of course, that poor old Natasha Richardson sustained a terrible head injury while skiing and died. And if this worries you, then you are perfectly welcome to dress up like a sperm. Likewise, you may choose to equip your children with hard hats – I do – but the idea that the law will be used to force everyone to follow suit is madness.

The good news, of course, is that it hasn't happened yet. So go to France and ski topless, at high speed, knowing that if you fall, you have a win-win choice. Either you can do the decent thing and accept it was your fault. Or you can sue and win such an enormous amount of damages that, single-handedly, you can reduce Nicolas Sarkozy's credit rating to an even more amusing B minus.

22 January 2012

We've got a million words for sex but not one for best friend

We all learn at a young age that the Eskimos or the Inuit or the indigenous Canadians or whatever it is they like to be called these days have several thousand million words for snow.

But, while I hate to ruin your day, I'm afraid it's a myth. They have the same number of words as we do: one.

However, the Sami people of northern Scandinavia – or Samikins, as they prefer to be called – can choose from hundreds of words to describe what is falling from the sky.

And I'm not surprised. I'm at the top of Sweden as I write and the snow is wondrous in its ability to change from one minute to the next. As I look out of the window now, I'd describe it as 'not see-through'. Earlier today it was 'sideways'. Later I'm going out and it will be 'a bloody nuisance'.

Of course, this is natural. I bet the Timbuktuians have many words for 'sunshine' in the same way as Arabs have several for 'sand' and we in Britain have many for 'rain'. Cats, dogs, drizzle, light, soft, heavy, shower, downpour and so on.

Each person in the world needs to spice up his or her life by having new, intricate ways of talking about things that happen often. It's why I have many ways of describing 'James May'.

It's said that English is fairly easy to learn, chiefly I suppose because, unlike the French, we don't insist that tables are female and that telephones are male. But I'm not sure that this is so, because for every word in the English language there are almost always a thousand or so more that mean pretty much exactly the same thing.

Heroin is a prime example. Even though it is used by only a tiny fraction of the population, it is also known as H, horse, black tar, brown sugar, junk, smack, gear and food. That's like nuclear physicists having a million words for the additive used in the manufacture of fuel rods.

When you say someone is homosexual, it's fairly clear what's meant. So why do we have so many other words that mean exactly the same thing? Furthermore, we have only one word for 'red' but several dozen for 'excrement'.

Army people are particularly good at dreaming up new ways of expressing themselves. Often they use acronyms that take longer to say than the words they have replaced – 'IED', for example, is more of a tongue-twister than 'bomb' or 'mine'. Then they will say they have you 'five by five' when they mean 'I can hear you'. Or 'on point' when they mean 'in front', or 'Your ego is writing cheques your body can't cash' when they mean 'You really are a ghastly little show-off.'

It is of course wonderful, great, marvellous and indeed super that we have so many ways of saying things, emoting and expressing ourselves.

It's especially useful for newspaper sub-editors whose first choice of word won't fit on the page. Famously one tabloid sub shouted across the newsroom: 'Does anyone know another word for Wednesday?'

There isn't one, of course. But strangely, in a language in which there is usually so much choice, there is also only one word for 'friend'.

The person whom you call when your wife has walked out, your car has broken down and you need picking up from Scotland at four in the morning is a friend. Whereas the person who is a good laugh but pretends to be a recorded message when you are in trouble is also a friend.

At work you know plenty of people whom you would see

socially only if there had been some kind of devastating plague and everyone else in the world were dead. Somehow, though, they are all friends, as are the people who clutter up your Facebook page. Even though you have never actually met half of them.

I recognize that we have 'acquaintance' to describe those whom we don't know well. But I'm not talking about that. I'm talking about people whom we do. People whom we see regularly. Having only one word for that wildly disparate group is as daft as having only one word for 'biscuit'.

Of course, you may say that 'mate' does the job of differentiation quite well. But that's not strictly true. I have plenty of good mates but I don't know their phone numbers. So I couldn't call them from Scotland at four a.m. Strangely, the ones I could call are not mates at all. They're something else; something that in the English language cannot be explained.

The sort of loyal, faithful soul who would leap in front of a bullet to save you and sit and listen to your woes for the rest of time, pausing only to make you cups of tea, is like the smell of a dead mouse, or the bit of west London between Wormwood Scrubs and Holland Park, or the noise made by hip-hop musicians.

We've been so busy dreaming up new names for cocaine and Piers Morgan that we have been ignoring the fact that some things in life still don't appear in even the largest dictionary. What, for example, is the word for the cheese-like substance airlines put in their sandwiches?

We have a million words for the act of sex – and we even have one to describe the antics of a dog with worms, dragging itself along while sitting down – but if I asked you for a single word for the sensation of having to be happy with something that actually isn't quite good enough, you'd be stumped. We experience it every day with our phones and our computers and even our houses. But nobody's bothered thinking of a word to describe it.

It's not just us, either. Irish has no word for 'yes'. The Warlpiri Aborigines of Australia cannot count beyond two. And in the Amazonian Amondawa language there's no word for time.

It seems, then, that our language is full to bursting with words we don't need and a bit light when it comes to things we do. And on that note, I'm off to fix the thingumajig on the bottom of my boiler near the whatsit.

29 January 2012

Carry on sniping at the rich, Ed, and I just might steal your seat

Obviously, it is important during times of economic turmoil to keep the Labour party as far away as possible from the purse strings. So, I suspect every right-minded person in the land breathed a massive sigh of relief when the unions rode roughshod over the rank and file and selected the completely unelectable Ed Miliband to be their leader.

'Good,' we all thought. 'The silly little man can flounder about in the background while people who know what they're doing set about rebooting the system.'

Last week he was being particularly stupid, suggesting once again that banks should be forced to get cleaners and postboys to choose how much executives should be paid. Really, Ed? Seriously? Do you think that would work?

I only ask because, years ago, Neil Kinnock was on the BBC's *Question Time* discussing a proposed increase in VAT, when a member of the audience leapt angrily to her feet and said: 'It's all right for you. You must be on £90 or £100 a week.'

She genuinely thought that the then leader of the opposition was earning £5,000 a year. And that this was a fortune. So how would she react today if she were appointed by Barclays to sit on the board and pass judgment on bonuses of five million or ten million quid?

She'd have a fit. They'd end up with a postal order for £2.75. Then they'd move to Frankfurt. And Britain's financial services industry would be finished.

The trouble is that thanks to the hysteria surrounding Fred

Goodwin – why doesn't he just change his name by deed poll to Sir Fred? – and Stephen Hester turning down his £1 million of share options in Royal Bank of Scotland, Miliband genuinely seems to have struck a chord.

People really do believe that other people should not be allowed to earn very large sums of money. I don't understand this. Soon the Facebook chappy Mark Zuckerberg will be worth $28 billion and that's fine by me because it makes absolutely no difference to my life whatsoever.

It's the same story with other high earners, such as the editor of the *Daily Mail*. If his pay were slashed and he had to move into a small house, the only people affected would be him and his immediate family.

And yet, people have got it into their heads that if rich people are paid less, it will somehow make them feel better. That's a hateful state of mind.

It's like a gang of ugly people roaming the streets throwing acid in the faces of those who are beautiful. It's like breaking the legs of those who are good at sport because you are not. It's like having cancer and hoping everyone else develops it as well.

David Cameron is scorned by Miliband and by people who leave comments on newspaper websites for being privileged. They say that because he has never had to burn his furniture to keep warm, he doesn't understand what it's like to be poor.

Well, I've never been to the South Pole but I know it's bloody cold. I've never been burnt at the stake, but I know it would be horrid. I've never been shot either but I know it would hurt. You don't need to have experienced something to understand what it means.

Anyway, it's not like a privileged person can help it. It's something they're born with, whether they like it or not. So how dare Miliband suggest that someone cannot do a job because they came into the world in an elegant pram with a silver spoon in their mouth? It's the same as saying they can't do a job because they were born with one leg, or ginger hair, or a black face. It's obscene and Miliband should be ashamed of himself.

But he isn't. He's consumed with envy and rage and he must be stopped before the stupid and the gullible put him into No. 10. Happily, I have a plan.

Miliband is the MP for Doncaster North and it's hard to see how he has any empathy with this former mining community. His mum is Polish. His dad was born in Belgium. He was born in London and educated at Oxford. He taught for a year at Harvard. It's entirely possible he had not even heard of Doncaster until he was twenty-seven.

So what we need is an independent candidate to stand against him. Someone who was not just born and raised in Donny but someone who can stand up and say, in an authentic Yorkshire accent if need be, that every single person in his family tree, right back to the middle of the eighteenth century, lived and died in the area.

Maybe their grandfather on one side could have been a popular family doctor in Sprotbrough. Maybe his or her grandfather on the other side could have run a pub, such as the Royal Oak in Tickhill. Obviously, whoever takes on the job must be able to say they have some mining stock in their genes.

In other words, we are looking for someone who wasn't just parachuted in to a safe seat but who understands and likes the place. Someone who didn't go to Oxford or Harvard but cut his teeth at a journalism college in Sheffield and later on a local paper in neighbouring Rotherham.

Sadly, the only person I can think of who fulfils all these

requirements is me, and I really don't want to give up my day job. It is more fun to drive across Italy in a Lamborghini than it is to smile while on a sponsored jog to raise money for a new youth centre. And yet . . .

I'm not suggesting for a moment that I could topple Miliband. Doncaster North is a Labour party fortress and the pages of history are littered with the carcasses of idiots from the world of television who thought they'd like to be an MP. And yet . . .

Someone has to do something to keep Miliband away from the nation's important decisions. And wouldn't it be fantastic to watch his little face the moment he realized his party had won the general election. But he had lost his seat.

5 February 2012

Having to sell the family silver – it's comedy gold

According to recent research, the average British Johnny worker takes six and a half days a year off sick. And, plainly, this is ridiculous. Nobody is ill that often. So what is he doing that's more enjoyable and more enriching than going to work?

Obviously, after you've phoned your line manager in the morning and made a selection of coughing noises, you can't very well go shopping or to the pub because you might get rumbled. This means you are confined to your house, alone. And what exactly are you doing in there?

Obviously, if you are under twenty-five, you are playing computer games and looking at pornography on the internet. But the figures suggest that in the past twelve months skiving has become very popular among the over-fifty-fives. Last week I think I found out why.

It started off as a normal cold, a bit of a sniffle, and a general sense that the central heating had gone haywire – one minute roasting the house to the point where the floor polish was melting into puddles and the next turning it into an igloo. Needless to say, all the women I met were very sympathetic. 'I suppose it's man flu. Ha. You should try giving birth. Then you'd understand the meaning of discomfort. My baby came out sideways and I was back at work fifteen minutes later. So get your own soup, and if you want to feel better, chop some logs.'

At first I soldiered on very bravely, and it was only because I talked of nothing else that people realized I was ill at all.

But then something strange happened. Normally a cold turns into a tickly cough and a runny nose, but mine didn't.

All the usual symptoms decided to pool their resources in my right ear. My cochlear nerves developed a cough, my tympanic membrane became inflamed and the gallons of snot and mucus that normally come down a patient's nose were channelled into my Eustachian tube until it felt as if my head would burst. Imagine pumping a trillion gallons of crude oil into a condom and you get the idea of what was going on in there.

I was rendered completely deaf to anything happening in the outside world. All I could hear was things happening in my own mouth. Breathing, the production of saliva and the large quantities of blood seeping from under my teeth. The pain was very bad.

A doctor suggested I perform the trick that you do when a plane is coming in to land. Holding my nose and trying to blow out. Well, I did it so hard, bits of phlegm shot at high speed out of my tear ducts. But my ear remained resolutely blocked.

I went to a chemist and bought every single thing it had. Lemsip. Nasal spray. Gum. Tampons. Cotton buds. Nothing worked.

I went to a hardware shop and bought a plunger, which I used on the side of my head. That didn't work, either.

I thought about trying a small bit of dynamite. The pain at this stage was so bad, I wanted to tear my own eye out to reduce the pressure.

By lying on the floor and screaming, I managed to convince friends that I was in a bad way, so they summoned a specialist, who said that he could drain the fluid but only by cutting a hole in my eardrum. That didn't sound a very good plan so I did the next best thing. For the first time in seventeen years

I phoned in sick and went to bed. And there I discovered a morning television programme called *Cash in the Attic*.

The idea is simple. Each day we are introduced by a woman with lovely diction to an elderly couple who have had a few personal problems. He has trouble with his knees. Her mum's ill. They have regional accents and, unlike those who take part in ITV dating shows, do not have any convictions for aggravated burglary. We therefore like them and feel sorry for them.

They tell us that to cheer themselves up they need £600 for a golden wedding anniversary party or a trip to the seaside or some other activity from the 1950s. To help them realize this dream, an expert descends on their house, snouting about in the loft for bits and bobs that could be converted into money at an auction. Grandad's old pipe. A boyhood collection of cigarette cards. A vase they'd bought together on a long-forgotten holiday in Tenby.

The tension is palpable. You know the couple. You've heard their sob story. You can feel the hope in their hearts as the auction begins. And then the despair as the first lot, a chipped teapot, goes for £1.72. And the next for £3.85. And the third doesn't sell at all.

It's tragic. They are selling the trinkets that bind them together as a couple. They are waving goodbye to their history, and at this rate they won't be able to afford even so much as the bus fare home. After every lot the host asks how they feel, but you already know. 'Very, very sad.'

It's the funniest show I've ever seen and I can quite understand why so many people aged over fifty-five are staying at home to watch it. After half an hour I was still weeping with laughter and had completely forgotten about my illness. I was cured and badly in need of more *Cash in the Attic*, so I went on the internet.

You might imagine that watching someone lose everything was a one-off. But no. It seems that the same thing happens every week. People sell off their things and get almost nothing in return. They'd be better off if they'd been burgled.

Cash in the Attic, then, is a show that proves mostly that you have no cash in the attic – just a lot of broken record players and things without plugs. But it's so addictive that already I'm planning what illness I can develop next week.

Lou Reed told us the perfect day was feeding animals in the zoo. He was wrong. The perfect day is a bowl of chicken soup, a packet of digestive biscuits and the spectacle of a woman in towelling trousers selling her collection of antique thimbles for 65p.

12 February 2012

Listen, officer, that gravy boat is the key to Whitney's death

Of course, we have no idea why Whitney Houston died last weekend. We cannot be certain about her state of mind or what toxins may have been coursing around her arterial route map at the time. All we know for sure is that she was found in a bathtub along with a towel, hair ties and a gravy boat. I suspect that the gravy boat is a clue. Because I had what might be termed a 'session' the other night, and as a result I arrived back at home a little rubbery. My legs wouldn't do quite what they were told and I have a dim recollection of having to repeat – several times – my address to the taxi driver.

Once through the door – this was tricky as there appeared to be many locks, none of which would stand still – I needed many things. Beans on toast was a big priority, along with a can of Coke, or as a friend of mine always calls it, the 'black doctor in the red ambulance'. This, I hoped, would settle my tummy, which appeared to be entirely full of sick.

I also needed my chilled floor tile. This may sound a bit strange but I have kept such a thing in my fridge ever since I realized that when you are in a bad way, it's refreshing and comforting to place your face on a cold floor. The trouble with doing this, of course, is that you usually fall asleep and wake in the morning feeling terrible. That's why I keep a floor tile in the fridge. So I can have the feeling of a cold floor while being in bed.

Ah, bed. That's what I always want most of all when I've had a few. Crisp, cool, cotton sheets, quietness and a sense that soon the spinning and the nausea and the pain will be buried deep under a comforting, numbing cloud of unconsciousness.

At no point have I ever thought, 'Right, what I need now is some gravy.' And even if I did have a hankering for a spot of Bisto, I'm not certain I'd have the gumption to decant it into a boat.

And even if I did, I'm fairly sure I wouldn't then think, 'Mmm. I know. I'll go and eat this in my bath.'

Mainly this is because we know from Jim Morrison that taking a bath when you are the worse for wear is jolly dangerous. You would be better off climbing into a hornets' nest or playing slapsy with a venomous snake. No, really. I have in front of me a chart showing some recent figures of how those who died unexpectedly in America went to meet their maker, and it's surprising.

You might imagine that since the soundtrack of American life is gunfire, that many people die in a hail of bullets, and you'd be right: 230 people were shot by baddies and 270 by the police in the same year. Then there were 55 who were pushed, fell or jumped from a tall building, 185 who died while jogging and 36 who went west as a result of a foreign body entering their being through a 'natural orifice'. In other words, 36 people died with a vacuum cleaner up their bottom.

A predictable 26 were killed by dogs, 395 were electrocuted (not by the state), 9 were killed because their nightclothes melted, and 55 by coming into contact with hot tap water. As you might imagine, the list is long and amusing, but there is one sobering fact: 341 people died in the bath.

Since the bath is warm and relaxing, we have to assume that few of these died from heart attacks. And I presume too that those who decided to share their bath with a toaster or an electric fire would be listed under 'suicides', which means that the vast majority of the 341 must have drowned.

I'm sorry, but how is that possible? It's not like the surface is very far away or that you can become entangled in weeds. Nor are you likely to be swept away from the edge by currents. Unless you are Donald Trump, perhaps.

So how does it happen? Do you fall asleep and slip under the water? I find that hard to believe because most people wake up when their ears hear a rustling outside or their noses detect a funny smell. So it stands to reason we would come to if our lungs noticed that, instead of air, we had suddenly started inhaling water.

Of course, when we are drunk we lose many of our senses. Young girls lying half-naked on the streets of Cardiff on a Saturday night testify to this. But not noticing that your knickers are on display is a far cry from not noticing that your lungs are filling up with soapy water. I suspect, therefore, that to die in the bath you have to be massively drunk. Monumentally out of it. So far gone that you have somehow mistaken a gravy boat for a bar of soap.

We can therefore speculate that Whitney Houston was intoxicated when she climbed into her bath last weekend. And judging by various reports, she was in this sort of state quite often.

Which brings me on to all the things her friends have said since that fateful night. They've all talked, with watery eyes, about how honoured they were to have known her and what good times they had together. And I must say, as I sat through the Grammys, listening to all of them weeping and wailing, I thought, 'Hang on a minute. If she was such a good friend, how come you allowed her to get into such a state that she was bathing with a gravy boat?'

And it's not just Whitney, either. Michael Jackson. Keith Moon. Jim Morrison. John Bonham. Phil Lynott. Elvis Presley. The list of superstars who've died, fat, drunk or alone in a puddle of effluent is enormous.

Nearly as enormous, in fact, as all the people who eulogize about them afterwards. People who claim to have been friends but who simply can't have been. That's the sad truth about superstardom, I guess. You end up with a lot of money and a lot of drugs and a lot of staff. But no one to make sure you're okay.

19 February 2012

Lord Lucan must be dead – no one can escape YouTube

Many years ago I interviewed a conspiracy theorist who maintained that Neil Armstrong could not possibly have walked on the moon. He was extremely convincing. First, he said America was lagging far behind Russia in the space race at the time and, as a result, it needed a public relations coup. And then, with the motive covered, he became technical, explaining that whoever took the famous photograph of Armstrong on what he maintained was a soundstage in Nevada must have been at least 8ft tall, and that cameras couldn't have worked because there was too much radiation, and all the shadows were wrong.

He laid all the evidence before me and, I'll admit, I began to think he might have a point.

Of course, I pointed out to him that the whole world had watched the astronauts climbing down the ladder and on to the lunar surface but he smiled the patronizing smile of a man who is winning and said that, actually, we'd only seen it on TV. We hadn't been there. And neither had they.

All I could do was say, rather hysterically, 'B-b-b-but, they had . . .', and that's no use as an argument when your opponent is talking about how they'd have been killed by the Van Allen radiation belt. This is the key to any great conspiracy theory: have plenty of science at your fingertips and keep calm. Make yourself look reasonable and well read, and make your adversary look ill-informed and mad. Do that well and you could convince half the world no one ever walked on the moon because it's made of cheese.

This, of course, brings us on to Lord Lucan, who, on the evening of 7 November, 1974, re-enacted what sounds like a scene from a game of Cluedo by murdering his children's nanny in the basement, bopping his wife on the head with a piece of lead piping and then disappearing into thin air.

Since then he has been spotted – usually by lunatics – in various parts of the world: Australia, New Zealand, Holland, India and riding through the lost city of Atlantis on a horse that answered to the name of Shergar. Now comes a claim from someone who was close to Lucan, saying that he fled to Africa and that he has seen his children on at least two occasions over the years.

She seems to meet all the requirements of the conspiracy theorist. She has no apparent motive for making the claims: there is no financial reward. She knows more about Lucan than you or I do. And she is calm. However, I think I am in a position to make a counterclaim that makes more sense: Lucan is dead. I don't know how he died, or when, but it was certainly before 11 June, 1997.

It was on this date that a chap called Philippe Kahn took some pictures of his newborn baby on his mobile phone and then wirelessly transmitted them to more than 2,000 friends and family around the world. This is acknowledged to be the birth of instant visual communication.

It has grown so quickly that today it is impossible for anyone to do anything, anywhere, without being found out. There is, for instance, a clip on the net of James May in a forest in Romania, taking a leak. And if you listen carefully, you can hear me saying: 'James. I wouldn't do it there. You'll end up on YouTube.'

Last summer I tried to sneak away to Uganda for a couple of days. It was hopeless because even though most of the locals do not have access to a lavatory or a classroom, almost all have a mobile. Which meant that within five minutes of my leaving Entebbe airport, friends in England were calling to ask why I'd gone to Kampala.

I'm nothing more than the presenter of a motoring show on BBC2 but I've been photographed, Facebooked and tweeted in Syrian market towns, Russian strip clubs, African wildlife parks and Chilean deserts. My family never bother to text to see where I am: they just go online.

There are no secrets any more. BBC reporters may be banned from Iran but those in Tehran who wish to get their message to the World Service can do so with a pay-as-you-go Nokia. I wonder how far the Arab Spring would have got without YouTube. And how much time is spent at GCHQ just looking at online crowd scenes?

Of course, you could argue that Lucan is a peculiarly British story and that the people of a remote African state would not bother to photograph the face of a man with whom they were entirely unfamiliar. True enough. There are no 'Wanted' posters in Mrs Mbutu's post-office window and the local police do not have an e-fit of the errant peer etched on to their craniums.

But this doesn't make a jot of difference. The television show I make is not shown in France but do not think for a moment this means I can walk through the streets of a small Breton town without being spotted. Because on every street corner there's a camera-toting tourist from a country where I am known. Today you can run but you can't hide. And that's why we know Lucan is dead.

It's why we know too that Armstrong walked on the moon. Because 400,000 people were involved in the mission and, if it had been faked, it's inconceivable that one of them wouldn't have put on an electronic veil and gone online to say it was all done with smoke and mirrors just outside Las Vegas.

There's another reason, too. The Van Allen radiation belt. There was a time when, to research this, you would have to get on a plane and go to the Smithsonian Institution in Washington. Now you can find out all you need to know with a couple of clicks. And guess what. It's a band of radiation around the earth that can affect an astronaut's eyesight. So, if Armstrong really had been to the moon, it's reasonable to say his vision would have been damaged.

Well, now let me leave you, calmly, with this little nugget. After returning from space, 33 of the 36 Apollo astronauts who went to the moon developed cataracts.

26 February 2012

Those pesky stars just won't expose themselves any more

Everybody likes Sir Michael Parkinson. Everyone trusts him, too – me most of all. He often pops up in ad breaks to bring news of a life insurance plan that will pay for my funeral with enough left over to provide cash gifts for my family, and even when he's halfway through I'm reaching for the 'Yes, I'll have that' button.

I reckon that at a push he could get me to sign up for a coach tour of North Wales.

But last week we began to see evidence that age had started to eat away at his marbles. Because he wondered out loud and in print why there were no traditional interview shows on television any more, and why, with Jonathan Ross and Graham Norton, it all had to be played for laughs.

That is easy to answer. In the olden days newspapers reported news. They were filled with earnest stories from around the world and weren't interested in the opinions or photographs of those who earned their crust by being in *Are You Being Served?*

So, to keep themselves in the public eye, the people from *Are You Being Served?* had to appear on a chat show. They would beg to appear on *Parkinson* and they would work hard beforehand, thinking up amusing anecdotes and practising their lines. It was important to do this because if people liked them, they would get bigger parts and one day perhaps get a job on *Robin's Nest*. If they were really popular, who knows? They might become David Niven.

If you have been listening to the endless parade of tabloid

newspaper people who have appeared at the Leveson inquiry, you would imagine that this sort of thing still goes on today. And you'd be right. But instead of appearing on chat shows, people who are orange and have no discernible talent employ public relations people to plant pictures in the papers and the glossy magazines of them cuddling African children and giving money to tramps.

That is why, the argument goes, they can hardly complain when they are subsequently photographed fondling an *X Factor* hopeful or vomiting on a homeless person. If you use the press to climb over the parapet and into the public consciousness, then you belong to the press. And it can do what it likes with you.

However, people who are not orange and who rely on their talent to get work, rather than a PR man, are caught in the same net. There is a photographer on every beach, waiting to spot evidence of a bingo wing or orange-peel thighs.

The star takes someone out to dinner and they are snapped. They go home with them afterwards and it's front-page news. They get into a cab and we are told what sort of underwear they've chosen.

I don't know Daniel Craig. Never met him. And yet I know, just from skimming the *Daily Mail*, whom he is married to, where the marriage took place, how many times he had been married before and what he's doing at the moment. It's the same with Brad Pitt. If he'd been around in the Sixties, we'd know what films he'd been in and to whom he was married. But that's it. Today, we know he hasn't seen his granny for years and even what brand of cigarette he smokes. I reckon I know more about Brad – whom I have never met either – than I do about my own children.

So, if I asked him to appear in *Top Gear*'s 'Reasonably Priced Car', he'd think, 'What's the point? I could sit here, in my lovely Los Angeles home, smoking Marlboros and drinking a fruity burgundy with my lovely girlfriend, Angelina. Or I could get on a plane, fly to England, drive a drab little car around an airfield and then have a yellow-toothed buffoon ask me a lot of damn fool questions that are pointless. Because everyone knows the answers already. Because they read OK!'

The only way you can get an even vaguely interesting guest on a chat show these days is if they are on a publicity tour, promoting their new book or film or fitness DVD. They are dragged into the studio in chains, poked into the chair by a film company exec with a cattle prod and nailed in place to make sure they don't wander off or fall asleep.

They don't know who the host is, what the show's about or what country they're in. All they know – because off camera there's a woman with three BlackBerrys and an agitated face tapping her watch – is that they've got only five minutes before they have to catch a flight to Germany to go through the whole rigmarole again. And then on Tuesday it's Uruguay.

Of course, the host could sit back and ask about their relationship with their father – a Parky trick – but there isn't the time. And on the part of the interviewee there isn't the inclination either. Plus, the modern audience isn't interested in a man's soul. Just his manhood and where it has been.

That's why I have such huge respect for Graham Norton and Jonathan Ross. I've tried to do what they do and it's bloody difficult. Seriously. You try keeping the viewers happy and entertained while talking to someone who doesn't want to be there, has nothing to say, feels worn out and is deeply aware that tomorrow the *Daily Express* is going to run pictures of him snogging a horse.

And there's no point being rude or refusing to talk about

their 'important' new project. If you do that, in future the film company will simply book all their big stars on to a rival show. You'll end up with Mr Motivator, Fred West's cleaning lady and Christine Hamilton. If you want the big names, you have to massage their egos, you have to show clips from their new DVD and you have to provide the laughs. Because if you don't, you've had it.

That is what Michael Parkinson has to understand. The talk show is dead. It was killed by OK! and the army of paparazzi who trawl the streets bringing us news of Sienna Miller's underwear.

4 March 2012

Three men go into a bar . . . and I couldn't hear the punchline

Tell someone you suffer from insomnia, and invariably those who do not will reply by saying they never have any trouble getting off to sleep – 'Head hits the pillow and I'm out like a light.'

This is spectacularly cruel because, as Ben Elton once observed, when someone in a wheelchair says they can't walk, you don't reply by saying: 'Crikey. I can. I can also hop and skip and jump.

'And now, if you'll excuse me, I'm going to dance with that pretty girl over there. And maybe later we shall have sex, which I bet you can't do either.'

What we *do* do when we meet someone in a wheelchair is steel ourselves to make absolutely certain that we treat them exactly the same as anyone else. We outstretch an arm in greeting, even though there's a distinct possibility no such gesture will be reciprocated. We ask them how they are, even though it's plain to see they are not well at all, and can't reply anyway because they have tubes coming out of their nose.

We spend ages yabbering away to desperately ill children in vegetative states, assured by their parents that it's all going in, even though there is not one iota of evidence to suggest that's the case. We may not give up our seat to a pregnant woman any more, but we will move heaven and earth to help disabled people go about their business.

We design buses that kneel down. We install ramps outside public buildings. Taxis have bright yellow grab handles so they can be located more easily by those who are hard of seeing. We even host a separate Olympic Games for disabled people. And you know what? A lot of us think it'll be better and more uplifting and more brilliant than the real thing.

But despite all this, despite our big hearts, there are still some disabilities that don't rock our compassion genes at all. Insomnia is just one. Gout is another. So is erectile dysfunction. And people with haemorrhoids? When we watch them walking around like cowboys and wincing when they sit down, we actually find it funny. Well, I do.

We don't laugh when someone has a hideous growth on their face. Not when they're looking, anyway. But when friends say they have piles, I'm gone. Lost in a sea of mirth, and inviting them to play a game of musical chairs.

Then there's deafness. We don't find this funny at all. There'd be no point because the poor soul with the wonky ears wouldn't be able to hear our taunts. Instead – and don't argue with this – we find it annoying.

The voice-activated devices in cars make my point especially well. You ask the electronic woman to set the satellite navigation system for home and she tunes the radio to a hip-hop station. Or says 'Pardon' over and over again. Soon you are seething.

And it's the same story with people. You say something to someone who's hard of hearing and it's deeply exasperating to have to say it again. 'Why? You have ears. I can see them. And maybe if you bothered to remove some of the hair in there, they'd work a bit better, you old bat.'

So we say what we've said again, as if we are Brian Blessed addressing people at the back of the Albert Hall.

Which is the same as picking up someone's wheelchair, with them in it, and hurling it down a flight of stairs because we have been momentarily inconvenienced.

I bring all this up because I've been aware for some time

that my hearing is not quite as good as it was. And how much sympathy do I get from the family? Absolutely none at all. My wife huffs a lot, claiming that I can't hear orders to feed the dogs or do the recycling but can hear someone saying, 'Would you like a glass of wine?' from three miles away. At least that's what I think she's saying. I can't be sure because, as I said, I'm a bit mutton.

Then you have the kids, who speak at 5,000mph, say the television is too loud and turn it down to a point where, to me, every show is basically *The Artist*. Richard Hammond is worse. When I don't hear what he's said – and it's hard sometimes because his mouth is very far below my ears – he just calls me a 'deaf old t***' and moves on to the next story I can't hear either.

And then last month I got a hole in my eardrum, which made everything worse. Well, not everything. Because at least I now can't hear what Vince Cable is on about. But it also means I just have to guess what people sitting to my right are saying. This is slightly awkward when you are at a dinner party, but very tricky indeed when you are hosting the chat-show segment of a TV programme and your guest is Slash, the guitarist formerly of Guns N' Roses.

Despite making loud music, he is very softly spoken, which in my world means he makes about as much noise as a mouse in lambswool slippers tiptoeing across a shag-pile rug. I'd ask him a question and I could see his lips moving but I had literally no idea what he was saying. Occasionally I'd pull a serious face, hoping he wasn't talking about the hilarious occasion when he set Axl Rose's trousers on fire. And sometimes I'd politely titter, praying to God he wasn't chatting away about his mother's funeral. Since he didn't try to punch me, I think I got away with it, but I won't know for sure until I see the interview air this evening.

The worst part of being deaf, though, is you lose your ability to find things funny. You can just about hear the first part of a story – the setup – but, for comic effect, the amusing ending is usually delivered quickly and quietly, which means you don't hear it at all. 'A Pakistani, a Liverpudlian and a Scot walked into a bar. And the Scot said . . .' That's as far as you ever get.

And let me tell you something. Losing your legs or your sight or your ability to sleep is terrible. But losing your ability to laugh? That's the worst thing of all.

11 March 2012

Even James 'Thunder' May couldn't make wind farms work

I predict that thirty years from now there will be just one wind turbine in Britain. It'll have been kept as a reminder of the time when mankind temporarily took leave of its senses and decided wind, waves and lashings of tofu could somehow generate enough electricity for the whole planet.

Schoolchildren will be taken to see it by newly enlightened teachers – in the way that today's children are invited to smirk at the Sinclair C5 – and then afterwards they will be shown a clip from last weekend's episode of the usually brilliant *Countryfile* programme to demonstrate just how silly the human race had become.

The normally trustworthy John Craven said with not a hint of doubt that climate change was fuelled by our love of cars, power, milk and lamb chops. Yup. He told us that cows and sheep produce methane, which is twenty-five times more damaging to the atmosphere than carbon dioxide, and must be fitted with a breathalyser as a result. Well, James May produces a lot of methane. I know because he's sitting next to me right now. Should we fit him with a breathalyser?

Craven also told us not to buy British tomatoes, which are somehow bad for the environment, and to eat instead South American bananas, which somehow are okay. It's all very confusing.

At the moment, you may be ambivalent about wind power. There are probably no plans to erect turbines near your house so you don't care, as long as your kettle works. You may have even heard from a Liberal Democrat energy minister who announced last week that living next to a bird-mincing, noisy monolith was good for you. Though what he meant to say was, 'I like seeing my name in the papers.' Fine, here it is. He's called Ed Idiot. I may have got the spelling a bit wrong but it's something like that.

The fact is that despite what Mr Idiot says, you will soon care very much about wind farms because the government is about to introduce a scheme in which big companies will be charged for emitting carbon dioxide. The idea is to encourage power companies to produce more energy from renewable sources. Of course, the cost of paying to emit all that CO_2 will be passed on to you. The result: your fuel bill is about to sky-rocket. Only last week the executive director of Which? took the unusual step of telling the government it was 'writing a blank cheque' with householders' money. How much money? Oh, about £1.4 billion by 2015–16.

And why? Simply to keep a few lunatics happy. And they really are lunatics. Over in California green enthusiasts are planning to carpet the Mojave desert with solar farms that turn heat into power to feed Wilbur and Myrtle's La-Z-Boy swivel recliner.

Sound good? Well, yes, but now some Native American lunatics have popped up to say, 'How can we make some cash out of this?' Sorry. I don't know why I said that. I'm muddling them up, perhaps, with Australia's Aboriginals, who always announce after every great mineral find that the land has deep religious, spiritual and ecological significance.

Anyway, Hiawatha reckons the solar farms will not only destroy the natural habitat of the desert tortoise and the horny toad but also irritate the gods. He says he wants to use the sun for power but not if it disturbs 'sacred sites, pristine desert, the turtles or the toad'. He then adds that he was placed on earth to be a guardian of 'harmonious equilibrium', and because of that, one green energy company has been forced to spend $22 million (£14 million) – of Wilbur and Myrtle's money – to ensure harmonious equilibrium prevails and the toad can continue to be horny in peace. Of course, this is normal. It is one of the things I enjoy most about members of the loony left. The reason they never get anything done is that they spend most of their lives arguing among themselves. It is hysterically funny and there was a prime example on *Newsnight* recently.

An angry man from the People's Front of Judea argued that climate change was the biggest problem in the world ever, and that we had to embrace nuclear energy if we wished to live beyond next Thursday. Then up popped an even more angry woman from the Judean People's Front, who said that to combat climate change we had to plunge into nature's bountiful larder.

She said at one point that we couldn't use nuclear power because it required too many state subsidies. Forgetting, perhaps, that wind power needs even more. And that uranium is just as 'natural' as wind.

What am I saying? She wasn't forgetting it at all. She wants us to use wind power even if it doesn't work. And perhaps that's what people like her are really after. A world with no electricity. 'What has electricity ever done for us? Apart from light, heat, warmth, better toothbrushes, iron lungs and Mildred's vibrator?'

As far as the Judean People's Front is concerned, a world without electricity will drastically reduce the gap between the rich and the poor. And it may have a point, because in the sixteenth century, before Michael Faraday ruined everything, Henry VIII had a broadly similar lifestyle to the people who mucked out his horses.

The problem with wind power is demonstrated well in

Denmark, which embraced the technology years ago. And as a result not a single conventional power station has been shut down. They're needed for the days when the wind doesn't blow, or blows too strongly. Worse, ramping them up and down all the time uses more energy than keeping them working constantly. So the Danes have paid a fortune to build wind farms that don't work, and, in return, their normal power stations are producing even more CO_2 than they did in the past.

And that's all I've got to say on the subject because I've just remembered I'm doing some shows in Copenhagen later this month and I don't want to be showered in Danish phlegm. It'd be disgusting because, of course, they don't have enough power to charge their electric toothbrushes.

18 March 2012

Smell my cologne: it's called Girlie Tosh pour Homme

Throughout history you were a child, and then you were an adult. You went from 'Baa, Baa, Black Sheep' to Brahms in an instant. But then in the early Sixties the word 'teenager' started to appear in dictionaries and a whole new species was created. A species that had money, but no mortgages to worry about or children to feed or bills to pay.

The creation of the word 'teenager' probably opened up the greatest marketing opportunity since Jesus rose from the dead.

Because now, between 'Baa, Baa, Black Sheep' and Brahms, there was a yawning seven-year gap into which some boogie-woogie could be inserted, along with a burger and Coke and maybe a pair of Levi's.

The trouble is that today every possible way of exploiting a teenager's naivety has been explored. As a result, some bright spark in a pair of thin designer spectacles and a polo-neck jumper has decided that it is time for a new type of customer to be created, a new breed that needs feeding with a whole new range of stuff it didn't know it needed. So he has come up with a concept called 'men'.

Up to now, it has been fairly simple being a man. Eat. Sleep. Mate. The only real complication was knowing which days you were supposed to make a lovely quiche lorraine and which days you were supposed to come home in a bearskin coat and engage in some rough-and-ready grunty-pumpy over the Aga. Certainly you never had to worry about what was written on the waistband of your underpants.

You do now, though. You are also expected to rub mud

into your hair, polish your nails, buy things to make your teeth shiny and white, and join a gymnasium to stay in shape. And gone are the days when you bought a wristwatch so that you could see what time it was.

Open any glossy magazine and it's full of chisel-jawed men advertising watches while doing something heroic and outdoorsy. Wear a Breitling and you are no longer Gareth Cheeseman from accounts. You are Clint Thrust and at weekends you race your Confederate Hellcat round the pylons in the Nevada desert. Wear an IWC and you are a deep-sea diver. Wear an Omega and you are George Clooney.

Arrive at a film premiere these days and some silly little girl with a microphone will ask: 'Who are you wearing?' I'm not wearing anyone, you idiot. I'm wearing what was on the floor next to the bed.

This doesn't work any more, though. A man is expected to be sharp, to know how many buttons he should have on the cuffs of his suit jacket and not to wear a shirt with a breast pocket.

It gets worse. On a recent British Airways flight I plunged into the in-flight shopping magazine, where a note from the editor said that because spring was in the air I should treat myself to a new fragrance. There were many from which to choose.

At work, apparently, I should use Acqua di Parma, which enables me to smell 'clean, fresh and professional'. What!? How can you smell professional? It's not a concept that has any known aroma. It's like smelling shy, or indifferent, or sad.

Then there's Eternity for Men, which is 'ideal' for rugged types as it smells of the sea. What sea? The Mediterranean? The Caspian? Or the little pool outside my holiday cottage? That's full of sea and has the ability to induce nausea from a distance of a thousand yards.

Perhaps we would be better off with 212 VIP Men, which is warm and sweet with sexy notes of vanilla, sandalwood and tonka bean. What is a tonka bean? Well, I've taken the trouble of looking it up and the news is not good. It's banned by America's Food and Drug Administration, it causes liver damage in rodents, it is worshipped by practitioners of the occult, bits of it stop your blood clotting and it is used to flavour tobacco.

You want to wear that to impress the ladies at a nitespot in Peebles? Go right ahead.

But count me out. In fact, count me out of all this tosh. The BA magazine explains that I should layer my fragrances, starting with shower gel and then applying deodorant, aftershave, balm and eau de parfum. I don't have time for that. And I don't need a handy cut-out-'n'-keep guide on the differences between eau de cologne and eau de toilette because I don't want to smell like a German or a bog. I want to smell of whatever I've eaten or done. I'm a man, and scent is for women.

Shopping is for women, and that's what our friend in the thin spectacles seems to have forgotten. I realize, of course, some men like to waste their free time mooching about in town, having their hair cut and buying silly clothes. These people are called footballers, or restaurant critics. They have scrotums but they are not men, really.

A proper man would have to think long and hard if offered the choice between selling his children for medical experiments and going into a cubicle to try on a pair of trousers. Trying on trousers is, without any question or shadow of doubt, the worst thing that can happen in a man's life. It is waterboarding dentistry with added cancer.

Look at a man in a supermarket. He is a fast-forward blur of activity, buying only what he needs at that precise moment, and then getting the hell out of there. Supermarket shopping for a man is like pulling off a plaster – it's best done as quickly as possible.

How many men have you ever seen in the Bicester shopping village in Oxfordshire? None. This place is a little slice of heaven on earth for women, but for me it's one of the circles of hell – a street full of stuff that doesn't fit.

So the marketeers can push as hard as they like with their idea of getting men to waste their time and money on sandalwood and mousse and fabric and handbags. But really they'd be better off targeting dogs. Men will only shop for noise-cancelling headphones. And we have some of those already. So leave us alone.

25 March 2012

A cheap booze ban will just drive your pooch to hooch

Presumably because no one from Foster's or Strongbow has thought to give the Conservative party a suitcase full of money, the government is drawing up plans to end the sale of cheap alcohol. This will make super-strength cider more expensive than petrol, vodka more pricey than myrrh and gin, quite literally, a mother's ruin.

Hilariously, people in V-neck jumpers think this new law is designed to combat the hordes of young girls who go into Cardiff on a Saturday night and wake up in the morning with heart disease, chlamydia, fat thighs and twins. But I'm afraid they've got the wrong end of the stick.

The law is designed primarily to prevent the downtrodden masses from getting so drunk that they fail to turn up for work the next day at the munitions factory. It was always thus. When the breathalyser was introduced here in 1967, an Old Etonian acquaintance of mine was overheard on a pheasant shoot, speaking to his local chief constable. 'It's a bloody good idea,' he said, before adding, in a nudge-nudge way: 'Of course, you won't be stopping anyone in a dinner jacket, will you?'

Frankly, the end of cheap alcohol and two-for-one strong lager offers will do nothing to prevent the passage of the port decanter clockwise around the M25 but it will make life just a little bit more complicated on either side of the M8. Because, unable to afford the traditional passport to inebriation, poor people will simply start making their own booze.

It'll be like prohibition in America, and that's a worry

because have you ever tried moonshine? No, of course not. You wouldn't be sitting there, reading this now. Unlike many other extremely powerful drinks, it is very moreish. And that's a problem because after two sips you start to hallucinate. I had a small glass in North Carolina last year and can report that if it catches on here people will be going to work imagining they are on the bridge of the Battlestar Galactica. I know I did. After another small glass I became convinced Richard Hammond was a Cylon and tried to kill him.

There's another problem, too, which came crashing through my front door last weekend. Our hayloft has no hay in it. Instead, we have vats in which thousands of sloes spend several months being marinaded in gin. Then, last Saturday, while you were out in the garden annoying your neighbours with your new strimmer, we were decanting gallons of the resulting pink refreshment into pretty little bottles we buy from the internet. It's one of the things the *Guardian* has not yet discovered about Chipping Norton: it's twinned with Tennessee.

Anyway, the discarded fruit was deposited on the compost heap, friends were invited over and the drinking began. It was a wonderful night with much laughter and, later, a Chinese takeaway to try to soak up some of the sick. Unfortunately, as we enjoyed life in the kitchen, our dogs were out in the garden, snouting around for tasty treats. A rabbit, perhaps, or their favourite snack – a nugget of horse poo. This time, though, they caught a whiff of something even more interesting and delicious than manure. It was coming from the compost heap, so off they trotted and – joy of joys – it was like the pudding counter at a Harvester. Thousands of wonderful sloes, all gooey and soft. They ate the lot.

Have you ever seen a drunk dog? It is funny beyond belief. A drunk human sort of knows why he can't climb a simple step but a dog does not. A dog cannot understand why its legs have stopped working properly and why it has four noses. You can see the bewilderment in its sad little eyes as it lurches about, leaning on trees for support, walking backwards and wagging its head. I laughed so hard that some of my spleen came out of my ears.

Unfortunately, while you may be tempted at this juncture to fill your dog up with Cointreau to see what happens, I must point out that this is police state Britain and you would be contravening Section 7 of the Animal Welfare Act 2006. A few years ago a Bristol man was given 150 hours' community service and banned from keeping warm-blooded animals for a year after he was found guilty of giving his bull mastiff two-thirds of a can of Stella Artois.

The reasoning's simple. You can take away half your average Brit's liver and three weeks later it'll be as good as new. But dogs are like Native Americans. One sip and you will be faced, as I was, with an invoice from the vet for the use of his stomach-pumping facilities.

The problem, however, is that I did not feed my dogs alcohol. They stole it. And now that cheap alcohol is going to be banned, I suspect that vets will be seeing a lot more of this sort of thing. Because at present beer is either sealed in a tin or sealed in you.

Furthermore, a bottle of gin has a screw top that would defeat the most determined dog. But when people are boiling up sacks of potatoes and every garden shed in the land is a steaming still, booze will not be sealed. It'll be in buckets and bathtubs, an easily reachable treat for the family pet.

So a ban on cheap booze will have several effects. All of them unpalatable. The poor will be forced to stay at home on a Saturday night, drinking potato juice from an oil drum. This means the pubs, kebab shops and nightclubs they used to visit will close. And there'll be no upmarket replacements because the rich won't dare go out in case they're attacked by a drunken dog.

As I've said many times before, it is the job of a government to erect park benches and replace the bulbs in street lamps. If it tries to do anything else, such as deciding who puts what in their mouths on a Saturday night, the moonshine-addled poor will go mad, the rich will be eaten, the country will become peppered with ghost towns and your West Highland terrier will end up with an ASBO.

1 April 2012

Exploding Art Snob – it's the best Hirst masterpiece yet

I've been to church. I've seen *Mamma Mia!*, the musical. I've played Monopoly. I've sat through a double chemistry lesson. I've even been to Lord's. I am therefore an expert on boredom and how deeply it can affect a man's ability to be rational.

Some people are able to fall asleep when they are bored. But in me it triggers a reaction in the liver, which starts to produce bile. This brings on a dull ache in the pit of my stomach, and then, if the boredom doesn't stop, the pain spreads, coursing around my arterial system like a superheated river of fire.

This is known as impotent rage. Inwardly, I curse at the man who dreamt up the periodic table and the idiot who thought it would be a good idea to turn Abba's songs into a story on the stage. How dare they steal my time from me like this? I am not given to violence as a general rule but when I am bored I can survive the agony only by imagining how the person responsible would look without a head. This is why I am not capable of going on a guided tour of an art gallery.

Once, I went to see the *Mona Lisa* at the Louvre. Then, having seen it, I decided it was time to go to the Zinc cafe for lunch. The guide, however, had other ideas and for thirty minutes talked non-stop about the bloody woman's smile. Then we moved on to the background and why Leonardo da Vinci had made it all wonky. 'Because he wasn't a very good artist?' I suggested. She didn't hear because she was droning on about every single detail of every single thing that ever happened in Italy in the sixteenth century.

I suspect this is why the *Mona Lisa* is guarded by bullet-proof glass. To stop bile-fuelled visitors smashing it up to silence the guides.

I don't mind a bit of art. I once spent an enjoyable thirty seconds looking at Picasso's *Guernica* when it was still at the Prado in Madrid. And a full minute enjoying Turner's *Rain, Steam and Speed*. I must say that Diego M. Rivera's epic mural at the Detroit Institute of Arts is very good. That sustained me for a full five minutes.

What I cannot abide, though, is how art is intellectualized and analysed to the point where I want to club someone to death. Why is the Mona Lisa's smile smudged? Oh for crying out loud. Maybe his brush skidded. What was on Constable's mind when he was painting *The Hay Wain*? Who cares? Being promoted to sergeant, probably.

All of this brings me on to Damien Hirst, whose retrospective exhibition opened in London last week. I quite like his stuff. I have some of his butterflies and I enjoyed his diamond-encrusted skull enormously.

However, those of an artistic disposition plainly don't like Hirst at all. Every report I've seen about him starts off by telling us how much money he has made and how this is disgusting. Why is it disgusting? Who says an artist is not allowed to be successful until after he is dead?

I know the whole country has become infected with a terrible hatred for anyone who is successful, but the loathing reaches new heights when the person is an artist.

'Look at you in your big house, you bastard. Why aren't you in a squat, eating LSD and cutting your ear off? You're not an artist. You're a businessman.'

Arty types also ask whether what Hirst produces is art. I do not know the answer to this but if the experts are reduced to gibbering wrecks by a can of soup or a woman with a smudged smile, then why is a cow's head covered in flies not worthy?

I think *The Hay Wain* is a terrible picture. It may work all right on an old lady's coaster but I'd rather have one of Hirst's chemist shop displays on my wall than a £2-billion Constable Turner greetings card any day of the week. And I'm sorry, but in my mind the Ferrari 275 GTS is an easy match for anything Rembrandt ever did.

Watching serious arts people dismiss popular efforts is like listening to some dismal mouse of a woman who has written about life in a Burmese laundry claiming that what Jilly Cooper does is not literature. It just is.

Then we get to the big issue. How much of Hirst's work is actually Hirst's work? This is the snide aside we are asked to ponder after we've been told the rich bastard is just cashing in on other rich bastards.

Apparently, Hirst has a workshop in which a team of craftsmen – and, I presume, butchers – is called upon to produce his stuff. This is a terrible con, we're told. But is it?

I only ask because, back in the Renaissance, Leonardo started out helping great artists of the time with difficult bits of their work. And when he became a master himself, he also used people to do the stuff that was boring.

Strangely, this brings me on to what many believe was the world's first electronic computer: Colossus, the machine that was used to help break the Nazis' Lorenz code. It was built by an engineer called Tommy Flowers, who worked at the Post Office Research Station in Dollis Hill, London. Heard of him?

No. But I bet you've heard of his fellow codebreaker Alan Turing. Today he is revered as a genius. A bit of the Manchester ring road is named in his honour and some like to believe the Apple logo is a homage to the man who, persecuted for his homosexuality, took his own life by biting into a poisoned Granny Smith. Steve Jobs, Apple's late boss, once said: 'It isn't true but, God, we wish it were.'

This is the thing about Hirst. Did he apply every single diamond to the skull? Did he cut that cow in half himself? Did he kill the shark? Probably not. And does it matter? Does it matter how rich he is? Do you care whether it's art or not? If you like what he dreams up, no.

8 April 2012

Where's the Dunkirk spirit? Doing a runner to Australia

So, would I ever emigrate? Well, if I were given limitless funds, the morals of Silvio Berlusconi, a large house full of lesbians on the Italian lakes, a private jet to shuttle my friends back and forth, some skin that didn't burn every time the sun came up, a sudden effortless gift to speak foreign languages and a capacity to deal with extreme boredom, then, yes, I would be delighted to leave Britain and spend the rest of my days under some wisteria, drinking wine and eating cheese.

However, last week a survey revealed that very nearly half of British people would be willing to up sticks and emigrate with nothing more than what they had in the bank and a stick or two of Ikea furniture.

Frankly, I find this weird. Of course, there are one or two minor irritations with Britain and one big one – the smoking ban – but as a general rule it's a country that works pretty well. We have a climate of such miserableness that we don't spend all day at work wishing we were at the beach, we have free healthcare, our friends are here and, unlike any other nation in the world, apart from South Africa, we have mains sockets that don't zap us every time we want to charge up a mobile phone. Why, then, is 48 per cent of the population either actively planning to emigrate or seriously considering it?

The answer, I think, is to be found on page 141 of a new book called *What It Is Like to Go to War*. It's by a chap called Karl Marlantes, who was educated at Yale and Oxford before joining the US marines. In Vietnam he was awarded the

Navy Cross, the Bronze Star, two navy commendations for valour, two Purple Hearts (some kind of Love Hearts, I presume) and ten air medals. His first novel, *Matterhorn*, is by far the best book I've ever read.

In his latest effort he talks about loyalty, saying he obviously had none for the men under his command since he was asking them to follow idiotic orders to charge a hill. So why did he stand up and say, 'Let's do it'?

He reckons his loyalty was to a mythic projection called the unit. 'It has a thousand specific names,' he says. 'It's the Marine Corps, the legion, the 82nd Airborne, the Gordon Highlanders and the Oxfordshire and Buckinghamshire Light Infantry.' In short, he ordered his men to charge the hill because of 'all those flags, all that history, all that dying'.

I think he makes a very good point. Because we can be sure that, while flying combat missions over Libya last year, Tornado pilots from the famous Dambusters squadron will have wanted to do a good job for the benefit of their senior officers, the Libyan rebels and their political masters.

But I bet that in the back of their minds they mostly wanted to do a good job to honour the ghosts of Guy Gibson and those bomber boys who smashed the Möhne and Eder dams and made the squadron famous.

We don't just see this loyalty to history in war, either. You sense when you watch Wayne Rooney play for Manchester United that he wants to win for the fans, himself, the lovely Coleen . . . and all those who died in the Munich air crash.

When I turn up for work at the BBC, somewhere not quite at the back of my mind is the need to do a good job for the spectre of Lord Reith.

Of course, when you are working, fighting or playing for your 'unit', you need to have a sense of pride about what that unit has done in the past. You don't dwell on its failures.

Rooney does not start every match remembering a far-distant 7-1 drubbing by Accrington Stanley. When I think of the BBC, the first thing that comes to mind is not *Nationwide*'s skateboarding duck.

But this is exactly what we are told to do when we think about Britain. We are a country that raped the world in the name of greed. We sent the Cossacks back to the Soviet Union after the Second World War. We enslaved a continent. We starved the Irish. Every time Tony Blair stood up, it was to apologize on our behalf for some heinous crime of two centuries ago. US marine commanders don't do that. They don't spur their men on by saying, 'We got our bottoms kicked in Vietnam.'

That's what happens here, though. What are the battles that we all remember most clearly? Hastings. The charge of the Light Brigade. The American war of independence. Arnhem. Notice a common thread? They're all battles we lost.

Then there's the whole issue of what it means to be British. For hundreds of years that was the easiest question of them all: we were polite, fair-minded and aloof. We went to work on big red buses, in bowler hats. We had a queen and beefeaters, and when times were hard, we didn't grumble.

What are we now, though? How would you define our 'unit'? It's pretty tricky. We're a nation of bankers, Simon Cowell, football hooligans, royalists, Muslims, tea shops, benefits cheats, Elgar, pearly queens and Polish plumbers.

The French work tirelessly on maintaining their spiritual history and their ways, which is why most people in France are proud of their country. You don't get Nicolas Sarkozy campaigning for re-election by saying, 'We are the surrender capital of the world!' It's the same story in America, where you can be black, white, rich, poor or Donald Trump – it doesn't matter because everyone subscribes to the American way. And as a result, the only American who has ever emi-grated is Gwyneth Paltrow.

At the Olympic opening ceremony, I bet you any money there's not a single thing we recognize as being typically Brit-ish. We don't even know what 'typically British' is any more. We're a unit embarrassed by our past, uncertain about our present and frightened by our future. Which, I presume, is why nearly half of us would rather be Australian.

22 April 2012

Welcome to the fifty-fourth series of *Top Gear*. I'm seventy-seven, you know

Alarming news from the pointy bit of London. According to various financial wizards, millions of fiftysomethings will have to stay at work until their arthritic fingers are bent double and their whole face is one giant liver spot.

Pensions experts say that if you want to enjoy a reasonable standard of living in your retirement, you need an income of around half your gross working wage. For a man thirty years ago, that typically meant keeping your nose on the grindstone until you were sixty-four. Today the average retirement age for men is sixty-five.

But because of all the gloom, analysis suggests that people will soon have to stay at work until they are at least seventy-seven. And at that age what jobs, exactly, are these poor victims of the system expected to do?

Certainly I don't want a surgeon to operate on any member of my family if he arrives in theatre on a mobility scooter, with a worrying wet patch on the front of his trousers. Nor would I put a seventy-five-year-old in charge of a deep-fat fryer. Bomb disposal is right out as well.

The human body is now a longer-lasting item than at any point in history, but by the time it is seventy-seven years old, chances are that there is something wrong with it. And I'm sorry, but how would you feel if your trial judge were suffering from the early stages of Alzheimer's? Or your computer repairman had Parkinson's? Or the ref turned up at Old Trafford with a guide dog?

It is great if a hale and hearty septuagenarian with a fine

mind and bouncy legs wants to work as a lollipop lady, but forcing someone who is tired and ill and a bit mental to go out and earn a crust demonstrates to me that the whole system is properly broken.

After forty years of commuting and dealing with office politics and bringing home the bacon, it's only right and proper that people should be able to put their feet up. I cannot imagine for one moment how horrible it would be for me still to be earning a living by driving round corners too quickly and shouting when I'm seventy-seven. It'll be a young person's job by then, and rightly so.

I have dreamt for some time now of the day when I can wake up without an alarm and spend my hours pottering about in the greenhouse, killing insects and wearing a jumper with holes in it. No more deadlines. No more five a.m. starts. And, best of all, no more James May.

However, today I'm not dreaming about it any more. For reasons that are far too dreary to explain, I'm not actually working at the moment. I'm in a period of temporary retirement. And it is without any question or shadow of doubt the worst thing in the world.

I spend all day inventing things to do, and then inventing reasons why it's better to do all those things tomorrow. I look in the fridge every half an hour to see if by some miracle I missed a plate of cold sausages on my previous sixteen visits. I look at stupid things on the internet. I read instruction manuals. And I thank God for the Leveson inquiry. I've watched it so much I've even developed a crush on the girl who sits over Robert Jay's right shoulder. Each morning I speculate on what she may be wearing that day.

It's not just the boredom, either. It's the expense. Yesterday I thought it would be a good idea to have the interior of my car retrimmed. Then I went out and bought some garden furniture. I spent most of this morning looking at old Mercs on a website, and unless someone gives me something to do soon, I know I'm going to buy one.

Then there's the drinking. If I'm out, I'll have a glass or two of wine with lunch. But I've no one to go out with because they're all working. So I have a glass or two on my own. Then, since there's no reason not to finish off the bottle, I do. Then I go back on the internet and buy something else that I neither want nor need.

It's no good expecting to survive on half your usual earnings when you are retired. You will need ten times more than Bill Gates just to make it through till lunchtime.

Of course, it is possible to keep busy without a chequebook. Mostly this involves going for a walk. And pretending to be interested in all the things that you see. On my last foray into the countryside I spent fifteen minutes examining the latch on a gate. Then I photographed a flower that I'd found so that I could look it up on the internet when I got home. It's just ticking away the moments that make up a dull day, as a wise man once said.

Naturally, for me, this period of inactivity will end and I'll go back to work. But in a real retirement you are simply filling time until a doctor shoves a tube up your nose, looks at his chart and uses the worst word in medicine: 'riddled'.

Retirement may conjure up visions of lemon barley water and grandchildren and a nicely tended garden by the sea, but actually it's a period of catastrophic boredom that has only one ending: death.

You should bear that in mind tomorrow morning when the alarm goes off and you have to trudge through the rain to the bus stop so that you can spend all day dealing with broken photocopiers and emails from people who have electronic diarrhoea.

You may imagine on the way home, when you are forced to sit next to a lunatic on the train, and it's late and you've spilt jam on your suit, that it would be nice to put your feet up one day. Well, mine are up now – and it isn't.

We should therefore rejoice at the economic turmoil that means we now have an excuse to keep at it until we are seventy-seven. Because even if your job is emptying the lavatories at an Indian army base in the tropics, it's better than not having a job at all.

29 April 2012

Heston's grub is great – but so what if your date is ugly?

I'm sure you will be interested to hear that at a glittering ceremony in London last week a herd of food enthusiasts announced with much trumpetry that the best restaurant in the world is a place called Noma in Copenhagen.

Not as far as I'm concerned it isn't, because I went to have lunch there last month and it was shut.

So we ended up at another top restaurant, where, for starters, we were given Kilner jars full of steam. How loony is that?

Another restaurant to feature high up the list of excellence is Mugaritz, in San Sebastian, where, provided you are not blown to pieces by a Basque on the way, you are served 'edible stones'. This is ridiculous. Of course all stones are edible, except perhaps for the ones that you find in Donald Trump's kidneys. But I can't see why you would want to put one in your stomach. Or pay for it.

There is a madness in the world of restauranteering at the moment. I've been a few times to Dinner, Heston's services in Knightsbridge, and while I think the food is absolutely unbe-grigging-lievable and the service even better, it is bonkers to make meat look like a tangerine and to make ice cream with nitrogen.

It's photo-opportunity food, really. Fun once in a while, but it has as much to do with reality as those split-to-the-crotch frocks that actresses wear on the red carpet.

So, to bow down before the genius of Heston Blumenthal, or a man who has the balls to make people pay for steam or stones, is absolutely fine if you are a food enthusiast or a silly rich person, but why publish a list of best restaurants as though it were somehow definitive? Because if you are working on the tills in the Dunfermline branch of Asda, it sort of isn't.

Those who compile the list may turn round at this point and say: 'Aha. But you, Mr so-called Clarkson, work in an industry that spends half its life giving out awards.' You're right. I do. And giving awards for cars is daft, too.

This year's European car of the year is a hybrid called the Vauxhall Ampera, and while I agree that it's a fine and noble choice if you are a climate-change fanatic with no sense of style, it is emphatically not fine if you are Elton John.

Film awards make no sense either. This year the Oscar for best picture went to *The Artist*, which I enjoyed very much indeed. But a fifteen-year-old lout with a fondness for vandalizing headstones and stealing cars would probably describe it as 'a bit boring'.

Every single night of every single year the Grosvenor House hotel in London is filled with Jimmy Carr, who is presenting Geoff Stokes with an award for being the best fertilizer salesman in the north-west. Geoff isn't, though. It's just that his company has bought more advertising that year from the organizers.

BAFTA, or to give it its other name, the Islington Appreciation Society, seems to reckon that *Made in Chelsea* is better than *Downton Abbey*.

But surely that depends on whether you are an elderly snob or a teenage airhead. Choosing between the two is like trying to decide whether you would rather be a petrol pump or a tree.

The fact, then, is this. Apart from the Rose d'Or television festival, which is usually wise with its choices, all awards are a senseless waste of human endeavour. But at least with cars and television shows and films everyone is eligible to chip in with their ten penn'orth. Because we are all exposed to these things every day, we can listen to what the experts say and then make up our own minds.

Eating out, though, is different. Being told that the best restaurant in the world is in Copenhagen is of absolutely no use if you live in Swansea, it's 7.30 p.m. and you're feeling a bit peckish. Then the best restaurant in the world is the kebab joint round the corner.

The food revolution is getting completely out of hand. Steve Hackett is about to start a tour of Britain, which is huge news, but it's lost in the hubbub of chitchat following reports that someone called Ferran Adria, who used to have a caff in Spain, is about to open a tapas bar in London.

Similarly, we are expected to pause for a moment to reflect solemnly on the news that Danny Meyer is thinking of setting up shop in Britain. So what? He's a bloody cook, for crying out loud, and he will probably charge you £400 for a bit of limestone served on a bed of steaming helium.

The problem, I think, is that these days far too much emphasis is placed on the food. I know one well-respected restaurant in London where everything tastes and looks like something else.

You order pigeon because you like pigeon. It arrives at the table in a banana fancy-dress costume and tastes like rabbit. And I want to grab the chef by his swarthy Latin mutton chops and ask him why he has ruined my dinner.

Now I just order something from the menu that I don't like, knowing there's a good chance it'll taste like something I do.

It gets worse. I ate at a restaurant the other day where the menu said, 'Chicken, flattened by a brick.' Seriously now. Do we really need to know how the creature died? 'Pheasant. Shot in the face by a drunken Freemason.' 'Deer. Run over by a Toyota.' Is that what you want?

My point, I suppose, is this. Food is only a small part of what makes a dining experience great. Acoustics are just as important. So is lighting, especially if you have an ugly date. But by far and away the most important thing is the company.

The best restaurant in the world, then? It may be in Denmark. That's what the experts say. But really it's the one where your friends go.

6 May 2012

One hundred lines, Miliband Minor: 'I must not show off in class'

Recently a number of people in suits were summoned to appear in front of a panel of other people in suits in a fantastically expensive and time-consuming attempt to find out exactly who listened to Sienna Miller making her hair appointments and precisely what sort of horse David Cameron prefers.

Interestingly, some of the people in suits said one thing while others said quite the opposite. Which means that a panel of politicians has had to try to work out who has been telling porkies. Fine. But then what?

You may imagine that if you tell a bare-faced lie to members of Her Majesty's elected government, your liver will be removed and your head placed on a spike in the Brent Cross shopping centre. There's even been talk of offenders being locked away for the rest of measurable time in a deafening room under Big Ben. But it doesn't quite work that way.

To find out how you are punished, we need to go back to 1957 – the last time a non-politician faced being reprimanded for contempt of parliament. Inevitably it was a journalist, the fearsome John Junor, who had wondered in his newspaper's editorial why extra petrol was being allocated to politicians during rationing. (To feed the generators in their duck houses, probably.)

And what was his punishment for this heinous crime? Was he hanged? Incarcerated? Deported? Or is that what the famed mace is for? Did they use it to stove in his skull?

No, actually. In fact, he was summoned to the bar of the

House of Commons, which is quite literally a white line across the floor, where he was made to say sorry. I'm not kidding. They took one of the most powerful newspaper people of the time and made him stand on the naughty step. And that makes me wonder. Would the use of primary school punishments work today?

At present there is no way of punishing a banker who has been greedy. We know that what he's done is wrong. And, in the wee small hours, he knows what he's done is wrong. But how can he be made to pay for his sin? At best he can be drummed out of the lodge, made to resign from the golf club and stripped of his knighthood. But that's about it.

We see the same problem in broadcasting. If I make a mistake, can Ofcom take away my children? Fine me? Put me in prison? No. Time and again I read in the *Daily Mail* that I've had my 'knuckles rapped' for 'sparking' some kind of fury. But the truth is, nothing of the sort ever happens. I don't even get a call from the headmaster.

And, who knows, maybe I might be rather more careful if I really did face having my knuckles rapped with a blackboard rubber. Maybe a banker would be a bit less willing to lend money to someone who couldn't pay him back if he thought that he might be forced to stand in Threadneedle Street wearing a dunce's hat.

And then we must move to Greece, where last weekend many people voted for a party that wants to break out the retsina and party like it's 1999. You may think that, in a country that claims to have invented democracy, that's their right.

But since their blinkered stupidity means the rest of the world has been thrown into a state of economic panic, there's no doubt in my mind that they should all be made to stand outside for a while.

I definitely think this kind of school-room justice would work in football. At the moment the yellow card is the premium economy punishment.

A barely noticeable uplift from a straight free kick but a long way from the club-class red. A yellow card doesn't mean anything. But what if the offender were made to go and stand in a corner while sucking his thumb for ten minutes? There would be far fewer late tackles, I bet.

Then we have weather forecasters. They tell us it will be a lovely day tomorrow and then bounce back the following evening showing not a hint of guilt that the picnic you organized on their recommendation was washed into the River Test by hailstones the size of small Toyotas. Would it not be a good idea, if they've made a mistake, to force them to deliver the next evening's bulletin in their school uniform? Certainly I'd like to see ITV's Becky Mantin do this.

It's in public life, though, that the humiliation would work best. All last week Ed Miliband was being foolish, acting up in front of his friends by saying his party had nothing to do with the country's woes and that the current leaders are interested only in millionaires. It was constant party political sound-bite diarrhoea, and there's only one punishment that would work. He needs to be put on silence. And Ed Balls, the fat-faced henchman who sits next to him in the debating society? Make him hold his hand out, palm upwards, and get the serjeant at arms to hit it with a ruler.

And what of the man – he exists somewhere – who chaired a meeting about Britain's naval requirements for the next fifty years and said: 'Yes. I agree. Even though we have no planes to put on the deck, we shall spend £10 billion of someone else's money building two new aircraft carriers'?

Why is he not summoned to the office of Philip Hammond, the defence secretary, and made to write out,

1,000 times: 'I must not order very expensive warships that can't possibly work.'

Other options under my new regime are detention on a Saturday afternoon – I think Theresa May could do with a couple of hours for the Heathrow immigration debacle – and the one thing that used to bring me up short in my school days: the threat of my parents finding out that I'd been smoking while eating in the street, with village boys, in home clothes.

This is what we do with George Osborne. We simply tell him that if he doesn't stop making silly mistakes in class, we shall write to his mum.

13 May 2012

Girls, gongs and JR – if only I'd worn a jockstrap

All awards ceremonies are the same. You sit on an uncomfortable chair for seven hours, watching an endless succession of orange people you don't recognize getting gongs for their contribution to God knows what, and then, when it's your turn, you either have to look pleased that someone else has beaten you, or you have to bound on stage and, through gritted teeth, say that you couldn't have won by yourself. When, in your heart of hearts, you know you could. And indeed have.

The hugely prestigious Rose d'Or festival in Switzerland is different, though. Very different. As different as the petal of a cornflower is from the crankshaft of an American monster truck.

I was there because *Top Gear* had been picked for a gong. And the first indication that the evening might be a bit unusual came when I opened the obligatory goody bag. At this year's Oscars the nominees were given tickets to go on safari in Botswana, a watch, beauty products and a testicular check-up. In Switzerland I was given a tube of toothpaste.

I was then ferried in a smallish Vauxhall to the red carpet, which was a teeming mass of guests, none of whom seemed to have understood the dress code. Either that or in Switzerland 'black tie' means 'anything you fancy, up to and including army boots and a jockstrap'.

Feeling a trifle overdressed, I was ushered by an enthusiastic PR type with a clipboard to a waiting camera crew. The interviewer, a deliciously pretty Swiss girl, plainly had not the first clue who I was. But I'd been presented to her so she had to say something. And what she said was: 'Eeeeerm?'

Since there was no suitable answer to that, I was guided by my elbow to the make-up room, where an enormous German woman pointed to a small pimple on my nose and said to everyone within 500 yards: 'Wow. That is a big spot.' She set to work with a trowel, and fifteen minutes later I was on my way to the green room.

Here I expected to be surrounded by the greats from international television. Simon Cowell. Jay Leno. Piers Morgan. And that madwoman from *Homeland*. But the only two people I recognized were Larry Hagman and Kim Wilde. As we chatted, I was fitted with an earpiece and a microphone and then I was pushed on stage.

It wasn't what I was expecting. Instead of a lectern from where I could deliver my acceptance speech, there was a sofa, adjacent to a massively breasted woman behind a desk. I took the applause from the very large audience, checked out the position of the cameras and sat down.

Now I don't know why, and with hindsight I see it was extremely arrogant, but I assumed the big-breasted woman would speak to me in English. She did not. To my dismay, she addressed me in one of the many languages I don't speak: German.

Happily, a rough translation of what she was saying started filtering through my earpiece. Unhappily, I couldn't make out any of the actual words. So in my right ear I had the Swiss woman speaking in German, and in the left one I had an unseen translator speaking in inaudible tinny English. Small wonder the United Nations is so useless at getting anything done.

Just as I thought things could not get any more confusing, she produced a pair of blacked-out spectacles, told me to put them on and then played Prince singing 'Little Red Corvette'.

You may remember that scene in the movie *Lost in Translation* when Bill Murray appears on a Japanese chat show and has no clue what's going on? Well, that's how I felt.

Mercifully, I was soon allowed to remove my glasses, and there in front of me was an Australian girl from the second *Transformers* film carrying my award. There was applause and then a man with a clipboard took me backstage, past Larry Hagman and back to my seat.

It wasn't over. No sooner had I sat down than that man with a clipboard was back. 'Schnell, schnell!' he said. 'You must go back on stage.' Once there, I was given a massive bunch of flowers and told to stand at the back for reasons that were unclear.

Then they became clear. The big-breasted woman announced the arrival of a newcomer. The audience went wild. And out tottered an elderly gentleman, who began to make a speech. Well, when I say a speech, it wasn't really. A speech has peaks and troughs. It has pauses and moments of light relief. This had none of those things. It was as if he'd been invited on stage to read out every single entry on Wikipedia. Or to count from one to one billion.

After twenty minutes of standing under the hot lights, with my face planted in a hay-fever factory, and wishing I'd opted for the jockstrap rather than my heavy suit, I started to feel quite dizzy. But still the man was droning on. And I know enough about how autocues work to know he wasn't even a third of the way through.

I tried to focus on something important. At first I wondered why the autocue was being projected in widescreen. Then I worked it out. In German, when 'Danube steamship company captain' is one word, you can't have a 4:3 screen or nothing will fit. Having solved this riddle, I started to see if it was possible to will yourself to death.

Luckily, before I succeeded, a woman I did not recognize leapt up from the front row of the audience, thanked the man and took an award from the *Transformers* girl, and that was that.

Afterwards, Larry Hagman was confused. He'd flown all the way from Los Angeles and hadn't won anything. I had, though, so I decided to hit the after-show party. Here a slim and well-dressed Dutchman invited me to spend the night with him 'disco dancing'. I made my excuses and left.

Back in my room I watched Swiss television. It's not like ours in any way. Which is probably why they gave a gong to *Top Gear*.

20 May 2012

I'm desperate to be a German – call me Gunther Good-Loser

You would have thought that after fifty-two years of being absolutely useless at absolutely everything – except perhaps the word game Boggle – I'd have learnt how to be a good loser. And yet I'm deeply ashamed to admit that I haven't.

Vince Lombardi, the famous American football coach, once said, 'Show me a good loser and I will show you a loser.' And that's the trouble. He's right. And I don't want to be a loser. I can't bear it. I can fix something that looks nothing like a smile on my face and I can extend my hand in a show of gracious defeat but, inside, it feels as if I'm on fire.

I lost a close game of table tennis recently to the very tall man in glasses who appears on the television show *Pointless*, and I was gripped in the aftermath by an almost uncontrollable need to stab him in the liver and jump up and down on his bleeding body shouting 'bastard'.

It was much the same story when I watched England lose to South Africa at the Stade de France in Paris five years ago. The etiquette of rugby provides no place for unsportsmanlike behaviour, so when the game ended I dutifully turned to the enormous Boer behind me and said, 'Congratulations.' But, like the 'p' in 'ptarmigan', there was a silent bit. And it was this: 'But I hope when you get home they put a burning tyre around your neck, and the necks of the entire team who have beaten us, you big, thick-necked, southern-hemisphere ape.'

Conversely, when Jonny Wilkinson kicked that last-minute drop goal to clinch the 2003 Rugby World Cup for England,

I spent an hour ringing random numbers in the Sydney phone book and laughing fanatically. This means I'm not a good winner, either. I fear this may be a British disease.

Let us examine the case of Colin Welland, the former *Z Cars* actor. When he won an Oscar for his screenplay for the film *Chariots of Fire*, he held it aloft and told the assembled moguls that 'the British are coming'. Which was inappropriate and, as it turned out, entirely wrong.

Then, later, when he failed to win a Bafta for the same film, he was caught on camera slumping back into his seat and looking as though someone had just launched a surprise sword attack on his scrotum.

When a sporting event finishes, I want close-ups of the losers. I want to enjoy their pain. Sir Ferguson is, we're told, similar to this. Even though he rarely fields the best team in the world, he is a consistent winner, partly because of his capacity for hard work and partly because of his unparalleled experience. Mostly, though, the reason his team win a lot is because the players know that if they lose they will be attacked in the dressing room afterwards. Losing is what defines us. When we think back through our military history, what names leap out of the fog? The American war of independence. The charge of the Light Brigade. Arnhem. In Britain we remember and worship John McEnroe for his tantrums and Paul Gascoigne for his tears. Gore Vidal could have been talking about us when he said, 'Whenever a friend succeeds, a little something in me dies.'

The *Daily Mail*'s website is a massive hit mainly because that is its mantra. In England success and those it envelops are to be ridiculed. Winning is a bad thing.

Was I alone in thoroughly enjoying the last day of the Premier League season? Because we had almost an hour of unbridled joy watching the anguish on the faces of Manchester City fans as they thought the title had gone to Manchester United. And then some icing on the cake when the boys in red realized at the last moment it hadn't.

I'm so unpleasant, in fact, that when a sporting event finishes, I never want to see the winners running around looking happy. I want close-ups of the losers. I want to enjoy their pain. And instead of the winning team being paraded around on an open-top bus, it should be the losers. That would make for much better television.

Unless they are German. The best losers . . . in the world.

It would be easy, and stupid, to suggest that they've had enough practice in recent times but, truth be told, in very recent times they haven't really had any practice at all. Motor racing. Industry. Football. They are alvays ze vinners. They even have the only eurozone economy that's growing.

Last weekend, though, it all went wrong for them. Bayern Munich lost the European footballing crown in a penalty shootout to Chelsea. Which meant that the big German team's fans had to trudge home alongside a joyous army of boys and girls in blue.

I tried – really, I tried – as the game finished, to organize my face into the right shape. It needed to be proud and happy. But not smug or boastful. The effort was wasted, though, because every single German I met was a model of decency und kindness.

Many pointed out the irony of an English team beating a German side at penalties. And how it was quite correct that we should get lucky once in a while. Others shook my hand. Most were quick to say, 'Well done.' And I could see absolutely no evidence that inside they were dying or on fire. There were no balled fists. They were sad to have lost. But happy for us that we'd won.

This is extremely admirable. It's a state of mind I wish

I could achieve in those white-hot moments of despair when the ball goes out, or I pick up a 'Q' at the last moment, or I land on Mayfair, or I get shot in the head by a Nazi zombie.

My inner McEnroe wants to be a Roger Federer, something the Germans seem to have achieved. I don't crave their shorts or their jackets or their moustaches. But I do crave their sportsmanship. I crave their decency. I crave their niceness. I want to be a German.

Because then I could take on the columnist Jane Moore at Boggle. This has not been possible in the past because she is reputedly very good at it. And I fear she would win. And then we'd never be able to speak again. Because she'd be dead.

27 May 2012

Go on, troll me – but leave your name and address

Britain's gold-medal-winning swimmer Rebecca Adlington has announced that during the Olympics she will not be looking at Twitter or any other similar site because she gets upset by remarks about her appearance.

What kind of person looks at a picture of Ms Adlington and thinks, 'I know what I'll do today. I'll go online and let the long-legged, blue-eyed, world-beating blonde know that her conk's a bit on the large side. And then afterwards I'm going to leave a message for Uma Thurman saying she's got thin hair'?

You may think that if this is happening there must be a lunatic on the loose. But you'd be wrong. There are, in fact, tens of thousands of lunatics out there, all of whom spend their days going online to insult a selection of people they've never met.

When a newspaper prints a picture of a pretty girl, comments are invited from readers, all of which follow a pattern. Savagery. Just last week the television presenter Melanie Sykes was described as a 'sleazeball' for finding a boyfriend. Somebody called Hilary Duff was accused of having a 'man's shoulders'. And Keira Knightley was told she looked like a 'famine victim hours from death'.

My wife has been subjected to this as well. She was photographed recently while out running, and you simply wouldn't believe how much bile this prompted. One person was so cruel that I was tempted to go round to her house and cut her in half with a sword. I also wanted to set fire to her photograph albums and boil her pets.

But therein lies the problem. She's anonymous. She's known only as a stupid user name – 'Fluffykins' or some such. She could be in Birmingham or Hobart. She's a microbe in a fog of seven billion particles and she knows it. Which is why, as I write, she's probably telling Bruce Forsyth he looks like a Russian icebreaker. With a moustache!!!!!

Would she walk up to a person in the street and say, 'God, you're fat'? No. And yet she sees nothing wrong with getting the message across just as clearly on the internet. Because that's the sad truth. The only people who read these comments are the people to whom they refer. And they are powerless to reply.

If I say something that offends you, either here or on the television, you know where I am. You can find me. You can shove a pie into my face or throw manure over my garden wall. These things happen and, in a way, it's to be expected.

But the person who ignores Adlington's remarkable achievements in the pool and concentrates only on her nose? She has no idea who they are or where they live.

This has to stop. And we know it's possible from the recent conviction of a Newcastle University student who was given two years' community service for bombarding the football pundit Stan Collymore with racially abusive tweets. This showed that if you are a racialist and you use the n-word, you are not anonymous and the police can find you.

We should be able to do the same. Easily. When people call from blocked numbers in the middle of the night to sing unpleasant songs, I should be able to get their number from Vodafone in a heartbeat. When Adlington is abused for having a daggerboard on the front of her face, she should be able to locate the culprit with a couple of clicks. His name. His address. The name of his boss. The lot.

Fans of the internet boast about its openness but, actually, it isn't open at all. It's a web of secrecy, full of dark corners that can be probed only by government agencies, and sometimes not even then. There are tens of thousands of lunatics out there, and the problem could be solved at a stroke if they were forced to step out from behind their user names and bask in the ice-cold glare of retribution.

This is not just a solution for Adlington. It's a solution for Lord Justice Leveson as well. For what feels like the past 200 years this poor old man has been made to sit in what appears to be *World of Sport*'s old studios, listening to a bombastic man in silly spectacles questioning every single person who has ever been, met or seen a politician, journalist or celebrity.

He is charged, among other things, with trying to recommend a code of conduct to which newspapers must adhere. But whatever he comes up with is pointless because clamping down on newspapers in the digital age is like worrying about a cut finger when you have rabies.

Newspapers are already covered by the laws of libel, which don't affect those on the internet to anything like the same degree. Because even if you can find the online culprit, what's the point of suing a penniless fat man who lives with his mum and spends his day spouting bile from his porn store in the loft? Even if he did turn out to be loaded, you're still up a creek with no boat because the only people who read his bile were you and your immediate family.

Privacy? There's a big debate here, too, but again I must ask why. Why is it not possible for a newspaper to dig around in your dirt when 'Buttcrack775483' can go through your bins and your knicker drawer – even your stools, if it takes his fancy – and describe exactly what he finds on his blog, knowing that he will get away with it?

I'm not suggesting for a moment that you should not be allowed to laugh about the vastness of my stomach. Within certain bounds of reason, you should be entitled to say pretty much what you like about whomsoever you like. But only if you do so in full view.

In short, we need to get rid of web anonymity. And if there's one recommendation I'd make to newspapers, it is this: only accept readers' comments if they are prepared to divulge their name and address. That way, we could choose to visit the person who thinks it's hilarious to make fun of Rebecca Adlington. And give him a comedy nose as well.

3 June 2012

Kaboom! It's my turn to play fantasy climate change

Ray Bradbury died last week. So now the author of *Fahrenheit 451* and *The Martian Chronicles* is up there in the firmament with all the other great science-fiction writers: Jules Verne, H. G. Wells, Isaac Asimov, Douglas Adams and Arthur C. Clarke. There's still a demand for science fiction, of course. *Doctor Who* remains popular among children and *Prometheus* is doing good business at the cinema. But in print? Well, you may imagine, if you spend any time at all in the bookshop, that all anyone seems to write about these days are mentally unstable Scandinavian detectives and women being lightly whipped.

In fact, though, you're wrong. Science fiction is thriving; only today it's all being written by global-warming enthusiasts.

Global warming was invented by Margaret Thatcher as a blunt instrument she could use to bop Arthur Scargill and his sooty miners over the head. But it didn't really catch on until the name was changed from 'global warming', which sounds comforting and pleasant, to 'climate change', which has unstoppable, apocalyptic overtones. With its new handle in place, science fiction had its modern day Martian.

Soon we were reading about how carbon dioxide, an invisible, odourless gas, would cause London to drown in a sea of its own making, turn Italy into a desert and generate flies the size of toasters that would ravage Africa. Al Gore was the new H. G. Wells and your patio heater was a Dalek.

One of the best stories to emerge from the period came

from a chap called Bill McGuire, who is professor of geo-physical and climate hazards at University College London. Back in 1999, he said that one day a volcano on La Palma in the Canary Islands would erupt and that this would cause a rock the size of the Isle of Man to crash into the sea. The immensity of the splash would generate a 500ft tsunami that in a matter of hours would decimate North America's eastern seaboard and wipe all life from the Caribbean. It's happened before, he said. And it will happen again.

Sadly, in 2004, researchers from Southampton University concluded that, if La Palma's volcano does erupt, it'll cause nothing more than a bit of mud to slither into the Atlantic.

Undaunted, Bill started on a new work and last week, at the Hay literary festival, he revealed it to a waiting world. It's a monster. He says that soon, climate change will bring about an age of geological havoc including tsunamis and something he calls 'volcano storms'.

Volcano storms were first charted by Pliny the Younger during the eruption of Vesuvius in AD 79 and were seen most recently when Eyjafjallajokull blew up in Iceland. Few things are as scary, because inside the choking black ash cloud you have a forest of lightning, with jolts of raw power two miles long surging out of the volcano's vents. And this terrifying, end-of-days spectacle, according to McGuire, is coming to Surrey very soon.

Like all the best plots, his theory that global warming can affect the fabric of the planet is based in fact. After the last Ice Age, Sweden literally bounced upwards by 1,000ft and it's still rising by nearly half an inch a year. So it stands to reason that one day the weight of the ice and snow that cover Greenland will diminish to a point where it's no longer sufficient to keep the world's largest island buried in the mud.

When that happens, and it will be sudden, the elasticity of

the earth's crust will cause it to *boing* upwards by perhaps more than half a mile. And you don't need to be a member of D:Ream to know what kind of a mess that will make of the northern hemisphere. A wave of biblical proportions will wipe out not just Iceland and Canada but most of America's eastern seaboard and all of Europe down to the Alps. The Empire State Building will crash into the statue of Jesus in Rio and the Arc de Triomphe will end up on Mont Blanc.

This is fantastic stuff. Scary. Possible. And we haven't even got to the clincher yet, because McGuire says that as all the snow melts, the sea will become heavier and that will cause fault lines to shift all over the world. Japan. Mexico. Chile. All gone. The man is talking here about an extinction-level event. And the word is that when the film rights are sorted, Denzel is earmarked for the lead.

Better still, at Hay, he delivered his cataclysmic view of events to come in much the same way that *The War of the Worlds* was first played on the radio. Seriously, as though it were fact. Very, very clever.

The only problem is that I think his story needs a bit of a lift between the moment when Greenland bounces into the clouds and the last man on earth drops dead. I'm thinking of that audience-pleasing moment in the movie *Deep Impact*, when a small meteorite arrives out of nowhere and flattens Paris.

And I have an idea. Let me run it past you. Like Greenland, Alaska will also bounce upwards when the weight of the ice currently pressing it down into the ooze reaches a critical point. And, as we know from all the recent eco scare stories about fracking, the very rock on which this great state is founded is full of methane and natural gas. That makes it a gigantic bomb. A bomb that will explode thanks entirely to you in your suburban house with your patio heater and your insatiable appetite for turn-on-and-offable gas.

I think you'll agree that this is a scary story. But I think the scariest part is that McGuire is actually employed by the government as an adviser. It actually takes him seriously. Worse – Westminster sorts take me seriously. Only last week, an MP called Ed Miliband quoted something I'd written in this column while making a speech about Scottish independence. On that basis, he will be back on his soap box this week warning citizens not to go to Anchorage because it's about to explode.

10 June 2012

They've read Milton, Mr Gove, now get 'em to rewire a plug

It has been a tense week. With my elder daughter sitting her A levels, the boy facing his GSCEs and the youngest doing common entrance, it's been seven days of American civil rights, worry, tears, the battle of Trafalgar and many heated arguments about the best way to do long multiplication. It's been like living in a never-ending pub quiz.

And to what end? Oh sure, the right results will be a passport to life's next chapter and will help to propel their schools up the league tables. But the awful truth is: none of my children can wire a plug. Nor can they change a wheel, reattach the chain on a bicycle, darn a sock, make a Pimm's, build a bonfire or mend a broken lavatory seat.

Of course, schools have always taught children stuff that doesn't matter, on the basis that parents have always been able to impart information about stuff that does. But parents can't do that any more because we don't know how to reattach a lavatory seat, either. And in my mind a boiler is powered by witchcraft.

This means a generation of children will soon be emerging into the big wide world, blinking in wonderment at all the million billion things that make no sense. Their fresh-faced little heads will spin, and their stomachs will sink in despair as they realize they know absolutely nothing of any relevance.

Will they be able to get a job as a hotel chambermaid? No. Partly because they will want more than the 5p an hour currently being paid to Mrs Borat, but mostly because they are not able to change a set of sheets. Street sweeping requires a rudimentary understanding of how a brush works. And plumbing? Forget it.

Every job I can think of requires a set of skills that no teenager in Britain has. Apart from the media. And by the time they are ready to start earning a living, that avenue will be gone.

Many may decide to go into business, which in the past used to be an easy option. If you had a product that people wanted to buy, and you sold it for more than it cost, then you would be sitting at the top table at the lodge within a matter of months.

It isn't like that any more. Today you start a business not because you want a fountain from which your family can drink. No, you start a business so that one day, as soon as possible, you can sell it.

Again, that sounds simple, but let me assure you that it really isn't. I've spent the past few months negotiating a business deal, and although I am not the most stupid man in the world, I haven't understood a single thing that has been said or done. It has all been gobbledygook, presented in a series of so many acronyms that it sounded as if someone were reading out the model names of every Kawasaki motorcycle ever made.

Each evening I'd call my accountant, who did his best to translate everything into primary school English. It was never any good because eventually it would go dark, and then it would get light and I would be forced by tiredness to say I'd understood when in truth I hadn't.

Are you familiar, for instance, with EBITDA? It sounds as though it might be a character at the bar in *Star Wars* but, in fact, it stands for earnings before interest, taxes, depreciation and amortization. It's critical you understand this in business but you don't, do you? Because you don't know what amortization is. And neither do I.

There's another issue with business that is not made clear on *Dragons' Den*. When you agree terms, you stand up and shake hands.

But then, the next day, the man with whom you did the deal has a completely different version of events in his head. 'No,' he'll say, 'you agreed to sell for 5p and give me your record collection.'

So then you have to employ some suits, who say that you should think more about EBIT rather than EBITDA unless, of course, you choose to use the DCF model. And then it goes quiet and you realize it's your turn to speak and all you can think to say is, 'Would anyone like a cup of tea?'

I haven't even got to the misery of tax yet. Not being Greek or Italian, I fully understand that a percentage of what I earn should go to the government. I recognize that if we want street lighting and a bobby on the beat and prisons, we cannot operate in a river of cash and hope the Germans will pay when our government cannot.

I can even work out how much I need to pay each year. Half of everything I earn. It's a simple sum. However, it turns out that in business, it's not simple at all, and don't ask why because you will then be plunged into a Scrabble bag of acronyms in which time slows down and your internal organs stop working.

To make matters worse, accountancy types actually seem to enjoy sparring with each other using nothing but letters. 'CGT?' one will say. 'Not with this PBT,' will come the snorted retort. After an hour you feel compelled to stand up and say, 'Are you dealing with my business stuff here, or are you playing out-loud Boggle?'

On the next series of Sir Sugar's *The Apprentice*, he should put those gormless marketing-speak idiots in a proper business meeting and then ask them to explain what just went on. It would be hysterical.

It's not hysterical, however, when it's your livelihood. It's bewildering and upsetting. And it's why I shall finish with an idea for Michael Gove, the education secretary, who suggested last week that kids must be able to spell 'appreciate' and do the twelve times table by the time they're nine.

This is all well and good for those who wish to follow the traditional path to university. But wouldn't it be a good idea to have other schools for those who wish to follow a path to somewhere called the world? Plug-wiring at nine a.m. Cook your own pie at lunchtime. And double EBITDA in the afternoon.

17 June 2012

Blow me up, Scotty, before I land on your Manx home

An Isle of Man-based company has stunned the nerd world by announcing that within three years it will be able to offer tourists a trip around the moon, and then onwards into bits of space where no man has gone before.

Passengers will be loaded on board one of four second-hand Russian re-entry capsules, and then blasted to one of two recycled Russian former space stations.

From here they will embark on an eight-month round trip through the final frontier.

Hmmm. Quite a few engineering types, including Sir Branson, are currently engaged in the development of space tourism and I'm not quite sure why, because almost everyone I ever meet says they'd rather spend their holidays in the No. 4 reactor at Fukushima.

They say space flight frightens them because if something goes wrong, there's no air. This, of course, is true but there is also no air in the sea and that doesn't stop anyone snorkelling. Plus space is not full of fish that will stick a spear through your heart, or inject you with a poison, or tear your leg off.

Also, space is not full of currents that will whisk you off to Venus, or people on jet skis who will run you down, or doped-up boatmen who will forget where they dropped you off and leave you out there until your tongue is the size of a marrow and you die a slow, agonizing death. Only a few humans have ever died in space. Plenty, however, have died in the sea.

I will agree that there are a few problems with space tourism. Cost is one. The Isle of Man round trip will be £100 million. And then there's the boredom. For a while the lack of gravity is undoubtedly fun. You can laugh at how everyone's hair is floating about like seaweed and spend an amusing few moments trying to convince your mates that the globule of liquid floating past their faces is tasty orange juice and not a drop of urine that somehow escaped from the lavatory.

But then what? On a cruise ship, you can stop off at the Virgin Islands for 'romantic cocktails'. But you can't do that in space. There's no Jim Davidson, either. You can't even sleep with the captain. You just have to sit there looking out of the window, at nothing at all, for half a million miles, wondering whether a Russian spaceship that's been recycled in the Isle of Man, where they have not invented the diesel locomotive yet, is really the right vehicle for the job.

It certainly sounds preposterous. But, actually, when you spend a few moments sucking the end of your Biro and thinking, you can't help wondering: is it? John F. Kennedy told us back in 1962 that we chose to go to the moon and do the other things, not because they were easy, but because they were hard. No one ever asked what the 'other things' were because they were too busy absorbing the central message: space travel, it's tricky.

I, however, am not so sure that it is. Because NASA showed us in 1970 that it was entirely possible to get a leaking spaceship from the middle of nowhere back to earth, into the atmosphere and gently into the Pacific using nothing more than the electricity needed to power a toaster, a slide rule, some duct tape and the cover of a flight manual.

We were also told that to go into space you needed to be a brave young man with the stamina of an Olympic marathon runner, the reactions of a cobra, the brains of an emeritus maths professor and the ability to hold your breath for seventeen weeks. Humans, they said, need not apply. For space travel you had to be superhuman.

But then in 1998, when the former Mercury astronaut John Glenn was seventy-seven years old, they put him up there without a second thought. And now we often find the International Space Station is full of portly middle-aged men and women who get frightened on a bus and who spend all day in the vast empty ocean, growing lettuces.

So, you don't have to be fit or clever and you don't have to be able to hold your breath for very long because the truth is that if something goes wrong, long before you suffocate, your blood will boil and your eyes will pop out of your head and your brain will burst.

However, there is one problem that does not seem to have been addressed by our friends on Fraggle Rock. It's a big one.

Had you been able to inspect the space shuttle as it sat on its launch pad, you might have noticed that the solid rocket boosters were carrying explosives.

The idea was that if something went wrong in the early stage of the shuttle's ascent and it was heading at several thousand miles an hour for downtown Miami, a man in a bunker at Cape Canaveral – a man who was never allowed to meet any of the people on board – would press a button. And blow it to kingdom come.

This, you see, is the trouble with rockets. Once they are lit, you cannot turn them off again. They run until the fuel is gone. So if something goes wrong with the guidance system and the rocket is heading back down to earth, there's nothing anyone can do. That's why NASA employed a man in a bunker.

If you watch footage of the Challenger disaster, you

will note that after the shuttle disintegrates, both solid rocket boosters spiral off and then explode at precisely the same moment. That's because the button was pressed to destroy them.

The Isle of Man government will have to think about this. And then it will have to employ a man whose only job is to blow up the spaceship and everyone on board. Because that's better than letting it crash into someone's house.

Although, I just have one request for the successful applicant. If it's heading for the headquarters of the Manx rambling association, leave it be.

24 June 2012

And your premium bond prize is . . . a seat in the Lords

If you were put in charge of a brand new country and told to organize a whole new system of government, you probably wouldn't come up with the House of Lords. 'Right. We've got some elected members in the Commons and now, to make sure they don't do anything stupid, we shall have another tier, which we shall fill with religious zealots, chaps whose great-grandads won a battle and various other odds and sods who only ever wake up when their bedsores start to weep.'

However, even though it makes absolutely no sense at all, the House of Lords has worked well for centuries.

It even continued to work when some of the inbreds were replaced by Muslim whales. It works so well, in fact, that Nick Clegg, who is the deputy prime minister, wants to change it. He's even made some suggestions that come straight from paragraph one, page one, chapter one of a book called *How to Let People Know You Are Mad*.

In short, he wants to cut the numbers in the Lords from 826 to 450, most of whom would be elected to represent a specific region. So far, then, he's just come up with a direct copy of the House of Commons. But since the elected representatives won't have the power to make law, what exactly will the job advert say?

'Wanted: a man or a woman – or a whale – to waste their lives listening to adenoidal dullards drone on about waste management on the Isle of Sheppey. The successful applicant must be willing to have his or her private life picked over in microscopic detail by journalists. On the upside, you'll get paid. But not much.'

I know exactly the sort of people who'll sign up for a slice of that. They're the people you find in any large organization, the sort who go to a lot of meetings and when there eat all the biscuits. They're people who never once in their whole joyless, friend-free, celibate lives contribute anything meaningful, constructive, imaginative, daring, fascinating or worthwhile.

They go on marches but half the time have no idea what they're marching for. They get involved in action groups. They wear protest T-shirts over their anoraks so they look stupid. They enjoy regional news. They disagree with shampoo. A lot have cats. All of them are a waste of blood and organs. Many are called Colin. And Nick Clegg wants to put them in the hot seat.

And it gets worse. Because when you've elected your Colin, you're stuck with him for fifteen years, which . . . let's do the maths . . . is pretty much adjacent to forever.

Naturally the costs involved are humungous and, frankly, how many elected representatives do we need? Because if his harebrained scheme goes ahead, we will have to vote for people to sit on a parish council, a borough council, a county council, the House of Commons, the House of Lords and the European parliament. We will be spending most of our lives in polling booths, choosing between candidates who are only united by their utter uselessness.

Suffice to say, I have a better idea. It goes like this. Instead of filling a House of Colins with a bunch of biscuit-eating nonentities, who left to their own devices would struggle to wire a plug, we use the computer that's used to pick premium bond winners to select eight people at random each week from the electoral roll.

Of course, it will be a nuisance for them to take a week off work, but on the upside, they will be brought to London and put up in a swish hotel. And all that will be asked in return is that they have a quick look over the bills being discussed in the House of Commons to make sure none involves reintroducing slavery or invading Portugal.

Humourless people in suits will suggest at this juncture that the second tier of government is rather more complex than that. And they may have a point. But it can't be that difficult because for hundreds of years the House of Lords has been run by a squadron of dribbling infantile buffoons who think they must be right because they talk more loudly than anyone else. And they managed just fine. Many managed even when they were fast asleep, dreaming – and not in a good way – of their old nanny.

Seriously. Who would you rather have doing the job: a man who thinks it's perfectly acceptable to wear a fur scarf on a hot day or your mate Jim from the builder's yard? Quite. We trust randomly selected juries on the important business of a person's liberty so, on the basis that most people can tie up their shoelaces and not get run over while crossing the road, why wouldn't we trust a similar system to apply the checks and balances in government?

A few moments ago I put this idea to Alastair Campbell who popped round for a cup of tea. I know. Strange. And what he said was, 'You're talking about a focus group.' As though this were a bad thing.

It isn't. These days, focus groups choose what we eat, what we drive, what we read, what we watch and how we furnish our houses. Almost nothing makes it on to the market without being presented first to a small group of people selected at random. Occasionally they let something daft through the net, such as cherry-flavoured Coca-Cola and the Toyota

Prius, but for the most part the observations they make are reasonable. Business trusts them. Shareholders trust them. So why shouldn't we?

Certainly I'd rather have a government's ideas checked for idiocy and recklessness by a small, cheap group of ordinary people than by 450 expensive Colins. Although, truth be told, the solution I'd most like to have is the solution we have now.

I understand, of course, why David Cameron allowed his tea boy Clegg to go off and work on House of Lords reform. Because if he's doing that, he's not mucking up something more important. But now that we've seen what Cleggy has in mind, it's probably a good idea to take his mind off it with another idea. Can't he be made to clean the silver or something?

1 July 2012

Cheer up, Mewling Murray, you've made it into *Boohoo's Who*

Last weekend all the tabloid newspapers were full of huge headlines wishing Andy Murray well as he prepared to become the first British man to win Wimbledon for 3,000 years.

This was odd. Normally tabloids are extremely good at judging the mood of the nation but on this occasion they were well wide of the mark. Because I couldn't find a single person, in real life or on Twitter, who wanted the miserablist-in-chief to win. There's a good reason for this. He'd had the bare-faced cheek to plough through the entire tournament playing nothing but tennis.

There had been no hopping, skipping or clowning around of any kind. He was a man with the personality of a vacuum cleaner and in post-match press conferences the sparkle of an old man's brogue. That's why we were all rooting for the man in the monogrammed blazer.

When the final was over and Murray had lost, I was praying he'd express his anger and disappointment by high-fiving his opponent. In the face. With a chair. That's what I'd do if I were ever to lose a game of Boggle. But what he actually did was blub, whimpering and mewling like a hysterical little girl whose puppy dog had gone missing. It was pathetic. And guess what. All of a sudden he became a national hero.

Why? We live on a solid little rock in the north Atlantic. It's cold. It's wet. We admire the bulldog spirit. We keep calm and carry on. We get a grip. Crying? It's like eating a horse. Something foreigners do.

In America a stiff upper lip is something that only ever happens when intimate plastic surgery goes wrong. There is no American word for 'stoic'. Americans cry more often than they don't. The smallest breath of wind and they're all on the news, tears streaming down their blubbery faces as they stand beside their fallen-over wooden houses, explaining between heaving sobs how the good Lord has deserted them.

Even Germans cry, a point that was demonstrated by the enormous and manly Carsten Jancker, who broke down and wept when his side were beaten by Manchester United in the 1999 Champions League final. Finns? Yup. The former racing driver Mika Hakkinen took himself off for a little weep when he thought a mistake had cost him the world championship. And Italian men cry a lot, too. Probably because most of them aren't actually men.

Here, though, things have always been different. A man could come home to find his wife in bed with the plumber, his dog nailed to the front door and his business a smoking ruin, and still he could be relied upon to put on a brave face and think of some suitable understatement to make it all seem not so bad.

It is impossible, for instance, to imagine a tear in the eye of Nobby Stiles or W. G. Grace. I bet Earl Haig had no tear ducts at all. Or Arthur Harris.

And certainly when my father-in-law was surrounded by overwhelming German forces at Arnhem, there is no suggestion that he broke down and wept. He just blew up another tank.

In Britain lachrymosity has always been seen, quite rightly, as a sign that you are not really a proper chap. That you may be someone who bowls from the other end, or a colonial. But, oh dear, that's all changed now.

Every night on the news in recent weeks fat people who've watched far too much American television are to be found standing in front of their moist sofas sobbing as they explain how the flood waters came all the way up to their knees. It's sick-inducing and should be banned from the airwaves. People aren't allowed to bare their breasts on the news. So why should they be allowed to bare their souls?

It gets worse. Nick Faldo wormed his way into the nation's hearts by crying after he won a stupid game of golf. And the only reason we feel sorry for Paul Gascoigne is that he let us see his feminine side during a football match against Germany. Nowadays a little tear on television can win you not just the love of a nation, but also a lucrative advertising deal and a lot of sex with women who think you are all gooey and nice.

Well, that's what they say. They argue that the tear-stained face of a man is a sign that he likes to eat celery and that he gives half of his salary each month to a home for distressed kittens. They say that this is a good thing. They also say they don't want us to come home at night in a bearskin and demand our wicked way. And that isn't true, either. Women want a crybaby in the house in the same way that men want their wives in a pair of Y-fronts.

That said, I can cry. I cried in *Born Free* when Elsa was released into the wild, and I'm told by my mother that I was inconsolable in a film in which Norman Wisdom went to bed with a horse. But as an adult? Well, when our pet Kristin Scott Donkey died I had to go for 'a little walk', and I'm afraid I get quite sniffly in *Educating Rita*. But that's it.

And rightly so. Because, as Britain changes, it is very difficult to think of one single defining national characteristic. We don't wear bowler hats any more. Benny Hill is dead. And our army is now smaller than the Padstow Tufty Club. All we have left is a stiff upper lip.

Which brings me on to the citizen test that all new boys have to pass if they want to become British. At present it's full of irrelevant questions about the number of parliamentary constituencies, what quangos do and who is allowed to vote.

There should be one question only.

When is it acceptable for a grown man to cry in public?

a) Never.

b) Whenever he is upset by something.

Anyone who ticks b) should be taken directly to Heathrow and put on the next flight to abroad.

15 July 2012

We're all running as Team GB, the grim bellyachers

Soon the waiting will be over, and we shall be able to find out whether a Kenyan man we've never heard of can jump further into a sandpit than an American man we've also never heard of. Plus we shall be able to see Russian women with scrotums like tractors hurling hammers about the place. And with a bit of luck, one of the triangular-torsoed diver boys will bash his head on the board. As you may have gathered, I'm no fan of London's forthcoming running and jumping competition, and in recent weeks I've joined in wondering why its officials, among others, should be given one lane of a dual carriageway while 8 million Londoners have to hutch up in the other.

However, even I am now starting to grow weary of the salivatory anticipation that the Olympics will be a soggy festival of incompetence, and that the wall-to-wall television coverage is bound to be ruined by Fearne Cotton saying 'wow' a lot.

When any other Third World country is asked to stage an international event, it doesn't actively hope for it to be a failure: Inner Mongolia, for instance, is hosting this year's Miss World and no one in the local press is saying that all the competitors are sure to get a nasty bout of genital itching.

Here, though, things are rather different. A lone American athlete arrived last week and tweeted to say his first impressions of London weren't good. And somehow this was seen as proof that the whole event was turning into a fiasco.

Of course, what we should have said is, 'Why? What

happened? Were you barked at by a furious immigration official and made to go to the back of a two-hour queue because
you'd accidentally said on your visa waiver form that you had
committed genocide? And then did you climb into a taxi that
had no legroom at all and was being driven by a non-English
speaker who had no idea where he was going? No. Well, shut
up, then, you disgusting little ingrate.'

Then came news that some of the on-site cleaners were
being asked to share a shower. Like everyone who goes to a
£30,000-a-year public school such as Eton. Not that you will
have noticed this little nugget because you were too busy
watching *Twenty Twelve* on your iPlayer.

Meanwhile, a hastily organized select committee was trying to find out why Nick Buckles, the G4S boss, had
announced with just two weeks to go that he'd been unable
to find enough guards to sit at the back of the stadium,
smoking.

But instead, a Labour MP called David Winnick, who
couldn't even do up his tie properly, shouted, 'If I demand
over and over again that you admit it's a humiliating shambles, can I appear on the front of all tomorrow's papers?'

Where was he going with that? And why didn't poor old
Mr Buckles, with his Bay City Rollers haircut, simply tell the
publicity-hungry moron that a much better question would
have been, 'Why did so many of Britain's 2.5 million
unemployed people decide they'd rather stay on benefits
than put on a high-visibility jacket and do a job?'

Whatever. We now get to the hated Olympic lanes, which
have been provided in the hope that visiting journalists are
made to feel so warm and fuzzy that they go home and
encourage business leaders to open an office here.

Do we see it that way? No. What we see instead is one tiny
little mistake on one tiny little road where one lane is for

buses and one is for someone from the *Kampala Gazette*. And for this, apparently, Seb Coe's head must be amputated.

There's more. One woman went to the papers to say that her son hadn't been allowed to wear his expensive training shoes while practising in an east London gym because they hadn't been made by Adidas, one of the Olympic sponsors. Well, yes, I too despair about the commercialization of sport, but the truth is that without Adidas and EDF and BMW, there'd have been no stadium.

Not that we need one, scoffed the cynics, because no tickets at all have been sold for any of the basket-weaving events. And anyway, it's just going to be a white elephant for the rest of time unless Bernie Ecclestone can be persuaded to remove the Monaco race from the grand prix calendar and replace it with an event through the streets of Newham.

By Wednesday last week the hysteria and general sense of impending doom had reached such a pitch that observers were quoting a German magazine that claimed the Games would be a washout because of the weather. And instead of saying, 'Well, yes, but at least the Queen won't storm out if Usain Bolt wins,' we took this as yet more proof that Britain is seen around the world as a useless, wet rock full of tax dodgers, benefit frauds and cheating bankers.

Even Boris Johnson, London's mayor, jumped on the bandwagon, saying that because the swallows were flying backwards and the cotoneaster berries were a little paler than usual, the whole of east London would be soaked for the duration of the Games. Really? Because the weather fore-casters say that the jet stream is moving north, that sunny skies are on the way and that as a result the beach volleyball girls will be allowed to perform naked as usual.

I'm not saying the Games are bound to be a triumph, but I am heartily fed up with the mongers of misery who think they'll be a rain-spattered orgy of mud, incompetence, striking bus drivers, disgruntled staff, angry Americans, corporate greed and empty stadiums. And that the army is almost certain to shoot down a patrolling Eurofighter with one of its Fisher-Price ground-to-air missiles.

We need to think positively. We need to imagine that the opening ceremony is rather more than a celebration of diversity and sustainability. We need to picture a bright summer sun glinting off all the gold medals our athletes have won. In short, let's enjoy the hope now and deal with the despair later.

22 July 2012

Stop, or I'll shoot . . . about 100 yards off to your right

Many people in the civilized world were a bit surprised when they heard that the good Christian folk of Denver, Colorado, had responded to the cinema killings by rushing out the next day to stock up on sub-machine guns.

Firearms permit applications were up 40 per cent.

What were they thinking of? 'Right. Good. I have in my belt a Mac-10, so now if I'm interrupted while out for a romantic dinner with my wife, or walking the dog, I shall be able to kill the assailant before he kills me.'

This is extremely unlikely. Gun-toting maniacs tend not to announce their intentions with a shouted warning. Which means that by the time you have located your weapon, withdrawn it from its hiding place, taken off the safety catch, aimed and pulled the trigger, you're already fairly dead.

And even if by some miracle you aren't, have you ever tried to hit a target with a gun? It's pretty much impossible, even if the target is an American. Once I was given a machine gun by a member of the army and asked to hit, quite literally, a barn door from a range of perhaps fifty yards. The first round was successful, but thereafter I was mostly spraying the sky while stumbling backwards with my eyes closed and my face all screwed up as if I were sucking hard on an unripe lemon.

There is no metaphor that quite captures the sheer violence of pulling the trigger on an automatic weapon. One second, it's as still and as silent as a rock. The next, you are attached to a living thing that is trying desperately to break free from your grasp. If you are a trained soldier, you can just about deal with this. If you are an overweight solicitor out for dinner with your wife, you will end up blind, deaf and surrounded by the thirty bodies of all the people you've just shot by mistake.

It's interesting. Since the *Batman* shootings, a handful of teary Democrats have been saying that automatic weapons with large magazines should be banned. In other words, they want to ban baddies from buying precisely the sort of gun that can't actually hit anything.

Mind you, a pistol is not much better. Only recently a deeply worrying man in North Carolina took me to his outdoor shooting range and asked me to 'double tap' one of his Osama bin Laden targets. So, aim carefully at the man's heart, fire and then straight away put the next round in his head. Seen it done in a million films. Simple.

It isn't, actually. The first carefully aimed round grazed Mr bin Laden's shoulder. The next hit a bush several hundred yards to the right.

Americans must know this. Many are descended from cowboys and gunslingers. So they must be at least aware that in the hands of an amateur, in the heat of the moment, a gun is about as useful as a pencil sharpener.

Politicians must know it too. So Mr Barack should simply explain that in the olden days, when there were Indians and Frenchmen and bears rushing about, it was fair enough to keep a Winchester above the fireplace. But today it's ridiculous.

He doesn't say this, though. After the Aurora massacre, instead of announcing an amnesty or a change in the law, he mumbled something about the need to address violence and explained that every day and a half the same number of young Americans are shot to death as died in Denver. It was a presidential shrug.

That's because asking a working-class American male to hand in his gun is like asking him to hand in his penis. Mr Barack knows that Bud and Hank won't vote for him if he takes away their right to have a machine gun. Which gets us back to the question: why would you want one in the first place?

Well, first of all, you grew up in the Cold War. You were taught by your leaders that when the bad guys have intercontinental ballistic missiles, you must have intercontinental ballistic missiles too. Plus the constitution says you can have a gun to defend yourself from the British.

But there's more to it than that. It's because guns are fascinating. If someone came round to your house today with a 9mm Glock, I can pretty much guarantee that if you have a functioning scrotum, you will want to handle it. And if the person in question has some bullets, you will want to go outside and shoot at a tree.

This probably has something to do with mating. When you have a gun in your hand, you are the most powerful person in the room. Which means you're like those birds that appear on natural history programmes with their feathers all puffed out, making themselves look manly and virile in front of all the girl birds.

A gun is also a comfort blanket. You know that if it's just you, with your weedy little arms, versus a bad man with a gun, you stand no chance at all. However, if you too have a gun about your person, there's a slim chance that as you blast away at all the furniture with your eyes closed, he won't stroll over, punch you in the face, take the gun from you and shoot you in the head with it. A gun doesn't level the playing field. But it does tilt it slightly back in your direction.

There's another thing. Guns are fun. I once spent a pleasant evening in the Arizona desert with a man who had a Mack truck filled from floor to ceiling with every kind of weapon you can imagine. He even had two 8,000-round-a-minute mini-guns mounted on his helicopter.

I was especially fond of something called a squad automatic weapon and spent many hours bouncing tracer rounds into the night sky until the desert actually caught fire. There's no reason, in a civilized world, why a member of the public should have this gun. And no reason why anyone should cackle and squeal with joy as they fire it into the void. But I did. And you would too. And that is the problem.

29 July 2012

Listen, Fritz, we'll do the efficiency now – you write the gags

Ben Elton is working on a new television sitcom about a health and safety department. Doubtless it will be full of high-visibility ear defenders and there will be many hilarious consequences. British health and safety is a rich comic vein. Or rather, it was before the Olympics came along.

I gathered with about 200 ocean-going cynics to watch the opening ceremony and as the lights went up on those little black and white children skipping around a maypole, all of us imagined the worst. We'd seen the knuckle-bitingly embarrassing handover in China.

We'd heard about the low-budget sustainable eco-plans for east London and we all knew, deep down in our stone-cold hearts, that Britain is a basketcase. We never get anything right. Only this time we wouldn't get anything right with the whole world watching.

Well, obviously we were wrong. It was a triumph and, as I write, the Games are proving to be a triumph as well. Furthermore, the trains are running on time, there are no strikes at Heathrow and London is quiet. This, I feel, is going to have a profound effect on not just Elton's new comedy but everything else too.

After the last world war, Britain lost its empire and slid into a soot-blackened well of dirt, discontent and despair. People lived in a monochrome world with outside khazis that didn't work, had no job and, as often as not, had a hideous lung disease. And it was here, in the misery pit, that our world-famous sense of humour was forged.

You knew your new Austin Princess wouldn't work properly. You knew the pubs would shut every time you were thirsty. You knew there'd be a power cut very soon and you knew that the little cough you'd developed yesterday was the onset of pneumoconiosis. And the only way to deal with it all was to have a laugh.

Think about it. How much comedy do you find in British literature that was written when we were rich and successful and ran the world? How many laughs are there in *Wuthering Heights* or *The Return of the Native*? Not many. We were known in Victorian times for many things. But being funny wasn't one of them.

However, when unemployment was running at more than 3 million, the miners were all throwing stones at policemen and your rubbish hadn't been collected for a year, Elton was bringing the house down in the Comedy Store and we were all gathered around the television, laughing our heads off at Frankie Howerd. Titter ye not. But titter we did.

When the people of other countries are displeased with their leaders, they chase them into drains or hang them from lamp posts. Us? We employ Ian Hislop to machine gun them with jokes. When John Cleese was unhappy with the service at a dreary seafront hotel, he didn't write an angry letter. No. He wrote *Fawlty Towers*. I spend my working life on TV praying to all the gods that ever there were that James May will catch fire. Because then we can all have a jolly good giggle.

Adversity and hardship are the cradles of comedy, so what are we to do now the Olympics have shown that, actually, Britain can be rather more than Belgium with a bit of drizzle? What if we're all inspired to succeed and everything we do from now on is equally well run and magnificent?

You really do sense this tide of optimism, certainly in London. Most of us watched that opening ceremony, with the inspiring semi-animated rush down the Thames and Kenneth Branagh as Isambard Kingdom Brunel, and we've all plainly decided Britain doesn't need to be rubbish at everything.

People talk about how the achievement will change the way other countries feel about us. Far more important is how it will change the way we feel about ourselves. That's what happened after Barcelona hosted the Games. Basking in a Ready Brek glow of pride, it went from a crummy little fishing port to one of the coolest cities in the world.

That could well happen here. The Olympics have injected us all with a long-forgotten sense of contentment, and who knows what effect this will have?

What if Terminal 2 reopens at Heathrow on time and all the passengers' suitcases end up on the correct planes? What if we build an aircraft carrier that can be used as a launch pad for actual planes? What if the people in charge of parking meters in some London boroughs scrap the pay-by-phone system, which doesn't work, and bring back the coin slot, which does? What if the banks examine what Sebastian Coe has achieved and think, 'Hey, chaps. Why don't we lend money to people who can pay us back?'

Where would that leave *Have I Got News for You*? Paul Merton may still be able to offer up some nugget about a squashed cat, but poor old Hislop would be castrated. And who's going to find Elton's new show funny if health and safety officers start to behave sensibly? Certainly I bet you would have found *Twenty Twelve* far less chucklesome if you'd known then what you know now.

If Britain becomes as well run as Switzerland, we could end up with a Swiss sense of humour. In other words, we'd end up with absolutely no sense of humour at all. You'd have John Bishop and Michael McIntyre and all the other observational comedians walking into empty theatres and saying, 'Have you noticed how all the trains run bang on time . . .'

The only crumb of comfort we can take from all this is that Germany is in a pickle. Thanks to the curious machinations of the European Union, various southern euro states have decided it's best if they sit under an olive tree all day and get Hermann to pay for all their public services.

As a result, Johnny Boche will soon be bankrupt. The country will have strikes and riots, and everyone's Mercedes will break down all the time. This could well mean that in the not-too-distant future, all the world's best comedians will be German.

5 August 2012

Arise, Sir Jeremy – defier of busybody croupiers and barmen

There were calls last week for the Cabinet Office to hand over the honours system to an independent body in the hope that more lollipop ladies could be knighted and more OBEs awarded to those who have done voluntary work in 'the community'.

Of course, this is yet another example of the drive to create a new people-power society in which the fat, the stupid and the toothless are encouraged to lord it over the bright, the thin and the successful. Already we are seeing its effects. A tiny number of morons decided that they would like very much to stroll through my garden, pausing a while to peer through my kitchen window, and now they can.

A noisy minority decided that Jonathan Ross should be driven from the BBC, and he was. And expensive public libraries are now kept open just because an infinitesimal number of internet-phobes from 'the community', chose to dance about outside with placards.

We turn firemen into heroes if they get their trousers wet and treat single mums like round-the-world sailors. David Cameron is an idiot, Boris Johnson is a buffoon, Richard Branson is a spoilt child. But the man who empties your bins is as wise as an owl and must be given a CBE immediately.

Unless this nonsense is stopped, we shall become like America and, having spent a couple of weeks there recently, I can assure you that this would be A Bad Thing.

We begin the shoulder-sagging saga in Las Vegas, six floors below a party that seems to have made the papers. I wanted to show my sixteen-year-old son how blackjack works, but although he was allowed in the casino, he was not allowed to stand near any of the tables.

The croupier had been issued with the power to enforce this law and as a result shouted, 'Back up!' as my son peered over my shoulder. In an attempt to defuse what appeared to be a life-or-death situation, I asked the boy to reverse slowly until he reached a point where the lobster-brained croupier was happy. Quite soon I noticed that he'd reversed perilously close to the table behind him, and I pointed this out to the woman. 'Okay,' she said, realizing the mistake. 'Forwards. Forwards. Forwards a bit more. Stop.' He ended up about nine inches from where he'd started.

Obviously it's a good idea to stop teenage boys gambling but the idea of using a stupid person to enforce this law doesn't work at all. A point that had been made a few days earlier at a hotel near Yosemite. When my eighteen-year-old daughter joined me at the bar for a refreshing Coca-Cola she was told, very loudly, that she needed to be twenty-one to sit there, and that she would have to join the half-hour queue for a table. So let's just get this straight: you can sit at a table and have a Coke but you cannot sit at the bar, even though the two places are 2ft apart?

The shouty barman agreed the law was stupid and that it would be ridiculous to deny a bar stool to, say, a twenty-year-old soldier who had just lost a leg in Afghanistan. But said there was nothing he could do.

Yes, Bud or Hank or Todd, or whatever single-syllable name you have, that's the problem. There is something you can do. You don't spend your evenings peering into the barrel of your Heckler & Koch machine pistol. You don't eat stuff that you know to be poisonous. You have nous. You have at least some initiative. Use it.

When on the balcony of a hotel room in Los Angeles, I was told by a bossy cleaner that she 'needed' me to extinguish my cigarette. Smoking on a balcony in Los Angeles is not allowed. But why? There was no one within 300ft. I was outside. I would place the butt in an empty beer bottle. But logic is a dandelion seed when the hurricane of state law is entrusted to someone with an IQ of four.

We went to an exhibition of Titanic artefacts. For reasons that are entirely unclear, all our cameras had to be left in a locker. But you can't use the lockers unless you can provide the idiotic ticket woman with photo ID. Can you think of a single reason why you need to prove who you are before being allowed to leave one of your own belongings in a locker? Me neither.

There was a similar problem with a zip wire my children wanted to try. Yes, they were tall enough and, yes, my cash money was acceptable. But before they were allowed to have a go I had to give written permission. And for that I needed photo ID.

What would photo ID prove? That my name was Jeremy Clarkson. But would that show I was the children's father? No, because they were not required by state law to prove who they were. The fact is this: ID was required because in totalitarian states such as Soviet Russia and North Korea and America it's important to know who is doing what at all times.

At one hotel we used there were two pools: a family pool that was full mostly of homosexual men, and a European pool where lady guests were allowed to remove their bikini tops. Strangely we weren't allowed to sit round the European pool even though we had photo ID to prove we were actually European.

After two weeks of being told by janitors, night watchmen,

cleaners and passers-by that we couldn't smoke near fruit machines, go barefoot in a shopping mall, park near a fire hydrant, drink in the street, take cameras to the Grand Canyon skywalk or make jokes to anyone in any kind of uniform, we kissed the tarmac at Heathrow and now see Britain in an all-new light.

Yesterday I was overtaken by a man in a sports car who had an unrestrained golden retriever in the passenger seat. And I rejoiced. Then, this morning, I applauded when I saw a cyclist jump a red light. And I have thoroughly enjoyed sitting with my children outside the Plough in Kingham, smoking and drinking and having a nice time. This is what should be meant by people power. The power for people to choose which of the government's petty, silly, pointless laws they want to obey. And which they don't.

2 September 2012

P-p-please open up, Arkwright, I need some t-t-t-trousers

We return this morning to a subject I've talked about before. It's a subject close to every man's heart: the sheer, unadulterated, trudging misery of shopping for clothes.

I buy my shoes at Tod's on Bond Street in London. Its window is always full of many attractive designs, and if I have a few minutes left on the meter I will sometimes pop in to buy a pair. But they never, ever, have anything in a size 11. The lady always comes back from a lengthy trip to the storeroom brandishing a pair of size 5s, asking cheerfully if they will do instead.

Which is a bit like someone in a restaurant ordering the vegetarian option and being asked if a nice, juicy T-bone steak will do instead. No, it won't. And now, thanks to this time-wasting, I have a parking ticket.

Shops never keep shirts in the size I want either, and every single available jacket would only really fit Ziggy Stardust. Trousers? Don't know, because I'm way too big to fit in the overheated postbox the retailer laughingly calls a changing room. However, if by some miracle you do find something in your size that you like, your problems are far from over because you have to pay for it.

When you buy £100-worth of petrol, you put your card in a machine, tap in your code and seconds later walk out with a receipt. When you buy £100-worth of trousers, you must stand at the desk while the sales assistant inputs what feels like the entire works of Dostoevsky into her computer. And then she will want your name and address so that you can be kept abreast of forthcoming clothing lines that won't be available in your size either.

And you can't get round the problem by going somewhere else because these days there is nowhere else.

This is my new beef. Every single high street and every single shopping centre in every single town and city is full of exactly the same shops attempting to sell exactly the same things that you can't buy because they don't keep your size in stock.

A recent trip to San Francisco has demonstrated that it doesn't have to be this way. I took my children to Haight-Ashbury so that I could talk to them about the summer of love and how Janis Joplin was about a billion times better than any of the talentless teenage warblers on their iPods.

At first I was a bit disappointed to find that the whole area had been turned into a vast shopping experience. The kids weren't, though. And soon neither was I.

The first shop was rammed with Sixties clothing and accessories. Purple hippie sunglasses. Vietnam Zippos. Joss sticks and curious-looking chemistry sets. There were posters of Hendrix and CND badges and I bought more in there, in ten minutes, than I've bought in Britain in ten years.

Then I found a shoe shop. It was selling shoes and boots the likes of which you simply would not find anywhere in Britain and it had in stock every single size you could think of. I bought many pairs. Then I bought two jackets that fitted, and then we decided to visit one of the many coffee shops. None of which was Starbucks.

Not a single one of the shops wanted my name or address when I bought anything. They had no intention of sending me exciting product information and they did not expect me to hang around while they updated their stock figures.

You hand over your card, provide the inevitable photo ID, sign your name and leave.

Of course, you may imagine that all of the hundreds of tiny independent shops in the area are being run by free-love people who arrived in San Francisco in June 1967 and who are therefore not interested in profit. You might imagine that as long as you worshipped at the altar of peaceful protest, you could barter for one of the chemistry sets with beans.

There was plenty of evidence to suggest this might be so. One shop was being run by a chap in his sixties. He wore his hair in a ponytail, with a pair of John Lennon glasses, a poncho and a set of groovy loon pants. Later, though, I saw him locking up his shop and climbing into a brand new Cadillac Escalade.

So why, if there's money to be made, have the big boys not moved in? Bloody good question.

Because that's exactly what's happened on the British equivalent of Haight-Ashbury: the King's Road in London. Back in the day this was a mishmash of small shops selling individually made items to Mick Jagger and Johnny Rotten. Now it's WH Smith, HMV, Marks & Spencer. It's exactly the same as Pontefract and Pontypool. Genesis has gone all Phil Collins.

The trouble is that there are only a few streets in London where the big multinational retailers want to be. This means the rents are six times higher on the King's Road than they are on Haight Street in San Francisco. One American chain called Forever 21 paid almost £14 million in key money to HMV to take over its lease on Oxford Street. And against that sort of financial clout, a slightly off-his-head jewellery designer with a fondness for growing beans and a laissez-faire attitude to payment is going to find himself priced out of the market.

The good news is, however, that I'm by no means the only person who shivers with despair at Britain's one-size-fits-nobody attitude to shopping. I'm not the only person who fumes with rage over the sheer length of time it takes to pay. And how the financial pressure to make every square foot count means stock and changing rooms are smaller than most lavatory cisterns.

Which means that one day the Starbucks and the Forever 21s and the Banana Republics will be brought to their knees. And the streets of our towns will be handed back to Ronnie Barker, who'll open all hours, sell us things we like and let us pay at the end of the week. In beads.

9 September 2012

Oh, my head hurts – I've a bad case of hangover envy

As you probably heard, the government announced recently that during the month of what it's calling 'Stoptober', it will run a nationwide campaign designed to make every smoker in the land stub out their last cigarette and quit.

I don't remember that being in the manifesto. And I certainly don't remember giving my permission for the Department of Star Jumps and Push-Ups to spend vast lumps of my money on a series of bossy television advertisements designed to make my life less pleasant. So, in protest, I decided to give up drinking.

Most nights, like many people of my age, I drink a bottle of wine, and this means that most mornings I have a bit of clutch slip until after I've had some coffee, a couple of Nurofen and some quiet time with the papers.

I'm comfortable with that. But I'm not really comfortable with the effects the booze has had on my stomach. Visually, it's a bit silly. It looks like I have the actual moon in my shirt. It's so vast that when I bend over to tie up my shoelaces, it squashes into my lungs so firmly that I can't breathe.

And when I run, it turns into a giant pendulum, sloshing from side to side so vigorously that sometimes I get the impression it may actually break free from its moorings. I needed to get rid of it, and if in the process I could stick a finger in the eye of a hectoring government, so much the better. I therefore decided to give up booze.

So the first night. I felt no need for wine. I'm not an alcoholic in the true sense of the word. But my hands felt a bit fidgety, like they'd been made redundant. They wanted something to do. They wanted a glass of something to nurture but what could I put in it?

Milk? Lovely. My favourite drink in the whole wide world. But even more fattening than wine and at seven p.m. it seemed wrong. Water? No. The stupidest idea in the world. It's just liquefied air. Something fizzy? Too carcinogenic. I thought about tea but I'm not old enough yet, and then discounted tomato juice on the basis that its primary function in life is to cure what I wouldn't be suffering from any more.

I went to the supermarket, where I discovered that all of the non-alcoholic 'beverages' are aimed either at people who want to stay awake, or who are four years old. It's row after row of idiotic lime-green labelling and contents that appear to have come from the props department of *Doctor Who*.

I was in despair until, at the last moment, I discovered a bottle of Robinsons lemon barley water. The taste of my childhood; Dan Maskell in a bottle. I took it home and it was like drinking the sound of a wood pigeon and a distant tractor. I was very happy.

The second night, I was going out and it transpires that no bar or restaurant stocks Robinsons barley water. So I had to think of something else.

I was still thinking several hours later, by which time my friends were unsteady on their feet and very garrulous.

And suddenly I discovered the biggest problem of not drinking in a society that does. When everyone else is drunk, they look stupid, they sound stupid, they laugh at things that aren't funny, such as a fart, and you start to hate them on a cellular level.

You begin to wonder what they would look like without heads, and because you are sober, the imagery is frighteningly clear.

Turning up in polite society and asking for a soft drink is like turning up and sobbing. It puts a damper on proceedings.

A meeting of friends is supposed to be light and filled with laughter. The last thing a group of happy people wants is one person sitting in the middle talking about the trauma of Syria.

If I was going to keep this non-drinking lark up, there is no doubt that the moon in my shirt would start to shrink. But, on the downside, I would lose all my friends and I would have to come to terms with the fact that never again would I have a great night out. No, really, I mean it. Can you think of a single memorable evening you've ever had when you weren't absolutely blasted? Nope. Neither can I.

In fact, you won't really have a night out at all because such is the pressure to drink, to join the herd, to find a fart funny, that it's a thousand times easier to decline the invitation and stay at home. Which is why for the next four nights I did just that, with my barley water, watching television and enriching my life not one bit.

I learnt something else as well. It is possible to suffer from hangover envy. In a morning, as you're doing a bit of light skipping, you see your friends clinging on to trees and street furniture, looking like a pile of laundry, with faces the colour of ostrich eggs.

This should be uplifting. It should make you feel good as you *boing* along the street with a zip in your step and sparkling eyes. But, in fact, it makes you crestfallen. Because at four a.m., when you were asleep, which is the same as being dead, they were very much alive. They were making memories in police cells and on inappropriate girls, and you were at home snoring the snore of a dullard. Waking up feeling fresh is like dying with a clear conscience and a healthy bank balance. It means you've wasted your life.

So here we are, ten days into my non-drinking regime. It's nine p.m., I have a glass of wine by the laptop and some friends have just invited me over – I'm going and I don't plan to be home till two. So when *Top Gear* returns to your screen, know this: yes, it will look like I've got a planet in my shirt, but I will be smiling the smile of a man who's happy with his life. I will be smiling the smile of a man who's had a drink.

16 September 2012

If breasts are no big deal, girls, don't get them reupholstered

In the past week I've been mildly startled by the attitude of many women, who've said they cannot understand why someone would take photographs of a girl sunbathing topless, why a magazine would pay money for the right to publish them and why Buckingham Palace should have used the courts to try to prevent further images from reaching a wider audience. All have said the same thing: 'Breasts are no big deal.'

On the face of it, that's true. How can they be a big deal when half the world has them? Well, I'll tell you how. Because the other half can't really ever think of anything else.

In a list of stuff that matters most to a man, breasts appear at No. 4, between oxygen and food.

Breasts fascinate us. We cannot imagine why women don't spend all day at home playing with them, because if we had them, that's what we'd do. It's why we were all so keen to have a look at what sort the future queen has. Would they be angry, sad, milky or pointy? Would they look like deflated zeppelins or dried fish? Or would they not really be there at all?

Often we are told by women that when at work or out socializing, they are heartily fed up with men who talk to their chest rather than their face. Well, I would like to say here and now that men do not do that. I would like to. But I cannot. Because on occasion we do. We can't help it.

In the same way that women could not help having a quiet moment with their laptop if they thought the internet was hosting a full-frontal picture of George Clooney.

Of course, since the invention of clothing there have been many attempts to desexualize the breast. In the 1960s, *National Geographic* magazine was undoubtedly seen as a weighty and learned tome full of many interesting facts about the world and its people. Not to me, it wasn't. It was a girlie mag.

Later, women's liberationists argued that by burning their bras they were freeing themselves from the shackles of history and propelling themselves through the glass ceiling. And this received a great deal of support from male observers, all of whom were equally keen for bra-less women to be seen anywhere.

Today new mothers are often to be found in crowded places breastfeeding their infants. They could go behind a tree or to a quiet spot, but by popping one out in public they send a clear message: This is not a sex toy. It's a food dispensary unit, so stop staring.

Yeah, right. Telling us to stop staring at a breast is like telling us not to stare at a burning airliner. It isn't possible.

The Duchess of Cambridge is probably fearful that she is the first senior royal to be seen in public in such a state of undress.

Not so. Queen Mary II was painted topless, and in France, scene of the current brouhaha, Charles VII's mistress would constantly swan around court with her breasts on show. It was the fashion then.

You might like to think that things changed in Victorian times but evidently not. The Victorians were idiotically prudish and got it into their tiny minds that the ankle and the shoulder should be concealed beneath many layers of velvet, steel and wood. Despite this, it was absolutely fine to turn up at a Brunellian reception for the monarch herself in the sort of top that even Kate Moss would find 'too revealing'.

So men have been exposed to breasts for centuries. Many of us were brought up on them. We see them every day in the nation's bestselling newspaper, on the internet and on even the coldest Saturday night in Newcastle. We see them on the beach when we go on holiday and in the office on a hot day. Breasts are simply everywhere. They should be about as sexual as moths. But they aren't.

Let me pose a delicate question. In the sort of exotic South Sea societies that used to appear in the *National Geographic* magazine, it is still completely normal for women to be topless as they go about their daily business. So does this mean that during lovemaking sessions, their boyfriends and husbands treat their breasts like their noses and ignore them? It's possible, I suppose, but I very much doubt it.

What's more, if breasts are no big deal, why do women buy bras that lift and separate and do all sorts of other things besides? Why queue round the block to have your breasts reupholstered?

It's because you know that, in fact, your breasts are a big deal. Mrs Mountbatten-Windsor knows it too and that's why she was so mortified to find them in the press and plastered all over the internet.

Those pictures should not have been taken and they should not have been published. And it is stupid to claim that she's to blame because she was in full view of the public road. Because that's only true if you were looking at her through a two-million-millimetre telephoto lens.

Happily, though, the argument brings me on to a solution. Doubtless one day the photographer who took the offending snaps will be identified, and when that happens he will become a public figure. According to his rules, that will make him fair game.

So someone should wait for him to go to the lavatory and

then snap away. If he chooses to complain about having a private moment appear on the internet, then we will simply argue that, at the time, he was clearly visible to anyone who happened to be on a stepladder peering over the top of the cubicle. And that he should have known better.

23 September 2012

Call me Comrade Clarkson, liberator of the jobsworths

In the past couple of weeks everyone in the country, except me, seems to have decided that Andrew Mitchell, the government chief whip, is a potty-mouthed snob who goes through life gorging on swan, goosing his housekeeper and shooting poor people for sport.

Last week the police released details of exactly what was said between officers and Mr Mitchell after he'd been told he couldn't ride his bicycle through the main gates at Downing Street. Mr Mitchell demanded that he be allowed to exit through the main gate whereupon it was explained to him this was not possible.

A police officer on duty said: 'I am more than happy to open the side pedestrian gate for you, sir, but it is policy that we are not to allow cycles through the main vehicle gate.'

At this point Mr Mitchell seems to have become angry, telling the officers they had best learn their effing place, that they were effing plebs and that they hadn't heard the last of the matter.

Hmmm. While his choice of abuse seems a bit weak, I sympathize with his sentiments absolutely. Because what petty-minded pen-pusher made this policy and why? What possible difference can it make which gate people use when leaving work? Why should bicycles use one gate and cars another?

These are the questions that matter. Except, of course, we already know the answers. 'It's security, sir.' Or maybe: 'It's health and safety, sir.' These are the catch-all responses from anyone in a uniform who thinks if he uses the word 'sir' as often as possible, we won't notice he's being a complete arse.

Only very recently I arrived at a department of the BBC, where I engaged in the usual good-natured banter with a security guard I've known for many years. I asked how he was. He asked after my family. We chatted momentarily about the weather and then, after I explained that I'd accidentally left my pass at home, he said he couldn't let me in. 'Security policy,' he said, with the good-natured shrug of a small cog that has never asked a bigger cog: 'Why?'

I felt it immediately: a hotness surging into my head and threatening to sever my tongue from its mountings, leaving it free to call the blithering idiot many cruel and unusual names. I began to imagine what he might look like without a head. And the noises he'd make if I staked him out in the desert with no eyelids.

This happens all the time. With traffic wardens who somehow can't see that I only popped into the tobacconist's for a moment; with airport security guards who think my youngest daughter is a dead ringer for Abu Hamza; and most recently in America with a moron who wanted photo ID before I could rent a luggage locker.

Then you have the imbeciles at the post office and various other large organizations who explain their company's stupid policy and, when they see you're about to boil over, point at a sign on their desk that says: 'The company will not tolerate physical or verbal abuse directed at our employees.' In other words: 'If you complain about our small-minded idiocy you will go to prison.'

So you stand there and you say, as calmly as you can: 'Why can you not deliver my parcel/fridge/important document?' And invariably you are told it is for security reasons. Or health and safety.

Actually, neither of those things is the reason. No. The reason the police officers in Downing Street, the nation's traffic wardens and the counter staff at the post office do not bend the rules even when they can see you're making sense is simple: they fear for their jobs. They've been told by their line manager what the policy is and they know that if they bend it even a little bit, just once, they will be sacked.

Things are different in Italy. Last week I flew back to Britain through Milan's Linate airport. And it was plainly obvious that the X-ray arch machine had been set to such a level it could detect tiny fragments of zinc in a lady's vajazzle, or bits of nickel in those hard bits at the end of a man's shoelaces.

We see this a lot with airport scanners these days and we know what the response will be. You'll be sent back to take off yet another item of clothing until you are butt naked. And even then, thanks to the cardamom in the chicken casserole you ate the night before, a man will want to rub his wand over your genitals. It's humiliating and disgusting.

In Milan, however, they do things rather differently. Someone would walk through the machine. It would beep. The security guard would note that it was a businessman or an old lady and would simply wave them through. I beeped. He looked at me. Saw no beard. Saw I had hands rather than hooks. And that was that.

Of course, he will have been told loudly, and usually by the Americans, that every single person getting on every single airliner is likely to explode at any moment, but Luigi uses his nous. And he has obviously worked out that if a terrorist organization is going to go to all the bother of blowing up a plane, it probably won't be the 11.30 a.m. commuter shuttle from Milan to London.

So why is Luigi allowed to use the power of reason when

Mr Patel at Heathrow is not? Simple. Because Luigi cannot be sacked.

Well, he can, but under the terms of Italian employment law, his employer must continue to pay his wages, his mortgage, his children's school fees and the grocery bill of his descendants forever.

I have no doubt at all that Mr Mitchell, a Tory, would fight tooth and nail to stop such communist laws being introduced in Britain. Which is why he will continue to be told by knees-knocking policemen that they can't let him cycle through the vehicle gate because using their common sense is more than their job's worth.

Simple solution. Introduce a system where it becomes less than their job's worth.

30 September 2012

If foreigners weren't watching, we'd be lynching bell-ringers

While on a tour of a factory in South America recently, David Cameron appeased the nation's meat-eaters by saying that at some point in the next parliament there might possibly be a referendum on whether Britain stayed in the European Union.

Isolationism is very popular at the moment. Not just with middle England but with the Scotch, too, and the Corns — everyone. If you gave people in Leicester the chance to form their own government and their own state, I bet you any money a majority would say, 'Ooh, yes please.'

Certainly the idea of Chipping Norton breaking free from the shackles of Westminster and Brussels is very appealing. There is little crime, so we wouldn't need a police force. Or an army. Many people own guns, so we'd easily be able to hold out should we be attacked by Stow-on-the-Wold or Moreton-in-Marsh. We have meat, trout and vegetables. We could trade jam for oil. And we have wind for power.

Taxes would be very low, since we would only really need a school, two doctors and a fire station. And we could introduce some new laws relevant to our way of life. We could make it illegal to be Piers Morgan or to harbour a badger. Campanology would be outlawed, too, along with motorcycles. On the face of it, then, life would be peachy.

To understand where all of this might end, you need to go back to the 1850s in what at the time was known as 'darkest Africa'. British explorers stumbled on a tribe living on the tranquil northern shores of Lake Victoria. People had been living there for tens of thousands of years, assuming that they were the only people on earth. They had never met anyone from another tribe, let alone an Arab or a white man. And it was interesting to see how their society had developed.

They had not invented the wheel or the plough. But they had invented beer. And they could carry it around in vessels woven exquisitely from reeds. They also had fine cloth and knew to wash their hands in the lake before eating. They had also come up with the idea of extreme violence.

If a child was making too much noise over lunch, it would be beheaded. If it got up without clearing its plate? That was a beheading offence, too. Beheading was their society's equivalent of the naughty step. It was also a cure for snoring, nagging or looking at someone in a funny way.

It could be worse, though. You could have ended up as one of the king's wives. They were kept bound on the floor and forced to drink milk for eight hours a day, non-stop.

This ensured that when the head honcho fancied a spot of rumpy-pumpy, the girl he selected would be nice and fat. Kate Moss? She would have been beheaded before she'd reached puberty.

Now remember, this was the middle of the nineteenth century. Elsewhere in the world there were steam engines and ladies with parasols taking tea in the park. People in India wore clothes made in Huddersfield. People in Louisiana drank tea from Ceylon. And yet in the middle of it all was a civilization in which you could be beheaded for talking with your mouth full.

What stopped it was the arrival of other people. People who said, 'Yes, cutting your daughter's head off is certainly one way of teaching her not to use her fingers at meal times. But have you tried a stern word, or a smacked bottom, because where we come from that works quite well, too?'

This argument is still relevant today. What do you think stops American police forces waterboarding pretty much everyone they take into custody? The answer has nothing to do with the inner goodness of a man's soul. It's the sure-fire knowledge that other people are watching.

Why do you think Robert Mugabe is such a monster? Because Zimbabwe is cut off. He can do as he pleases because he doesn't have people from other places raising an eyebrow and saying, 'Are you sure?'

Closer to home we have the Isle of Man. Because it's not really in the EU and not really part of the UK and because people from abroad are viewed by locals as Romulan stormtroopers, it was 1992 before they stopped birching homosexuals in front of a baying mob. And why? Because that's when satellite TV from other countries showed them that homosexuality wasn't a lifestyle choice and that birching was a bit last week. Maybe one day soon its idiotic government will also learn that it can't just go around confiscating people's gardens.

Most governments in the civilized world are constitutionally bound by checks and balances to ensure they don't do something idiotic. And what are those checks and balances? They usually have fancy names but, actually, they all boil down to the same thing: other people.

In Britain every single poll on the death penalty suggests that the vast majority of us would like to see the gallows reintroduced. And, of course, if we weren't in the EU, a government would be free to bring it back.

But what for? At first, it would be for premeditated murder and rape. However, with no one looking, how long would it be before we were hanging people for having a beard, or for shouting at meal times, or for being Peter Mandelson? How long before disaffected Muslim youths started disappearing?

And before child molesters and bell-ringers were hung from lamp posts by lynch mobs?

Take the case of Abu Hamza. Every fibre of your being wanted him gone and you didn't really care where. If he'd ended up becoming part of a new flyover on the M6, you'd have been relieved. But would that have been a good thing? Really?

We need to be in Europe, to trade with the Germans and holiday in France. We need to be Spain's checks and Sweden's balances. For the sake of decency and the advancement of science, we need to share ideas, to compromise, to be a team. We need to look after one another. Not the Greeks, though. They can get lost.

7 October 2012

Take another step, Simba, and you'll feel my foldaway spoon

When I was growing up I used to go on a great many bicycle rides and they were great fun. But, of course, you can't do that any more because today cycling has been hijacked by thin-spectacled men from the marketing department, and as a result it's become a 'lifestyle choice'.

This means you can't just buy a bicycle. You need lots of other paraphernalia as well.

You need what's called 'kit'. A helmet with a built-in camera, brakes made from materials that aren't even on the periodic table, some sideburns, a carbon-fibre boot mount for your car, some ridiculous energy bars and half a pint of special gel to keep your gentleman's area zesty and fresh.

And then, when you have all this, you will meet other people who've made the same lifestyle choice and they'll explain that their gel is better than your gel and that their energy bars are more energetic. So you'll have to throw all your stuff away and upgrade immediately.

It's the same story with fishing. Gone are the days when you could splosh about, netting sticklebacks. Now, you have titanium rods and a range of neoprene waders. If you want to hold your head up on the river, you'll be forced by your bank manager to sell all the natty golf-bag attachments you bought during your recent flirtation with the men of Pringle.

All you need to shoot a pheasant is a gun and some cart-ridges. But, of course, that's not true because today you need to turn up looking like a cross between King Edward

VII and Pablo Escobar. And in addition to the fancy-dress costume you'll need noise-cancelling headphones, leather wellies, some care-in-the-community fingerless gloves, a pair of yellow sunglasses, a Range Rover and the ability to talk for hours about the weight of the shot in your cartridges. This means the cost of each pheasant you bring down is approximately £1 million.

It doesn't seem to matter, though. For many men nowadays the thrill of buying a new hobby-related gadget far outweighs the thrill of actually doing the hobby. And absolutely nothing proves this more than a trip to see the big five in Africa.

I've just spent a couple of weeks over there with a handful of colleagues who I know from experience travel the world armed only with jeans and T- shirts. Unless they're in the Arctic Circle, in which case it's jeans, T-shirts and an anorak.

When they go to China none of them feels the need to dress up like Chairman Mao. When they're in Japan they don't wear kimonos and slippers. And in France none of them comes down to breakfast wearing a beret. But in Africa they all take leave of their senses and turn up dressed like the zipped and Velcroed love children of Bear Grylls and Joy Adamson. And that's before we get to the kit.

One night a hippopotamus came into the camp, and like any sentient being I was mesmerized by the stupidity of its ears and the idiocy of its noises. But no one else even looked up because they were all engrossed in Richard Hammond's new torch.

When it comes to holding my attention, a torch is right up there with a knitting needle or some lettuce.

But this one was somehow amazing because it had come from an African adventurer's kit shop. Along with Hammond's trousers, which had many pockets for his foldaway cutlery, his compass and, bizarrely, his massive knife.

Now I can see why you might need a knife when you are carving the Sunday joint or chopping vegetables. But why would you need such a thing in Africa? Do people really imagine that they will be attacked by a lion? It's nonsense because a) lions are too busy sleeping or having sex to attack people, and b) even if one did, do you think you'd have the presence of mind to unzip your special knife pocket, retrieve the blade and stick it into a bit of the beast that might somehow make a difference?

Hammond was not the only one to have succumbed to the marketing man's spell. Our minicam operator had plainly overdosed on the gullible pills because he arrived with a head torch that shone a red light.

'It doesn't attract insects,' he said from inside what looked like a beehive.

His other new toy was a hammock that featured a shaped bottom section and a ribbed mosquito net on the top. It had probably cost about £2,000 and looked very sleek and impressive. But as he climbed inside on the first night, he discovered as the rain started that while it kept the flies away, it was not waterproof.

Shoes were another big thing among the chaps. It seems that people in the outdoor pursuits industry have it in their minds that in Africa there is very little gravity, so to anchor yourself in place you need to be sporting footwear that weighs the same as a small house.

Plus, because they've also decided there is almost no friction in Africa, the soles must be made from chunky grooved rubber that appears to have come from the tyres of an earth mover.

Americans are very easily conned by the outdoor leisure

industry's marketing powers, which is why they turn up at every hippo watering hole looking as though they've just stepped off the set of *Daktari*. I realize, of course, that American tourists are always more interesting than whatever they're looking at, but in Africa's game reserves they are absolutely hysterical. I saw one with a canvas drinking canteen. What use would that be on a holiday where you are never more than 30ft from a fridge?

I'm not saying that all hobby-related kit is useless. Obviously you can't jump from a balloon in outer space wearing a blazer and slacks, and you can't dive to the bottom of the deepest trench in the ocean in a suit and tie. Sometimes equipment is necessary. But if you are going for a walk, or going on holiday, or going for a bicycle ride, trust me on this: it isn't.

21 October 2012

So, the Scouts came to earth in a reptilian space plane, right?

Many state-educated people have it in their heads that life for those in Britain's public schools is a deeply weird potpourri of silly uniforms, brutal sport and endless lessons about tax avoidance and the benefits of offshore slavery. In Latin.

I sympathize with all this, of course.

You see those Eton boys poncing about in their frilly shirts and their frock coats and because you have no idea what goes on behind the closed doors, you're bound to think they're all a bit mad, bad and dangerous.

It's the same story with Scientology. We have a vague idea that if you follow its principles, you will be able to fly an F-14 upside down and sleep with Kelly McGillis. On the downside, however, you have to believe that humans were transported to earth millions of years ago in a DC-8-like craft by a tyrant ruler of the galactic confederacy. This is hard to swallow, of course, because the DC-8 was a jet. And jets don't work in space.

At this point we should move on to Mitt Romney. I am told that it is not possible to take anything he says seriously because he is a Mormon and, of course, I nod sagely even though – if I'm honest – I really don't have a clue what Mormons do. Are they the ones who can have nine wives but no blood transfusions? Or is that the Jehovah's Witnesses?

You see the problem. We get snippets of information about these organizations and they worry us. Ignorance makes us afraid. That's why I have a morbid fear of the Freemasons. As I understand it, you may not progress beyond the rank of constable in the police unless you are a member. Which means that every single senior officer has to really believe that if he explains the secrets of the handshake, his tongue will be torn from its mountings and thrown in the sea.

This is why when I'm talking to a sergeant I'm always a bit frightened. Because, thanks to the small amount of knowledge I have about his lodge meetings, I think he is a loony.

But I reserve my greatest fear and trepidation for people who are, or who have been, Scouts. In the olden days, Scouting was very obviously a harmless pursuit. You'd see them in the woods from time to time, tying knots and rubbing sticks together, and then once a year they'd emerge from the tree-line and offer to rub grit into your car in exchange for a shilling.

Now, though, we never see them at all. However, like the ebola virus, they're still out there in their millions. And we have scant idea of what they're up to . . .

Their leader in Britain is a man called Bear Grylls, a survival expert who stays in hotels and likes to be attacked at night by friends and colleagues in wildlife costumes.

More importantly, we heard last week that Scouts are no longer permitted to use nicknames. That is very sinister. Scout chiefs say that nicknames can lead to bullying and argue that this is in some way a bad thing. I disagree.

Bullying gives a man a spine. It forces him to address his issues and work out what he's doing wrong. I was bullied for two straight years at school and I like to think it toughened me up and made me realize that you can't go through life being a hopeless, quivery-bottom-lipped, unfunny prig.

In the early days this is what Scouting was all about. It prepared boys for life as adults. It made them strong and practical. They knew what to do when they were attacked by a fox. They knew that if they worked they would be rewarded.

They also knew how to keep Scout masters out of the tent at night. So when you left the Scouting movement you were more of a man than if you'd never joined.

But now that your comrades are no longer allowed to call you 'Chubby' or 'Ginger' or 'Slob Boy', you will be weak and unprepared to deal on your own with life's little crises, so you will have to rely on the authorities to settle your disputes.

There's more. Jews, Muslims and Buddhists are all welcome but you are not allowed to join if you are an agnostic or an atheist. How mad is that? The movement's leaders argue that this is in the sprit of Robert Baden-Powell's demand that members believe in a higher power.

Hmm. So why are gays allowed in? I can't imagine he'd have approved of that. He didn't even like foreigners very much.

This is the big problem for Scouts. We hear about the hypocrisy and the nonsense. But other than that we know very little. So we fill in the blanks ourselves, assuming that in America it's a front for the neo-Nazis and that in Britain it's a division of the Liberal Democrats, only with more on-message sustainability and inclusivity.

Happily, however, I have a solution. Twenty years ago the Scouts' bob-a-job week was abandoned for fear that little Johnnie – known until then as Fatso – might fall foul of health and safety legislation or get sued by a little old lady for fire-hosing her cat to death.

There was an attempt earlier this year to bring it back. It was called 'community week' and it saw Scouts planting wild flowers and retrieving shopping trolleys from canals. But, I'm sorry, to take the mystery out of Scouting it's not good enough to have members in a faraway lock, doing what prisoners should be doing.

We need them at our doors, with pockets full of scrumped

apples, offering to clean our shoes and sweep the chimney for 5p. We need to encounter Scouts in our daily lives, helping old ladies across the road and petting guide dogs.

It's the same story, in fact, with all the world's esoteric organizations. Opus Dei, the Masons, UKIP, Tom and John at the Scientologists, Eton, the European Union, the Salvation Army. All of you. Come round this evening and clean my shoes. Not the Jehovah's Witnesses, though. I've had enough of you already. You can stay at home.

28 October 2012

This lanky git will call you what he wants, ref – you blind idiot

For the sake of English football Manchester United always need to win. Which is probably why, in last weekend's top-of-the-table clash, the referee set about sending the entire Chelsea team off for wearing blue clothes. And then, when that didn't work, he awarded a goal to a player who was so offside he might as well have been standing in Bristol.

As a Chelsea supporter I was very cross about all this. Indeed I spent most of the game wondering what the ref in question would look like without a head.

Today, though, I feel rather sorry for the stupid, blind idiot because it has been alleged that during the game he made derogatory remarks about John Obi Mikel. It was also suggested earlier in the week that he had called Juan Mata a 'Spanish t***'. (Clue: not 'twit'.)

I would imagine that this sort of thing has been going on in football since someone inflated a sheep's pancreas and discovered that jumpers could be used for goalposts. But suddenly it isn't allowed any more. So the ref has been suspended and is being investigated for a racially aggravated offence by Plod. In other words, the sharp-elbowed group hug of inclusivity has now landed in the middle of a football pitch.

Football is not croquet. The stands are visceral and ugly places full of rage and hatred. And standing in the middle of it all, trying to keep order, is the referee. Until 2001 he was an unhappily married amateur called Keith who used a Saturday-afternoon kickabout to get back at everyone who had made his working week so dreary and miserable. I do not know a football referee. I've never even met one. And I bet you haven't, either.

Today Premier League refs are professionals on more than £70,000 a year. But, I'm sorry, that's not enough.

Dentistry is bad. You live in a fog of halitosis waiting for the day when you accidentally catch AIDS. And I can't imagine it's much fun being a North Sea trawlerman either. You spend all day in a fish-scented cloud of diesel smoke, vomiting, and when you get home a bureaucrat tells you to throw the six cod you caught back into the sea.

But worse than both these things – worse even than being a dentist on a trawler – is the job of a Premier League referee. No. 1) you have to wear shorts. No. 2) there is a very great deal of running about. And No. 3) every single person in the entire world would like to eviscerate you, in front of your family, on the internet.

Can you imagine what life would be like for a surgeon if he had to go through his working day with his assistants, his nurses and even his patient telling him loudly and constantly that he was useless, that he was bent and that he worshipped at the altar of onanism? 'Call that an incision, you effing w*****?'

Then there's the business of making mistakes. We all do that. I make millions, and so do surgeons, even when they are in a warm room, wearing long trousers and listening to the calming strains of Pachelbel's Canon.

A football referee, on the other hand, is not listening to classical music. He can't sit back in a comfy chair to ruminate over a steaming mug of tea on what he should do next. He is running at top speed, often in the rain, trying to keep on top of the action in a game that is played 20 per cent faster now than it was just five years ago. He is being told to eff off at every turn.

And then he thinks he sees something happen and must react without a moment's pause. I think I would be useless. I think you would be, too.

But Premier League refs are not. Because more than 92 per cent of the decisions they make are subsequently proved by slow-motion replays to be correct.

To achieve this level of accuracy, they train hard. Not just so they're as fit as the players they're monitoring but also so they can see like a bird. Seriously. They do eye exercises to improve both their peripheral vision and their ability to spot, through a fast-moving pack of tangled limbs twenty yards away, who's doing what to whom.

In short, then, the man in black must have the stamina of an athlete, the eyesight of a pigeon, the reactions of a kingfisher, the legs of a male model and an autistic indifference to the opinions of other people. And now, on top of all this, he must also behave like a vicar.

Last weekend Mark Clattenburg, the ref at the Chelsea game, was having an off day. He must have known this because 35,000 people, including my son, were reminding him very loudly, and with uprooted chairs. It is entirely possible that Juan Mata was reminding him also. So what's wrong with saying, 'Shut it, you Spanish t***'?

When Richard Hammond is being annoying, which is when he's awake, I refer to him as a 'Brummie t***'. He, in turn, often calls me a 'lanky t***', and both of us regularly call James May a 'boring t***'. No harm is meant by any of it.

But we are now reaching the point where, even on a football pitch during a vital game between the two best teams in the country, people are expected to address one another like promenading ladies on a Victorian pier. It's absurd.

And, of course, it's all the fault of a man called Ed Miliband who runs the Labour party. He is leading the charge to make it impossible to tease anyone because of their colour, their facial disfigurements, their religion, their size, the colour of their hair, their sexual orientation, the country of their birth or their sex. Only last week he added a new one: we can no longer poke fun at those who suffer from mental illnesses.

Of course we can't go around tipping people out of wheelchairs and hounding fatties to death. But there should be a distinction between genuinely unpleasant behaviour and harmless banter. Otherwise we end up with a situation where I can't call Miliband an 'adenoidal t***', but I can call him a 't***'. Which is why I just did.

4 November 2012

Chew on a Big Mac with fibs before you answer a survey

I think it was the much-missed Keith Waterhouse who invented the 'I have never' game. The rules are simple. You tell a group of friends something that you have never done in your whole life and those that have done it give you 10p.

Keith's sure-fire winner was 'I have never taken a dog for a walk'. But I could always retort with the incredible but true 'I have never bought anything from Marks & Spencer'.

And there are other nuggets in my repertoire. I have never seen a single moment of *EastEnders*. I have never seen any of the *Godfather* movies. I've never smoked a joint. And I've never been on a London bus.

The only problem with the game is that after about five minutes people are struggling to think of mundane things that they alone have never done. So things become sexual. And embarrassing, as ten people around a bottle-strewn table try to claim that they too have never had intercourse in a public place or by themselves in front of a computer.

Once, having been cleaned out by a chap who had never been to Scotland, I was so desperate I came up with, 'I have never used a tampon', knowing that half the table would have to cough up. Amazingly one man gave me 10p, though obviously I won't mention his name here – only that it begins with a J and ends in Ames May. Apparently he uses them to clean hard-to-reach parts of his cooker.

Anyway, a survey revealed last week that the smuttiness and tampon admissions are unnecessary because millions of people in Britain have never done anything mundane at all.

Some of the findings are not surprising: 37 per cent have never read anything by Shakespeare, 68 per cent have never been skiing and 36 per cent have never been to a football match.

But most of it is just too amazing for words: 23 per cent of the nation – that's more than 14 million souls – have never been on an aeroplane while an equal number haven't even been to France. Also 17 per cent have never wired a plug; 6 per cent have never used a mobile phone; 16 per cent have never sent an email; and 30 per cent have never ordered a takeaway cup of coffee. But for me the biggest surprise is this one: 19 per cent have never eaten anything from McDonald's.

Of course, we all know the problem that lurks behind Ronald's cheery grin. McDonald's is fundamentally evil. We don't know why we know this, but we do. Which is why whenever three or four protesters are gathered together, they head immediately for the golden arches.

It doesn't matter whether they are fathers fighting for justice, or anti-G8 communists, or students campaigning on behalf of Brian May's badger; all of them feel certain that their cause will be strengthened if they go and kick a hole through Ronald's windows.

It has been argued in the past that no two countries where McDonald's operates have ever gone to war with each other. And that's true. Apart from when America invaded Panama. And when NATO bombed Serbia. And Libya, obviously. And Russia bombed Georgia. And so on. 'You see,' scream the protesters. 'Evil!!!'

Then you have the comedian Robin Williams, who once said of his new son: 'I have a dream where one day he is saying, "I would like to thank the Nobel academy." And a nightmare where he is saying, "Do you want fries with that?"'

My children have had Big Macs in the past but now they are full of righteous teenage anger they would not have one again. This is partly because they know for sure that McDonald's is pouring acid into the sea and partly because company executives like to unwind after a busy day by clubbing puppy dogs to death.

Mostly, though, it's because they know as a fact that McDonald's has bulldozed the entire Brazilian rainforest to create pasture for its beef herds. Yes, that's right. It has severed the world's lungs to increase its filthy profits. This is the level of evil we are talking about here. Top baddies such as Blofeld and Osama bin Laden pale into obscurity alongside the corporate savagery emanating on a day-by-day basis from the company's Illinois headquarters.

And that's before we get to the damage done by its products. A Big Mac is a heart attack in a bun. A Quarter Pounder has exactly the same effect on your well-being as licking the debris at Fukushima. And a McNugget is basically a piece of battered excrement. Eat any of this stuff and you will swell up until you are the size of a Buick. And then you will burst, showering everyone within 400 yards with thick, yellow fat, and spiders.

However, the problem is that after a night out, when you are weary and hungover, there is nothing that hits the spot quite so well as a Big Mac and fries.

I have tried everything in these circumstances: pills; hairs of every dog I can think of; worcestershire sauce with a splash of tomato juice; and once an injection of vitamin B. All of them work – the injection works brilliantly, in fact – but none works quite as well as a Big Mac.

It's as comforting as your childhood teddy bear, and as tasty as the tastiest thing you ever put in your mouth. And when you've finished, and it's down there in your stomach, absorbing the sick, you know that despite everything your head may be saying, all will soon be right with the world once more.

I am plainly not alone in thinking this because in Britain McDonald's serves 2.5 million customers every day. Around the world it serves more than 75 burgers every second. To date it has sold more than 245 billion and that means, all on its own, the company has a bigger economy than Ecuador.

So when I read that almost one in five British people claims to have never had a Big Mac, I draw a simple conclusion. Either many millions of people are missing out on one of life's greatest pleasures, or Britain is home to a great many liars.

11 November 2012

Yes, siree – count me in for genocide and conservatory-building

Twenty years ago I would land at Heathrow after every trip to America and kiss the tarmac, thanking every god I could think of that I was back in the land of the free.

Back then in Britain we were allowed to smoke and smack our children and rush about the countryside on horseback.

Footballers could call one another names, children could cycle in home clothes, we could drink irresponsibly and park on a yellow line while we popped into the shop for some milk. We could use cameras to film school sports days, abuse useless counter staff and get on a plane with our toothpaste. It was nice.

America, meanwhile, was drowning in a thunderstorm of petty bureaucracy that meant every janitor was armed with a walkie-talkie and a gun and encouraged to shoot anyone who broke any of the laws, no matter how bonkers they may have been.

You had to wear shoes while shopping. It was illegal to deface signs telling you it was illegal to deface signs. You were not allowed to swim in the pool if you'd had a tummy upset within the past fourteen days. Drinking in the street was prohibited. And you were not permitted to take any smoking material on to federal property. You couldn't even use a police car park if there was a cigarette lighter in your vehicle. It was madness.

In Soviet Russia you were allowed to do everything but vote. Whereas in America twenty years ago you could vote. But do nothing else. And it's still bad today. In the summer my daughter was carted off by the police for smoking near a fruit machine while under the age of twenty-one. And we had to produce photo ID before being allowed to rent a locker. It was almost as though they'd studied the ancient British laws governing London taxi drivers and high sheriffs and thought, 'Ooh. They look good. Let's insist New York cabbies carry a bale of hay in the boot, and ban people from taking fish into a cinema in Colorado.'

And it's even worse if you are part of a television crew because you'll need a permit before you film anything. And even when you get a permit, there will be a problem. An example: you can get permission to film on Wall Street. But it does not entitle you to film any of the buildings. And have you tried to take a picture in this concrete canyon without any office block appearing in the back of the shot? It's pretty tricky.

Another example: you can close a street in Detroit but you must give every single business whose door opens on to the street in question several weeks' notice of the closure.

And if you don't, an angry policeman will arrive to tell you the mayor has chewed the district attorney's bottom and that the DA has chewed his bottom and that now he's going to chew yours.

However, I was in America last week and I have some good news. Because while the fools in state and federal government continue to cut away at every basic human freedom, people are starting to find ways round the nonsense.

There's a bar in Los Angeles where the roof does not quite meet in the middle. This means that, technically, it's open to the air and that means you can smoke. And at the fabulous Roosevelt hotel in Los Angeles, there is no smoking allowed anywhere. But no one stops you if you do. In fact, they'll even bring you a saucer, saying you can use it as an ashtray.

It gets better. Because although we were forced to have a highway patrol officer in attendance while filming on the road, he was empowered to let us do what we wanted. Which meant that last Saturday I went past him on State Route 111 in southern California doing 186mph.

So to sum up: they've made a law that requires me to have a policeman on site, and by doing so have enabled me to break the law he's supposedly there to enforce.

But it gets even better. We also wanted to film some aeroplanes that needed to be flying at 300mph about six inches off the ground. To make sure that didn't happen, the authorities sent along an aviation inspector, who turned up and promptly moved heaven and earth to make sure that it did.

Everywhere we went it was the same thing. Normally if you make one little mistake on your visa waiver form you are sent to the back of a three-hour queue. This time I'd made lots. I couldn't be bothered to rummage around in the overhead locker to find out what my passport number was so I'd made one up. I said I was staying at a Premier Inn. And that I had been on a farm, and in Africa and that I had done a bit of genocide. None of which bothered the Homeland Security chap one bit.

Plainly, then, everyone is becoming content to let the politicians huff and puff and introduce silly laws to appease tiny but very noisy minorities. Just so long as the people employed to enforce those laws don't. This is very cheery news because, of course, what happens in America happens here shortly afterwards.

At present we are in a mess. You couldn't shoot a badger. Then you could, but only if your shot was monitored by a government official. And then you couldn't shoot a badger again.

You couldn't build a conservatory on the end of your

house. Then you could, so long as it was less than 27ft long. And then you could build a chemical plant as well, and your neighbours weren't allowed to object four times – only twice. Provided they weren't smoking at the time, or under arrest for hugging a teenage fan thirty years ago, or for taking make-up samples home from work just before the police arrived to search the building for evidence of a crime they said hadn't happened.

It's time we started to behave like modern-day Americans and used our nous. These badgers are killing my cows. I shall shoot them. No one will be inconvenienced if I stop here for a moment to buy stamps. And if I'm warned by someone's employer that I face prosecution for telling counter staff they are morons, I shall write back saying they are morons too.

25 November 2012

Coming soon, *I'm a Terrorist . . . Make Me Lick Nadine's Toes*

Every so often someone with too much time on their hands works out how much of our lives we spend at work, or eating, or looking for cooking utensils that we haven't used for a while.

Well, last week, while waiting for yet another flight, I worked out that I spend, on average, twenty hours a month sitting around in airports. That's ten days of my year spent in a cloud of idiotic perfume, looking at watches and trying to make the Wi-Fi work. Simply so that I can get on what is basically a bus. And there's no point complaining to the authorities, because it's 'security, sir'.

This is the problem. So long as there is one man out there with a grudge and a stick of dynamite, governments have a perfect excuse to stick their fingers in your bottom, look at pictures of you naked and rummage around in your handbag. You can shout as much as you like, but it will make absolutely no difference.

If you abuse the staff, they won't let you on the plane. If you refuse to let them look in your underpants, they won't let you on the plane. If you ask them not to take photographs of your breasts with their X-ray cameras, they won't let you on the plane. It makes my teeth itch with rage. But happily, last weekend, I came up with a solution. We simply get rid of terrorism.

In the early seventeenth century the world was troubled by religious division. I know, I know. Hard to believe, but there you are. Anyway, some Catholic Brummies felt they were being persecuted by King James I of England and decided it would be best if he, his family and all his Protestant muckers were killed. They decided, therefore, to blow up the House of Lords during the state opening of parliament. And the Gunpowder Plot was hatched.

Unfortunately, from their point of view, there was much plague around at the time and, as a result, the state opening was delayed for more than six months, by which time the gunpowder had spoilt. So they went off to buy some more, and while this was happening one of the group accidentally told some of the king's men what they were up to.

The House of Lords was searched and in the undercroft soldiers found Guy Fawkes standing next to a big pile of wood. He claimed he was a servant and they went away. But the next day they went back and the idiot was there again. So they looked under his wood and found all the gunpowder, and that was the end of that.

Fawkes, then, was a terrible terrorist. Such a moron, in fact, that today people of all faiths celebrate his subsequent execution by burning his effigy, eating sausage rolls and keeping the neighbours awake with various loud noises. In short, our forefathers turned him into a figure of ridicule and as a result we've had a Protestant monarch ever since.

Today, though, things have changed. We put Che Guevara on a T-shirt and think he looked rather cool. People say that Osama bin Laden had kind eyes. We've dug up poor old Yasser Arafat to see if he was murdered. And in Northern Ireland former enthusiasts of terror are allowed to take up serious positions in the government.

This is all wrong. Instead we should rename Guantanamo Bay as the Che Correctional Institute because that would annoy him. Every year on 2 May – the anniversary of bin Laden's death – the free world should be invited to go round to one another's houses for a piss-up. And all those IRA boys should be put on floats, dressed as clowns and paraded around town centres so we can laugh at them and their failure.

Nobody would ever dream of giving a failed terrorist community service. But that's exactly the sort of humiliation I'm after. I'd very much like to see the shoe bomber cutting all the grass in Hyde Park. With nail scissors. And it'd be a hoot to make the underwear bomber clean all the stained glass in Westminster Abbey. With his tongue.

We could even bring back *It's a Knockout* and howl with Stuart Hall-style laughter as two teams from, say, the Real IRA and al-Qaeda splosh about the streets of Corby in yellow onesies and big shoes. We could then see them for what they are. Not ogres. Not heroes. Just sad, pathetic, misguided losers whose big idea ended in capture.

At present we see terrorists as swivel-eyed, hook-handed madmen with hearts of stone and nitroglycerine for blood. Wrong. The authorities should show us pictures of them naked. Crying. Begging for their mums. We need to see what they really are. Humans who've gone a bit wrong.

There's another advantage too. At present, Muslim extremists are told that if they explode in a shopping centre they will have a jolly happy afterlife full of many good things. This means that from their perspective there's no downside. But if the bomb fails to go off and they end up as part of an insect-based bushtucker trial on *I'm a Celebrity . . . Get Me Out of Here!*, they may well think twice about putting on the vest.

When you are a serious, religious, committed zealot, you do not want to spend the rest of your days sucking worms from between the toes of Nadine Dorries. Or working out how long we spend on the lavatory. And you certainly won't want to be remembered every year as an excuse to get bladdered on mulled wine. Ask Guy Fawkes about that.

I realize, of course, that none of my ideas will be taken seriously, which is why I have devised a back-up plan. All Western governments abolish, immediately, all security screening at all airports. Because nothing tells a terrorist he's failed more than a show of complete lack of interest.

Sadly, though, this won't be adopted, either. Because governments are interested in the contents of your bottom. Obama Barack wants to look inside your handbag. And airports like it too. Because the longer you have to wait, the greater the chances you'll end up buying a tin of horrible shortbread with a picture of Windsor Castle on the lid.

2 December 2012

Write in now, eel fanciers, and claim your million quid

It's very rare that we ever catch a glimpse of a newspaper editor. But last week there they all were, suited and booted and strolling down Downing Street in a scene that in their minds probably looked like a publicity poster from *Reservoir Dogs*.

Unfortunately, in my mind they looked like the sixth form on their way to be beaten by the headmaster. You had the speccy Potter boy from the *Guardian*, the one who looks like a young farmer from *The Times*, the rather suave one from the *Sunday Times* [Ed: Christmas bonus for you, Jeremy] and a diminutive urchin from the *Sun*.

The school bully – the man from the *Daily Mail* – was missing because he had a note from his mum.

Inside No. 10 they were told, more in sorrow than anger, that they must come up with a tough new set of rules for themselves or the headmaster would be forced to introduce even tougher ones himself.

In short, they were informed that they must set up an independent body that could a) hand out fines of up to a million quid and b) force them to write lines on the front page of their homework when they got their facts wrong: 'I must stop calling people murderers when they are not.'

To Grant and Clegg, the smaller boys in the school, this probably seems a good idea, but in reality there are going to be some serious problems. Because these guys are not sixth-formers. They are the editors of national institutions. And now they face being neutered by one of the biggest scourges of modern society – the pressure group.

Every single thing you can think of is represented by a pressure group. Trees. Haulage contractors. Bats. Shrubs. People with big ears. The Welsh. Great crested grebes. Oil companies. The royal family. I bet you there's even one for women who have supernumerary nipples.

At present an editor is free to place letters from such organizations in the bin. But when they threaten to go to the new independent body, and that body is able to hand out million-quid fines and force him to print humiliating front-page apologies, he is going to have to take them seriously. And that – from my experience at the BBC – is an absolute nightmare.

When I get a complaint letter from an individual, it is fair enough. They are entitled to their opinion and are allowed to express it. But when that individual has some official-looking headed notepaper and a website, he is a pressure group. And he is not expressing an opinion. He is expressing what he sees as a fact.

And he cares. Boy, does he care. He cares so much that once he has his teeth into your ankles, he will not let go until you are sacked and dead. And to make matters worse, he knows what to say in his complaint letters and to whom they must be addressed. He knows – because he is a pressure group and it is therefore his job – how to get any independent body to sit up and pay attention.

This means I have to go through life with a thousand tractor tyres on my back, spending 10 per cent of my day doing my job and 90 per cent dealing with someone from the Incontinent Society who was offended because the previous week on television I said I'd driven so fast I'd wet myself.

Several years ago a pressure group called Transport 2000 contacted the BBC saying that either *Top Gear* had to be pulled from the schedules or a new pro-bus eco-car show must be commissioned as balance.

Now if you wrote to the editor of the *Daily Mail* ordering him either to stop printing stories about the Duchess of Cambridge's pregnancy or to set up an anti-monarchist newspaper to provide readers with an alternative point of view, you'd either get no reply at all or a two-liner inviting you to go and boil your head.

But because the BBC is governed and monitored by precisely the sort of independent body that Lord Justice Leveson wants, Transport 2000 – despite its out-of-date name and its communistic outlook – had to be taken seriously. Very seriously. So for months, hundreds of man hours were wasted on analysing and studying its stupid suggestions. Before sense finally prevailed and they were rejected.

This is what the editors are going to face. Legally savvy nutcases with time on their hands, using every trick in the book in an attempt to force newspapers to toe a line, no matter how idiotic that line might be.

Yesterday I blew up an eel. No big deal, you might think. It was only going to be eaten by a Cockney, anyway. But next year, when the scene is shown on television, we can be absolutely sure that someone from the Eel Preservation Society will start the complaint ball rolling.

And even if that person is just one madman, living in his mother's loft, it will be considered by all the organizations that have been set up to make sure no one at the BBC ever upsets anyone ever. The editorial-compliance people. Ofcom. The BBC Trust. They'll pore over the complaint. They'll study the explosion in slow motion. They'll contact experts from other pressure groups to see if the creature suffered in any way. (Yes. It died.) And afterwards they'll write to me to say that I've just issued an 'unreserved' apology. Because a 'sincere' apology or a 'profound' apology won't do.

It's this constant pressure that explains why, with the notable exceptions of Harry & Paul, there are now no edgy comedians on the BBC. I spoke to one last week, who said, 'It just isn't worth it any more.'

And don't, for heaven's sake, think the committee set up to monitor and fine newspapers will be staffed by people such as you and me; people who'll strive to keep the pressure groups at bay and the fun ball rolling. Because that won't happen.

Instead it'll be run by hopeless do-gooders who in their ridiculous quest for fair play will ensure that there's no play at all. Which means that this time next year, no matter what paper you buy, it will be the *Guardian*.

9 December 2012

Of all the towns in all the world, Cold, Wet and Closed is best

Soon the nation's experts will settle down to decide what's been the best of everything in 2012. Best sports personality. Best frock. Best dog. And best moment.

Actually, scrub that. The best moment's easy. It was when those five rings of what appeared to be molten steel were lowered into the Olympic stadium and the whole country, as one, suddenly decided that it wasn't so bad to be British after all.

I've already named my best car; AA Gill will soon be revealing which chef did the best job of disguising the bodily fluids in his food; and you, in the meantime, will be in a frilly dinner shirt at a crappy hotel on Park Lane as a comedian with a vaguely familiar face presents some drunken halfwit with the award for 2012's best new packaging solution.

Rough Guides, meanwhile, has announced the ten best places to visit in all of the world. And No. 1 is Northern Cyprus, apparently.

Of course, this is nonsense. Northern Cyprus is just southern Cyprus, only with more soldiers and cheaper carpets. As a travel destination, it is in no way a match for Hue in Vietnam, or New York, neither of which is in the Rough Guides top-ten list.

Puerto Rico is, but that's madness. Unless you like staying in a hotel where the lifeguard has a sub-machine gun.

I'm not sure that north-eastern Iceland should be there either. Because if what you want is peace and quiet and rugged volcanic splendour, you can find that twenty minutes from Keflavik airport. Driving six hours to find something even better is like spending a day rummaging around in a box of Lego, looking for a more impressive yellow brick.

And I'm sorry, but Dresden? This is the world's fifth-best place in the same way that Angela Merkel is the world's fifth-best-looking woman. There are some fabulous towns in eastern Germany but Dresden isn't one of them. Yes, you get some beautifully restored cobbles but you also get a lot of bitter old men who hate you very much and wish the communists would come back.

However, the entry on the Rough Guides list that seems to have surprised most people is to be found at No. 7. It's the only place in all of the British Isles to get a mention: Margate.

Even the locals seem to have been taken aback, with one saying the town centre is full of yobs and amusement arcades and boarded-up shops. And there's more too: Margate is in Kent and, frankly, that's the least accessible place on earth. If you live anywhere else in Britain, it's easier to get to Yukon. Not that I'd recommend that either, unless you enjoy being bitten by mosquitoes.

However, I can see the logic of Rough Guides with Margate. Sure, it's not as visually impressive as Sydney or Hong Kong. And I am certain San Francisco has more restaurants. But put yourself in the mind of a visitor coming to Britain.

When we go abroad on holiday, we like to annoy our children by taking them to see the 'real' country. We like to find the restaurants where the menus aren't also printed in English and we want to drink the local wine. Even though we would get the same taste sensation by sucking on one of the blue tablets at the bottom of the urinals.

It stands to reason, then, that many people coming here would want to see the 'real' Britain. So where should we send them? Once, I sent some particularly nasal Americans to Loughborough, telling them they couldn't get more British than that. But what if you were taking it seriously?

A seaside town makes sense. Fish. Chips. Vinegar. Endless afternoons in the Cafe de Formica, rubbing condensation from the windows and kidding yourself that the sky is definitely getting brighter. Walks on the gritty sand in the drizzle. A mug of tea. And then off to an amusement arcade to shoot an alien.

There is simply nowhere else on earth where people do that to get away from it all. So I'd say to any visiting American: once you've done Stratford-upon-Avon and an open-top bus tour of Warwick Castle, and you are fed up with how Britain was, get a taste of how it is now with a trip to the seaside.

Margate would do nicely, for sure, but if you want somewhere that's a bit easier to reach from your overheated, Polish-run central London hotel, I think you can do better. Tenby, for instance. Or north Cornwall. Or East Yorkshire.

All of these places are still dripping with echoes of the past. You have hints of fishing and roll-out-the-barrel revelry. But most now also have hotels run by people who've been to London and know that nylon is no longer an acceptable bedding solution.

Back in the summer I spent a few days in Whitby and it was perfect. Cold. Wet. And mostly shut. I bought fish and chips and I ate them on a bench overlooking a forlorn-looking trawler. It plainly hadn't been out for months, because all you can catch in Whitby these days is chlamydia.

I loved it. I loved the wiggly little streets and the old cottages and the sea air. I loved the sound of the gulls and of the rigging in the sail boats, flapping about in the biting wind. I also loved the hotel I found just north of the town, a little bit of Knightsbridge wedged between the bleak moors and the rocky shoreline where I spent a couple of idyllic hours looking for sea creatures in slippery ponds.

We've all spent time in a seaside town such as Whitby. It's one of the few bonds that we all share. France has its cheese. America has its proms. Rwanda has days when the whole country goes out on the streets to clear up litter. And we have our seaside. It's our glue.

So, yes, since millions of foreign visitors come here every year wanting to know who we really are, it makes sense that one of the world's ten best places to visit is a town on the British coast. For me, that'd be Whitby.

16 December 2012

Help, I've lost track of world affairs in Bradley's barnet

When a televisual quiz show finds its feet and becomes popular, its producers get it into their heads that the audience would be much happier if the ordinary contestants with their terrible shoes and their ghastly jumpers were replaced by 'celebrities'.

So instead of Brian standing there, sweating slightly as he tries to win enough cash for some new decking or a short cruise, we have a bright orange woman whose name we can't quite remember trying to win money for injured rabbits and various other charities no one's heard of.

Shows to have gone down this route in the past include *Mr & Mrs*, *Who Wants to Be a Millionaire?*, *Weakest Link* and *University Challenge*. Most recently, we've been treated to a star-studded version of the rather brilliant *Pointless*. Which ended up being called *Pointless Celebrities*. And so it turned out to be.

One team was made up of two extremely enthusiastic young people who may have been in a soap opera, or one of Simon Cowell's singing contests, or perhaps a sex tape. But anyway, it quickly became obvious that they had put a great deal of effort into their appearance but none whatsoever into any sort of research.

Luckily, however, the topic that would take them through to the next round was easy: David Cameron. All they had to do was correctly answer just one of the following questions. Which famous public school did he attend? What's the name of his baby daughter? What's his constituency? What's his wife called? And for which former chancellor was he a special adviser?

Amid staccato bursts of shallow, forced, embarrassed laughter, they had to admit that, actually, they didn't know any of the answers, but that they were prepared to hazard a guess at the name of the public school he'd attended. 'Oxford,' they said nervously.

Now if I'd been the host, I'd have fixed them with a steely glare and wondered out loud what on earth had possessed them to appear on a quiz show when neither of them even knew the difference between a school and a university. Perhaps this is why I'm not the host of a quiz show.

But here's the thing. While I knew all the answers to the questions about Mr Cameron, I would make an equally enormous fool of myself if I were in their shoes and I was asked questions about *EastEnders*, which I have never seen, or musicals, which I studiously avoid, or Chaucer, the one man from history whom I'd most like to murder.

In the fairly recent past, it was not hard to be knowledgeable. So long as you had read a couple of Shakespeare's plays and you spent an hour each morning reading *The Times*, you were pretty well placed to hold your head high at even the most sophisticated dinner party.

Not any more. I spoke last night to an extremely bright girl. She was eloquent and fully up to speed with how pigs are farmed in Chile, but when it came to recent problems with the press, she had it in her head that journalists had paid the police to hack Milly Dowler's phone.

I encounter similar problems at work because when I introduce the Stig, I usually include a sideways reference to some report from the papers that day. And afterwards, we have to dub on the laughter because almost no one in the audience gets it. That's why you always hear people laughing so hard it sounds like their spleens are coming out of their noses. And yet the people in the back of shot look like they've just been told a theory about particle physics, in Latin.

The problem is that in the olden days, news was roughly divided in two. You had news about ragamuffins who had appeared in court. And you had news of natives being brought to heel in some far-flung corner of the empire.

Nowadays there's so much information coming from so many different places, we cannot possibly keep abreast of it. Syria, for example. I was really concentrating hard on the complexities of the civil war and what its effects on the region might be when, all of a sudden, *The X Factor* finished and suddenly I felt compelled to read up on the winner.

But before I even had a chance to discover his or her name, I found myself embroiled in a heated late-night debate on the American constitution and the rights and wrongs of being permitted to bear arms. Hard when your head is full of Alex Reid's sexuality. And Bradley Wiggins's haircut. And whether Aston Martin will do a deal with Mercedes.

Today the news agenda is so vast you don't absorb information. You simply skim along its surface. I read a fair bit about the plight of soldiers in Afghanistan and I was fairly clear on one thing: lots of them were being shot by local soldiers they'd helped to train.

But then at a recent military function I spoke to some chaps who'd actually been there and they assured me that this was complete rubbish. So how do I check this out? In the past you would turn to the BBC or the papers but almost no one does that any more. Which is why we end up with a head full of misconceptions, half-truths and flimflam about Kelly Brook's breasts.

Some have argued that Twitter would be the answer to all our prayers; that it would provide a balance of real-time information from people who are actually on the spot. You'd have news from the rebels in Syria and news too from President Bashar al-Assad. But the truth is that you can't really condense the complexities of the Middle East into a *Very Hungry Caterpillar*-sized crucible of just 140 characters.

And anyway, these days, if you speak your mind on Twitter or any other social networking site, you will wake at five the next morning to find half a dozen policemen ripping up your floorboards.

But the worst thing about any ether-based news delivery system is that no one's on hand to decide on our behalf what matters and what doesn't. Which is why we have two pointless celebrities going on television to demonstrate that, actually, they don't know anything at all.

And neither do I, if I'm honest. Except that it's Christmas this week. Have a happy time and see you on the flip side.

23 December 2012

Stand by, Earth, to boldly look where there's no point looking

As we speak, British boffins are busy building a remotely operated telescope high in Chile's Atacama Desert.

The optics have come from Austria, the mounts from America and the housing from a company in Cornwall that makes cat flaps.

When it is finished, it will be pointed at a randomly selected star to see if the light dims from time to time. If it does, they will know that orbiting planets are passing in front of it. And then they will get to work, measuring how much the light dims.

This will tell them if the planet in question has an atmosphere, and even what sort of atmosphere that might be. A lot of oxygen suggests it may be host to all sorts of plants and photosynthetic bacteria. If there is water vapour as well, then there might also be water on the ground and that could mean it is capable of supporting life.

There are, however, one or two slight issues with all of this. First of all, there are 125 billion galaxies. And there are probably 300 billion stars in each one. So the chances that our new telescope is looking at the right one at the right time are quite remote.

Second, we know that the earth is home to a great deal of oxygen and water but we keep being told by Prince Charles that it's the delicate balance of other things – such as the Ferrybridge power stations and the Dog and Duck's smoker-friendly patio heaters – that provide the conditions for life to flourish.

So even if the new telescope does spot a likely-looking planet, it may well be it has no ozone or a tiny bit too much methane and, as a result, the only life there is a walrus or a version of Esther Rantzen that has two heads and can only say 'wibble'.

It gets worse because even if the life in question does have digital sound and non-stick frying pans, it's very unlikely that its inhabitants speak English. Or even French. Over the years, scientists have pondered this problem, with many suggesting that maths would be the only way of conversing.

They've been wasting their time, though, because even the nearest star – apart from the sun – is about 25 trillion miles away and it would take 81,000 years to get there.

And there's no point using the radio to transmit all our prime numbers and theories about pi because the message would still take more than four years to arrive. And if there was anyone on the other end, they'd just think, 'Oh Christ, we've had a call from James May.' And not bother replying.

To sum up, then. There is only an infinitesimal chance that our telescope will find a planet capable of supporting intelligent life, and even if it does, we can't speak to the inhabitants. As a result, the whole exercise is a complete waste of everyone's time.

Except it isn't, and here's why. Back in the day, a bunch of Vikings set off across a seemingly endless ocean to seek out new worlds and new civilizations that they could rape. After 500 miles they must have thought, 'This is pointless.' After 1,000 miles one of the rowers must have stood up and said to the captain, 'Look, sir, I'm sorry, but I really want to give up.'

But they didn't give up. And after nearly 2,000 miles of rowing and sweat and toil, they bumped into America. Where there was no intelligent life, so they went back to Oslo.

More recently, Victorian explorers stomped about in

Africa being eaten by lions and catching malaria simply so they could find the source of the Nile. Before then you had Captain Cook who went off to find Australia, even though the world knew it wasn't there.

A Dutch explorer called Abel Tasman had been to the region in 1642. He had found Tasmania, New Zealand and later the Fiji islands, but many doubted there was any other large land mass. So Cook's mission was pointless and stupid. Except, of course, it wasn't.

Exploration against all the odds is still going on today. For the past few months, Russian, American and British scientists have been engaged in a race to explore a recently discovered sub-glacial lake in Antarctica. Though, sadly, the British team had to pull out over the Christmas period because its generators ran out of fuel.

Undaunted, the others are soldiering on in the belief that 52 million years ago the region was home to a giant rainforest and that some strange life forms have survived. I have to say that this is unlikely because the lake in question is buried under a slab of ice that's two miles thick. Which means there's no air and no sunlight.

'Unlikely', however, is not a good enough reason for quitting. Nor is 'pointless'.

Many years ago I was on board a plane that sort of crash-landed at a remote airstrip in the Sahara. It could have been in Libya or it could have been in Chad. The pilot didn't know because he was a bit drunk.

Anyway, we would be stuck for a while, so I decided to sit under the plane's port wing. After an hour or so, this became boring, so I switched to the starboard wing. And when this became dreary I set off on foot to have a look over the nearest horizon. Even though I knew for sure, because I'd already seen from the air, that I'd find nothing of any use at all.

Human beings like checking stuff out. When a child says he wants to go into the woods to 'explore', no parent says, 'What's the point? All you're going to find are nettles.' And it was the same when John F. Kennedy said America would send a spaceship to the moon. Everyone knew it was just a big dusty golf ball and that no good would come of it; but they went anyway, and who now thinks it was a bad idea?

I don't expect our new telescope will find a damn thing. I really don't. But let me conclude with this: many years ago, a friend lost his signet ring while swimming off Pampelonne beach in the south of France. The next day he set off on a completely pointless mission to find it. And he did.

13 January 2013

Dim staff and no stock: the key to hanging on in the high street

Three more teeth have been smashed out of the high street this month. Jessops, the camera people, went belly up and HMV, the purveyor of tunes and action films, called in the administrator, before Blockbuster, which wanted you to rent the same films from it, followed suit.

We're told they were casualties of the nation's new-found love affair with online shopping and renting. And this seems to make sense. Figures just out reveal that 9 per cent of all business in Britain is done on the internet. That's the highest proportion in the world.

It doesn't include me because I find online shopping a bit sinister. I have it in my mind that the moment I feed the details of my credit card into the system, someone in California will use them to buy a light aircraft. I know this is irrational but it's what I believe, and as a result I have never bought anything from someone I can't see.

There are other reasons too. If you buy online, your goods have to be delivered. Which means the streets of suburbia are now full of dithering van drivers getting lost and doing three-point turns and generally getting in everyone's way. This annoys me.

Plus, if your groceries are being delivered, you have to be in when they arrive. And if you also have to be in to receive your kids' birthday presents, your replacement toaster, your copy of *Madagascar* 3, your new shoes, a sex toy, a dog blanket and three hats, you will never find the time to go out. Which means you will become friendless and lonely.

And cross. Because, from what I can gather, supermarkets guess at what might make a suitable replacement if what you ordered isn't in stock. And usually they get it spectacularly wrong. Duraglit, for example, cannot be used to power a torch. And you can't make a salad with advocaat. Plus, as I like to point out to American barmen, I'll only accept that Pepsi is a substitute for Coca-Cola if they accept that Monopoly money is a substitute for cash.

Anyway, as you can see, there are many good reasons I choose not to shop online. But I must say that shopping for real is becoming increasingly difficult these days. Because most shops never have a single thing in stock, ever.

Shopping for shoes in Tod's, for instance, is like being stuck in Monty Python's cheese shop. Loafers? Nope. Brogues? Nope. Wellies? Nope. Lace-ups? Nope. Slip-ons? No, sir. Not today. I'm convinced the storeroom is full of nothing but sales assistants making coffee while pretending to look for the size you need.

Then you have Sony. I went there last week to buy a television and a PlayStation. The first branch I tried had closed down, and the second had neither in stock. How can Sony not stock a Sony PlayStation? Apple? Yes, it had the iPhone I needed, but no way of taking the data from the previous model and putting it on the new version.

So, after a wasted half-hour, we cancelled the credit-card transaction and I left empty-handed.

You will find this everywhere you go – shops that carry just enough goods to fill the window display and that's it. You want to actually buy something? Well, they ask a lot of damn-fool questions about where you live and whether you're transsexual, and then the gormless imbecile on the till tells you that what you wanted is still in its component parts, in Hamburg.

That said, there was one notable exception to all of this, one shop that carried a selection of goods and was staffed with extremely enthusiastic, knowledgeable and delightful staff. Its name was Jessops.

We are used, these days, to shop assistants being one step removed from plankton. Many have not mastered the art of speech, know nothing about what they're selling and would much rather you died of a heart attack than bought anything. Not in Jessops, though.

Let's be brutally honest. The sort of people who are keen on cameras and photography are deeply suspect. I imagine that most are mainly interested in pornography. But even when the Jessops people were presented with a man who plainly wanted a camera to take up-skirt shots of women in the supermarket, they remained as bubbly and as helpful as ever.

They were knowledgeable too. I went to the company's Westfield branch in west London on several occasions over the past couple of years – my kids do photography at school, in case you were wondering – and whoever served me could always explain whether one of the submenus on a Canon was better than that on a Nikon. They knew about f-stops and aperture priority. They knew about focal length and could advise on toughness. They had plainly been trained well and they were brilliant. And they always had whatever I selected in stock.

And where did the former chief executive of this fine chain of shops end up? Yup. HMV. Another well-organized shop, if I'm honest.

Now, I don't know anything about retailing, but I can see a pattern here. Run a shop well and it will go out of business. Run it on a shoestring with no stock and staff who can only just about manage to walk on two legs and you'll hang on in there. Just. But not for long.

Some say this is a good thing; that when all the chain stores have gone, the high street will once again become home to lots of little shops selling home-made biscuits. But in a world that worships cheapness and convenience, it's more likely that the high street will become home to nothing more than charity shops, pizza takeaway joints and *Daily Mail* photographers, prowling around looking for a drunk girl in a short skirt.

Eventually, Amazon and eBay will turn Stow-on-the-Wold into downtown Detroit and cause Hartlepool to drown in a sea of vomit.

Still, it's not completely the end of the world. Because many of the Jessops sales staff are now posting pictures of themselves and contact details in the windows of the shops where they used to work. They are, in short, selling themselves. And, frankly, they are probably the best things you can buy on the high street right now.

20 January 2013

Forget the cat and the pension, wrinklies, a gap year beckons

Round about now your teenage child will be queuing at the check-in desk for an airline you have never heard of, and flying off to a part of the world you have never visited, to spend a few months doing stuff you don't understand. It's called a gap year. And it sounds fun.

Now, when I grew up in South Yorkshire there was no such thing as a gap year. You left school at three o'clock in the afternoon and by quarter to four you were down the pit. Besides, 'abroad' was Nottingham, and 'university' . . . it was a place of learning for hoity-toity homosexuals. So it was on nobody's radar in Doncaster.

It certainly wasn't on mine. I left school, rather earlier than I'd planned, on a Thursday and by Monday morning I was starting work, on a picket line, outside the *Rotherham Advertiser*. And I spent the short gap in between buying a coat and a notebook.

Things seem to have changed, though, because most of my friends' children are currently cycling round Mexico before taking a trip to Cambodia via space. They're all turning their geography lessons into reality, in Israel, New Zealand and Canada. And it all seems to have been funded by light babysitting, occasional bar work and a one-off payment from some long-forgotten godparent.

Last weekend my daughter outlined her gap-year plans. She announced that she'll go to Cape Town, do a spot of work, buy a car and then drive it via various countries beginning with Z to Uganda. It would be the tip of Africa to the equator, the trip of a lifetime. And the total cost, so far as I can see, is about £7.50.

When she had finished outlining the route, where she would stay and what she would see, a deathly hush descended like a snowy blanket on the adults in the room. Sure, we had arranged our faces to suggest we were thinking of pitfalls she might not have considered and titbits that we, in our wisdom, could pass on.

But I know everyone in that room was thinking the exact same thing. And it had nothing to do with my daughter's wellbeing. It was this: 'Goddamn. I would kill someone's small dog to make a trip like that.' And it got me thinking. Maybe in society's haste to create a gap year, we've put it in the wrong place.

Eighteen-year-olds are vibrant and their brains are tuned beautifully to receive and disseminate even the most complex information. So it stands to reason that at this age they should be at work, dreaming up new ideas and making the world a better place.

It's stupid that they spend the sharpest year of their lives catching chlamydia on a beach in Thailand when they could be inventing batteries that rejuvenate themselves, and corkscrews that actually work.

Gap years, I think, would work better for older people. Now I'm not suggesting for a moment that you get up from the breakfast table and, after a brief trip to the cash machine, set off like the hero in a Leslie Thomas book, on an odyssey of beach bars, sultry girls, mad jobs, endless starry nights and no real sense of what the next day will bring. That would be absurd. You have a job in accountancy and responsibilities to your children and your family. So you can't just set off and drift about the world in a two-legged demonstration of Brownian motion.

Besides, you have a lodge meeting at the civic centre on Thursday so you can't very well be in Laos that day, lying on a hammock, drinking an ice-cold beer with an Australian girl called Sarah who's wearing a white, Flake-advert gypsy dress and not much else.

No. I'm not suggesting that a gap year would work at all well for people in their forties and fifties. But what about when you're sixty-five? What about a gap year between the drudgery of work and the mind-numbing tedium of retirement?

In the olden days you retired because you were simply too old and feeble to carry the coal to the surface any more. But today people pack in the day job with forty years of life left in their bones. And then what? They spend half their savings on a lousy cruise on a lousy ship round a lousy bit of coastline of what we used to call the eastern bloc. And then they come home to the floral-print conservatory and an eternity of watering plants and praying one of the children will ring that day.

They won't. They've got their own kids to worry about, and all the responsibilities of moving on and moving up. Listen to Harry Chapin's song 'Cat's in the Cradle' and forget about them. And forget about your savings, too. Leave them where they are. Hitch a lift to the ferry port in Dover and see what happens next.

At sixty-five you're showroom-fresh. You can play tennis and ski and scuba dive. So why don't you just bugger off and spend twelve months doing what you can while it's all still possible?

You know by that age what you haven't seen and what you want to see. You know what you haven't done. So go and do it. Bungee jump into the Grand Canyon and make love on a Tahitian beach. I know what you're thinking. What about the cat? How would I carry all my things?

Well, stop it. Kick the cat out. It'll be fine, and when it comes to luggage, take a leaf out of the teenagers' book. It doesn't matter whether my son is going skiing for a week, going to a party at the other end of the country or pheasant shooting in Outer Mongolia, he only ever travels with what he's wearing, a phone and a credit card.

And what's wrong with that? Someone always has a phone charger and a jumper you can borrow. And if you need a new pair of pants, which you will after you've worn them back to front on day two, inside out on day three and both on day four, get a job for a couple of days.

Or you could get an allotment, I suppose, and have Betty round for a sherry a week on Tuesday.

27 January 2013

Your next HS2 service is the 3.15 to Victorian England

As I see it, there are two clearly defined camps in the debate about the proposed high-speed rail link.

You have those who live more than five miles from the proposed route. They say it will be a wonderful piece of engineering, that it will make the nation proud and that it will bring untold riches to the north. And then you have those who live less than five miles away. They say it is stupid and wrong-headed and a complete waste of money.

Interestingly, both sides are wrong.

I have a great deal of sympathy with people who will soon have trains charging at 225mph through their kitchens. You sign up for a quiet life in the countryside and then you are told that soon your life will be ruined and your house value-less. Nimbyism is much criticized but it is an understandable reaction at times such as this.

Certainly if someone said they were going to locate the town tip in my back garden, or build a footpath right past my bedroom window, I'd fight like a savage dog to make the problem go away.

However, if we'd always put the needs of the few above the needs of the many, we'd still be in smocks, herding oxen. When Isambard Kingdom Brunel announced plans for his Great Western Railway, he faced a staggering level of resistance. But today we thank God he prevailed, or Bristol would still be ten minutes behind London and you'd have to travel between the two on a horse.

It was the same story with the M1. The chief engineer

spent months touring the proposed route, being shouted at by farmers and red-faced lords. But again we are grateful today that he was able to win them round. Or Leeds would be as inaccessible as space.

I like big engineering projects. They make my tummy do backflips. Often, when I'm on my way to Hull – it doesn't happen too often – I'll pull over and spend a few moments admiring the Humber Bridge. When it was proposed, it was considered stupid to spend millions linking Barton and Hessle, two settlements no one had heard of. And it probably was. But we ended up with what, to my mind, is the most beautiful bridge in the world. And that makes me feel all warm and gooey.

Which brings me on to the other side of the argument about HS2. The people who say it's a wonderful piece of engineering. Because is it? Really?

No French or Japanese person I've met lists the railway network as a reason for visiting their country. A big dam, yes. That would be tremendous. Or an elegant viaduct. But some track nailed to some sleepers and laid on a bed of cinders? My boat's unfloated, I'm afraid.

Part of the problem is that trains are a bit Victorian. Tub-thumping and puffing your chest up about a new railway line is like tub-thumping and sticking your chest out about a new steamship. Or a new woollen mill.

We're told that no one can know what life will be like when HS2 opens for business in 2026. Absolutely. But we can make an educated guess that the electronic revolution will have turned our lives completely upside down and that in all probability there will be no need to travel at all.

Which brings us on to the biggest problem with HS2. David Cameron quite rightly acknowledges that the north-south divide in Britain is getting so wide that unless something is done, we really will end up with two countries. I'm troubled by this as well but I fail to see how a railway line connecting the haves and the have-nots will help.

Last month I climbed on board a train in London and after just two chapters of my Jack Reacher book I was arriving in a northern town where there was some drizzle and a bit of graffiti. One chapter after that, I was in Liverpool. It was seriously quick.

But here's the thing. Even if HS2 shaves an extra thirty or so minutes off the journey, I wonder how many people in Kensington and Chelsea will wake up and say, 'You know what? Since Liverpool is only ninety minutes away, we shall move to the Wirral.'

It's even more bonkers when you view the situation from the other side of the coin. Because does anyone honestly think that Scousers continue to live and work in Liverpool simply because the current train ride to London takes too long?

At this point politicians tell us that a faster rail link would be good for business. Right. I see. But hang on a minute. What business?

One of the stations will be located at Sheffield's vast out-of-town Meadowhall shopping centre. So are we expected to believe that because Yorkshire is only seventy-five minutes away, people in Notting Hill will decide to forgo a trip to Portobello Road on a Saturday morning and spend all their hard-earned City bonuses up north instead? I'm struggling with that concept, if I'm honest.

And I also struggle to imagine that life will become any easier for those running the BBC's new northern headquarters in Salford. Today, even though staff in London are being offered up to £90,000 to relocate, many are refusing to move away from their friends, their families and their children's schools. And those who do go are finding that booking guests for their shows is difficult. Tom Cruise, for example, would travel to west London to promote his new film. But Manchester? Not a chance. And I can't see the situation changing just because the journey time is an hour faster.

And in the big scheme of things, what's the journey time got to do with it, anyway? People don't choose to live in Liverpool or Sheffield because of how near they are to London. It's just not relevant.

Most northern people I know hate London and care about its proximity only when their football team are playing Arsenal or Chelsea. If you live in Rotherham, you eat, socialize, drink and mate in Rotherham. What many don't do, however, is work. Because there are very few jobs. And I'm afraid to say that problem won't be solved by a big, noisy Victorian throwback.

3 February 2013

Oh, waiter, can I pay with this microchipped finger?

We have been informed by the government that we have three years to microchip our dogs. And that if we fail to comply, we will be fined up to £500. This is normally the sort of bullying nonsense that makes me want to spit tacks and vandalize a bus shelter.

But I've read the details and I'm alarmed to say that the new law seems to make sense.

At present more than 100,000 dogs a year are either dumped or lost, and these days the police are too busy investigating dead disc jockeys to cycle around the parish comparing those out-of-focus 'missing' posters on lamp posts with the forlorn collection of pooches they have in the station kennels.

We can hardly expect the RSPCA to help out, either. Well, we can, but sadly this once great charity is now little more than a branch of the Communist party, which would rather spend its money prosecuting people for living near David Cameron than help a little girl to find her lost Labrador.

In fact, the RSPCA seems to have rather missed the point of the chipping scheme, with a spokesman saying it will do little to prevent dogs from biting other animals such as hedgehogs, badgers or, horror of horrors, possibly even one of the charity's beloved foxes. This is true. Other things it will not prevent include barking at postmen and urinating.

However, those of us who are not mainly interested in resurrecting the ghost of Stalin can see there is one big advantage. The chip containing your details is inserted into a small glass cylinder the size of a grain of rice that is then injected into your dog's back.

So, if it's lost, the dog can be scanned in the same way that you scan vegetables at the supermarket and, hey presto, it'll be back in its own bed, drinking warm milk by nightfall. Brilliant. And, at the moment, it can be done free. It's so brilliant, in fact, that I started to wonder why, for instance, you could not insert a similar chip in your laptop and your phone or even your children.

You may argue, of course, that if a lost child is subsequently found, a chip is not necessary, because they are capable of telling their rescuers what their name is and where they live. But what if they're not found?

As we all know, your mobile phone is constantly telling anyone who cares to look where you are. So long as the battery is connected, it's a non-stop homing beacon. So why do Apple and BlackBerry not start selling parents the technology that can do this? Insert it into a child's back and when they wander off at the supermarket you can wave goodbye to the misery of spinning round and round in pointless circles and in just a few moments find out exactly where they've gone.

Naturally, it gets better. Because later in life, when they are sixteen and they say they are popping out to the library to catch up on some physics homework, you can determine whether this is true, or whether, in reality, they are doing 90mph in a mate's Vauxhall Corsa, on their way to the Duck and Sick Bag.

Indeed, as I lay in the bath last night, considering all the advantages of chipping children, I hit upon an even bigger brainwave: chipping myself.

I bet the government has already had many meetings about this. Because if every single person in the country were chipped, they'd know where we'd been, who we'd been with and how fast we'd driven home. Such a scheme would free up so much police time, they'd be able to investigate even more dead DJs.

But, of course, there's the pesky question of human rights. We don't necessarily want Mr Cameron to know where we were last night, so we may be reluctant to provide him with a means of finding out. And we may remain reluctant right up to the point where we realize the advantages.

For many years boffins have inserted electronic devices into our bodies to regulate the beat of our heart and alter our mood and even bring about orgasm. But this, I feel, is just the start.

Look at that tiny chip in your credit card. Why does it have to be mounted in a bit of plastic that one day, as sure as eggs are eggs, you will lose? Why can it not be sewn into the palm of your hand, which, unless you go shoplifting in Saudi Arabia, you will not?

There are other advantages, too. There's no reason why, when you pick up a product at the supermarket, its sensors cannot read your chip and automatically deduct its cost from your bank account. This would mean no more queuing at the checkout tills.

It's the same story at airports because the electronic chip in a modern passport would easily fit into your earlobe. You just walk past a scanner and – ping. You're in. And, of course, your other earlobe could contain details of your driving licence, which would cut the time it takes to rent a car from the current average of around sixteen hours to just a few seconds.

Pub landlords would also welcome the idea because at present they have to serve a six-year-old child with six double vodkas simply because they have produced a scrap of

ID, written in crayon, that says they're actually eighteen. But with chipping, he'd know.

You could have an electronic ignition key for your car sewn into one thumb and a complex laptop password sewn into the other. And never again would you forget to withdraw your card from the cash dispenser because you wouldn't need one. Simply insert your wedding ring finger into the slot and seconds later bundles of delicious money will pour forth.

You could even have a chip containing your medical records sewn into your genitals so that on one-night stands your partner would be able to determine whether you were suffering from anything they would rather not catch. The possibilities are quite literally endless.

It's been said for many years that your body is a temple. And that's fine. But I'd quite like mine to be a mobile phone and a credit card as well.

10 February 2013

Hello, sailor. Show me what Britain is really made of

As we know, everything run by the dull, penny-pinching hand of government is a bit rubbish. Walk through Heathrow and when you get to the customs hall, all the equipment is scuffed and the tables are held together with duct tape.

In a hospital the front-of-house staff may be cheery and the shop may sell all kinds of succulent-looking fruit but peep into the spaces where the public are not allowed and it's like peering into Eeyore's Gloomy Place. It's like nobody cares. And that's the trouble, really. Nobody does.

It's the same story with the police. Elsewhere in the world, they get snazzy costumes, flash cars and cool sunglasses. Here they rock up in a Vauxhall Astra, sporting a pair of trousers that have plainly been designed to fit someone else.

You just know that if the government had built the Shard it would have been quite a lot shorter and that the lifts wouldn't work. The government doesn't do fabulous. It does woeful. A point that was well made by the Royal Navy Lynx helicopter that recently came to pick me up in Stavanger in Norway.

To keep this ancient design even vaguely relevant, it has been retro-fitted with all sorts of radar equipment so now it looks like it's caught a terrible warty skin disease. But it took off, nevertheless, and half an hour later deposited me on the navy frigate HMS *Westminster*.

It's a little bit shorter than Roman Abramovich's latest yacht. And cost slightly less to build. And from the outside, it's not hard to see why. There's a bucket for fag ends, and a principal armament of just one 4.5in artillery piece. Or as a Second World War admiral would say, 'one peashooter'.

There are, however, several health and safety notices advising crew members on how not to get hurt. Which seemed to be a bit incongruous on a warship. But this is a government vessel. So what do you expect? Four functioning diesels, perhaps? Nope. Sorry. One of them was broken. Oh, and the previous evening it had sprung a leak. It might as well have been called HMS *Vulnerable*.

You could say that of the whole service because, if you exclude training vessels, the minesweepers and various other odds and sods, the number of Royal Navy frontline surface ships stands at eighteen. That's eighteen vessels – frigates and destroyers – you would recognize as a warship.

To put that in perspective, the number of surface ships sent to give the gauchos a thick ear in 1982 – and I'm not including the subs or the transporters or the service vessels, just the main warship flotilla – was twenty-five.

At the outbreak of the Second World War the Royal Navy had 317 surface ships. At the Battle of Jutland in 1916 it lost fourteen warships and 6,784 men in just one encounter. And still came home saying, 'We won'.

All of which makes you think, with only eighteen ships currently ready for duty, we couldn't even defend ourselves against Belgium. Or could we? Because unlike any other government-run operation, HMS *Westminster* is much better than first appearances would have you believe. First of all, there's the crew. One was just back from a spell with NASA. Another, who had a regional accent, could mend a gas turbine with his eyelashes. Sailors? Yes. But everyone who I spoke to was a top-class engineer as well.

And you should see how they operate on the bridge. Quietly. Like components in a brand-new laptop. Orders are spoken. They are repeated. Something happens. Have you ever been in a really busy restaurant in Turin? Well, this ship is the exact opposite of that.

And then you have the toys. What you can't see from the outside is the astonishing array of missile launchers. The 4.5in gun is only there to frighten a Somalian pirate. The real hardware is the Sea Wolf and Harpoon missiles, and the torpedoes. It's a smorgasbord of guided ordnance designed to make Johnny Baddie have a surprisingly bad day.

But they are nothing compared with what you find in the bowels of HMS *Westminster*. You go down and then down some more, through tiny hatches that feature standard-issue military-sharp edges, until you arrive in a below-the-waterline room that looks like an air-traffic-control centre. But it's no such thing. Because it's not designed to land planes safely. It's designed to land them quickly and at very high speed in the sea.

Then you move into the submarine-detection area. Same deal. It's a room built specifically to make the enemy submariner all wet and uncomfortable. And yet, like the bridge, it's as quiet down there as a chess tournament. Even at full speed. I know this because we went there. And Holy Mother of God . . .

Have you ever rented a jet ski while on holiday? Feels fast, doesn't it? Well, the *Westminster* is faster still. And then, as we approached 30 knots and we were playing Moses, the captain ordered a sharp turn to port. You'd imagine a ship this size would respond like an elderly dog. But no. One second we were heading north and then we were heading west and I was standing on the aft deck, wondering out loud how the bloody thing hadn't capsized.

You often see books that tell a man what he must do before he dies. Well, I've landed on a Nimitz-class aircraft carrier and flown an F-15 and been shot at while flying over Basra but I can tell you that the No. 1 must-have experience is a Type 23 frigate turning hard to port at almost 30 knots. It is absolutely hysterical.

As night began to fall, it was time to make port in Bergen. The sentries put on body armour and manned the machine guns, in case the Norwegians got any silly ideas. And we were nudged to a standstill by a local tug. When you have only eighteen warships in total, you can't risk dinging one in a parking accident.

As I disembarked, I couldn't help turning round for one last look. It may be a government vessel in a government navy. But I can tell you this. It does something no other government operation does: it makes you achingly proud to be British.

17 February 2013

Work on the accent, Brum, and Tom Cruise will be in for a balti

If I may be permitted to liken Britain to the human body, then Scotland is the brain, East Anglia is the stomach, North and East Yorkshire are the breasts and London is the heart that pumps vital nutrients and oxygen to the fingernails and the ears and Preston. Which leaves us with the garden shed we built years ago when we decided to take up metalworking: that's Birmingham.

In recent years it's been tidied up. Earnest locals have fitted funky new lighting and a bar. They've polished the lathe, too, and turned the vice into an amusing beer pump.

But still nobody's interested. We don't do metalwork any more. So, neat though it now may be, the shed remains rather unloved.

Early last week there were many big news stories to titillate the nation. A meteorite had crashed into Russia, a film had been made about Tom Cruise visiting a curry house last August in St Albans and people were very interested in the dramatic downfall of Oscar Pistorius. But even so, the eighth-most-read story on the BBC website was: 'Why does everyone hate Birmingham?'

Twenty years ago it was very probably the worst place on earth. If you fancied eating something that wasn't a curry, you'd set off on a long and fruitless walk that would culminate in you being vomited on. And then stabbed, for daring to get in the way of someone's sick.

There was only one hotel where you had even half a chance of not catching lice and only one nightclub where you wouldn't necessarily be glassed. Not that you could find either because a few years earlier someone had decided the city should have a series of underpasses. Unfortunately they'd got a bit carried away, so that visitors would turn off the M6, disappear immediately into a hole and not emerge until they were past Kidderminster. Birmingham, then, was difficult to find and horrible if, by some miracle, you succeeded.

The reasons for going? Well, Brummies were keen to point out that they had more canals than Venice. By which I think they meant more shopping trolleys in their canals than Venice. And, er, that's it. Birmingham was just an industrial city that had no industry any more.

Today, though, everything's changed. There are bars and nightclubs and Selfridges. And all the old industrial buildings have been turned into loft apartments for thrusting young executives. So why do we still have a problem with it? I realize, of course, that it takes a while for people to notice there's been a change. We still, for instance, think of Stella Artois as reassuringly expensive rather than a drink that causes you to beat up your wife.

But continuing to think of Birmingham as a wart is as daft as continuing to imagine that York is full of oxen. You simply can't not like the city any more. And it's hard to dislike the people either. Chiefly because they are usually more British than we'll ever be.

Show a Brummie a spectacular house and after he's arranged his face to register a complete and absolute lack of interest, he will say, 'I wouldn't want to hoover a sitting room that big.' Show him an amazing garden and he will say, 'I bet that takes a lot of digging.' Put his wife in a pretty frock and he will wonder what happens when she spills her balti on it. In short, a Birmingham person is born with an inability to say, 'That is amazing.'

The British have a global reputation for keeping their emotions hidden. But Brummies have taken this to a level that would flabbergast even the Duke of Marlborough. Their emotions are not just hidden. They are locked in a safe and buried under twenty tons of concrete, in a well, at the bottom of the garden.

You know Michaela Strachan? The bubbly, enthusiastic former children's TV presenter? She's not from Birmingham. We know this because she released a video called *Wild About Baby Animals*. If she'd been a Brummie, it would have been called *Not Bothered Either Away About Baby Animals*.

Of course, this refusal to find anything wondrous can be rather irritating. Especially when you are with a Brummie at the Grand Canyon and he's facing the other way, checking his text messages. I'm not saying who that was. Only that his name begins with R and ends with ichard Hammond.

However, when you see a party of Americans whooping and high-fiving one another about something as trivial as a tropical sunset, you crave the company of a Brummie, who'll wilfully face east and tell you he'd rather be in Moseley.

I'd be happy in the trenches with a Brummie too. Because the upside of his downbeat nature is that he doesn't find things spectacularly bad either. You get the impression a Brummie would be capable of sitting there watching a rat eat his gangrenous foot without moaning anywhere near as much as, say, me.

So. We go back to the original question. Why, if the city's improved and the people are stoic, does the rest of the country have such a problem with the place? Well, there's no easy way of saying this. But, um, it's the accent.

In the complex world of advertising, a Yorkshire twang is perceived to be honest. Which is why Sean Bean is used to promote every single thing. It's the same story with the

Scotch. *Gavin & Stacey* has made the Welsh accent funny and likeable, and now that Cilla Black has taken her mocking tones into retirement, posh is okay as well.

A Birmingham accent, however, makes you sound thick. If Einstein had been from King's Heath, no one would have taken the theory of relativity seriously. If Churchill had been a Brummie, we'd have lost the war. And if you don't believe me, just get someone from Castle Bromwich to read out the 'We shall fight on the beaches' speech.

That's why people hate Birmingham. It's because they think everyone who lives there is a bit daft. Happily, though, I have a solution. If the council really wants its city to thrive after the second phase of HS2 has turned it into an oxbow lake, it needs to stop giving the locals more bars. And send them for elocution lessons instead.

24 February 2013

As Russians say, manners maketh the British late

Time. It's now so precious that we will happily spend an absolute fortune making all the things we do faster, simply so we have time to do more things.

A decade or more ago, if you were suddenly consumed with a need to watch some online footage of a cat falling over, it took about a minute for your internet to load the film. This was a minute none of us could spare. Then we got the idea of watching it on the go. Luckily a conglomerate of international mobile phone companies had paid the British government £22 billion for something called 3G. This meant people had to wait only five seconds to see a cat falling over, and for a while we were all very happy.

But then we realized that in the modern world five seconds is far too long. So now phone companies have paid a further £2.3 billion for 4G, a service that delivers hilarious animal-related accidents almost instantaneously.

We see the same thing going on in lifts. We need a button that closes the doors when we're ready to go because we simply cannot wait four seconds for them to close by themselves. Rightly so. Two lift journeys a day could waste eight seconds. Which in a working week is forty seconds. In a time frame that vast we could have watched six cats falling over. And an amusing helicopter crash.

It's the same at our favourite supermarket. If the queues are too long, we will go elsewhere. Even if we know the next shop fills its burgers with horses, toenails and bits of mashed bat.

I know I'm more pathological than most about wasting time, but surely you too must froth at the mouth when you sit down to watch a DVD and you are electronically prevented from fast-forwarding through the legal disclaimers that precede it. This is lawyers stealing our lives. And we hate it.

It's strange, though. We fume in traffic jams and curse when people on pavements walk too slowly, yet we are prepared to waste hours and hours of every day gurning and engaging in idle chitchat with people we don't know.

The British middle-class obsession with good manners means we feel obliged to discuss the weather with our postman and our holidays with our hairdresser. We write ridiculously long thank-you letters to people we've already thanked verbally. In business emails we use words that aren't necessary simply because we feel the need to be polite, and if we want directions we always start out by saying, 'Excuse me. I hate to be a bother but . . .'

Been on a flight recently? The obsequiousness is now so rampant that it takes half an hour to make every announcement. 'Any bread items for yourself at all today, sir?'

I bring all of this up because I've just spent a week in Russia where manners don't seem to have been invented. When a hotel receptionist needs your passport, she doesn't say, 'Would it be possible to see your passport for a moment, sir, if it isn't too much trouble?' She says, 'Passport.' And if you can't find it within three seconds, she says, 'Now!'

When you order a dish from a menu that isn't available, there's no tiresome hand-wringing explanation from the waiter. He just says, 'It's off.' And if you are struggling to get your luggage through a revolving door, no one waits patiently until you've sorted the problem out. They repeatedly shove the handles until everything in your suitcase is smashed and your fingers have been severed.

When a British *Top Gear* fan wants my photograph, they spend hours explaining how their son watches the show on Dave and how he can impersonate me and how it's a religion in their house. Whereas in Russia they just say, 'Photo.' And if they don't happen to have a camera, you are told to stay where you are until they have been back to their house and got one.

Ever been stuck behind two British people while waiting for a ski lift? 'After you.' 'No, you were here first.' 'No, really. I'm sure you were.' 'Oh, it's okay. I don't mind waiting. It's such a lovely day.' 'Much warmer than last year.' After a while you are consumed with an urgent need to stab both of them with your poles.

Queuing is much easier in Russia – because no one bothers. You just walk to the front and if anyone objects – this actually happened – you pull out your wallet and show the complainant your credit cards. This is Russian for, 'I am richer than you, sunshine, so shut up.'

It's the same in what we call polite discussion. You don't dress up counter-arguments with subtle innuendo. Russians just say, 'You're wrong,' and move on. Here's one conversation I had:

'Jews are running the world.'

'I hear what you say, but I don't think that's the case.'

'You're wrong.'

'But there are plenty of examples . . .'

'I said, "You're wrong."'

Being British, it's all very upsetting. But after a while I started to realize that being impolite saves an awful lot of time and costs you nothing. When someone is wasting your evening with their harebrained nonsense, just tell them they are wrong and walk away. When you are in a butcher's shop, don't bother with small talk. Just say, 'Two chops,' and wait to be told the price. When someone is dawdling on the pavement, push them out of the way. And in a bar, don't try to catch the barman's eye. Just shout what you want from the back of the queue.

It certainly works on Aeroflot. Planes set off before everyone is seated, and when you are coming in to land, you don't get any rubbish from the pilot about the weather and he doesn't wish you a safe onward journey. You are told to sit up straight and to remain seated until the plane has stopped. Which no one does.

Back at Heathrow, the immigration official was very chummy. 'Been away long?' he asked politely. I saved two seconds by not bothering with an answer.

I felt terrible. Guilty as hell. But that's the curse of being British. That's why we need 4G and buttons that close the lift doors and high-speed rail links. Because they free up more time for writing very long thank-you letters and making small talk with the milkman.

3 March 2013